Finger on the Trigger's

by

Ross Bowran

Finger on the Trigger's
By Ross Bowran

This book was first published in Great Britain in paperback during April 2025.

ISBN: 979-8311097581

My Early Life:

I am from humble stock. Born in Edgware, London in 1965. My parents being devout Christians were grounded and decent, but they were quirky, somehow old fashioned. This was demonstrated by their insistence in all of us going to church on Sunday mornings.

I used to think that this was their way of washing away the weekly sins. I now think it was a method for intelligence gathering against the children, attempting to find a parenting strategy that resulted in blind obedience. Perhaps to the point of being challenging. I would frequently describe them as being a contradiction. Not just in values but more importantly in their worldly nature.

As a child I remember how my mother would preach complete honesty. Instilling in me the importance of truth. Unless it conflicted with her hand, in a game of poker, or gin rummy! She would often give the impression "white lies," were ok, as long as no one got hurt! It saddens me to admit that my parents unfortunately have passed away these last few years. I have a younger sister. Louise and an older brother. Scott, or rather, that is what our parents wanted us to believe. A standard middle-class family.

However, all my pre-conceptions surrounding this changed in the weeks culminating in dad's funeral. In amongst his keepsakes in an old miniature filing cabinet I discovered some paperwork that made me spring bolt upright. Amongst a collection of correspondence from a relative who had written from Germany as a P.O.W. During World War 1, was a collection of documents concerning me.

The first few envelopes were letters and correspondence about inoculation and medical treatment, then came my old school reports and my Army passing out parade photographs. There were community events, reminders of volunteer efforts I had contributed to. Trying to raise awareness and financial support for mum's charity, or some newspaper clippings of my sporting achievements, which he was obviously very proud of.

Quite unceremoniously I chanced upon a copy of not just my birth certificate, but also all my siblings too. I had discovered our secret! We are all adopted. Now call me "old fashioned," which I am not, but isn't it disgusting that all those years ago when our judgmental, church worshipping ass for a society came up with this pass the bastard plan.

When children born out of wedlock were deemed too much of a stain on the country's reputation, that mothers were simply prevented from being given a chance. Parenting was considered only for those on the moral high ground. Excess offspring, or unwanted children were farmed out like the runts of a litter of puppies. So, for anybody who is interested; this is why I hate the church. This is why I hate politicians, and perhaps most damning of all. This is why I hate society! The general public are forever playing games with focus on the ridiculous and insane belief that conformity is the best way forward. Have a long hard think and look around you. Who actually believes that our society is fairer or more progressive than the rest of the world?

I'll tell you the answer to that is nobody! I am just beginning to realise my entire life has been a lie. Where the politicians and boardroom sitters are concocting devilish propaganda and policies to make the average citizen feel like we're all pulling in the same direction. In reality, it's all part of a complex conspiracy. Allowing certain families and organisations constantly make steady gains. Whereas many of us, irreconcilably and unfathomably buckle under, agreeing to play our part, by sticking to the capitalist script. Making our meagre wages stretch to breaking point. I want you all to stop right now and consider this very uncomfortable truth.

The excesses of the last century are about to engulf us. Any possible advantage that Britain might have held over the rest of the world is long gone. All those years of economic and financial stability, combined with the military advancement or wealth distribution of empire and the slave trading. Not relevant. We never should have been allowed to behave that we did. When individuals were forced into class brackets, where entitled couldn't mix with riffraff. But despite advances in all these outdated and obsolete stereotypical behaviours. The majority of plumb-sucking Eton and Harrow alumni have all retained their wealth and influence.

With most historical families, relocated to tiny island nations or sympathetic despotic countries. Hashtag # Under the Radar! This would have to be rule one of a reconfiguration of the whole population. The current expansion and growth obsession of national economies must end. I'm not a rocket scientist or anything remotely highly educated or qualified, but even I can see that kicking a ball down the road is not going to solve the earth's problems.

For starters who thinks 8 billion is too many? I think one tool that will have to be considered is the mass sterilization of the human population. We could fashion it like Willy Wonka's chocolate factory. With a global lottery of golden tickets. the movement of Billions and secrets to float around the globe. Untouched and undocumented.

So how did we get to this place? It would be tempting to blame the various systems of government around the world. But I don't think that would be fair. One obvious shortcoming is the human tendency to imitate squirrels! Running around the garden and gathering food and nuts. Then finding some places for storage. Totally mirrored behaviour is demonstrated by us people. A bank account here, a house over there. We even play Top Trumps with our possessions or friends.

Have you ever watched this playing out in real life. Comparing the sports cars or yacht! Claiming to have the biggest bank account or property portfolio! Sad isn't it!

Fortunately, the recent pandemic and global economic downturn which fuelled unrest, has also provided a perhaps once in a lifetime opportunity. We are all currently living under the unenviable predicament of a looming election for the nation. It's always touted as a natural reset position. When everyone from corporations down to media moguls or politicians to stars have their theories examined. Economic claims and counter claims are thrown around in a fashion resembling a shark's feeding frenzy. Only to become forgotten the second the polling booths close! This is for me why politics can't be trusted. So how about starting a new democracy?

Now is a moment to slowly start re-evaluating our relationship with our ancestors and history generally. The difficulty is finding a sustainable direction which is fundamentally different to our past. Everybody somehow needs to agree a strategy. I think it should involve every single nation. I'm not talking about United Nations. Too over politicized, with an unwillingness to take decisive actions when required. In my fifty-eight years, I have often watched scenarios played out in the polished halls of the UN headquarters and seriously wondered how it is possible those so-called leaders and representatives are even allowed to participate.

Do I have all the answers? Unsurprisingly I don't. But I do have an increasing intolerance for the time wasters and functionaries that seem to be part of the idiotic brigade. Which to you and me are the policy makers. In Britain this includes Whitehall, the civil service and other institutions. I think collectively they like to be referred to as the diplomatic corps. The "entourage."

People who have no life skills but can provide "indispensable expertise" when it comes to functionary positions, such as legal services, advice on cultural and religious matters, regional or national peculiarities and language translation for different nationalities. But possibly hardest of all we need to be honest with the public! Like what happened in government when The Labour Party were voted out by the electorate.

After the Blair and Brown administration. The incoming officials found a handwritten note in the treasury saying, "I'm sorry there's no more money!" It was left by a Labour MP. A great deal of fuss was raised about this at the time. However, after all the hype and controversy surrounding it died down. I think the average citizen was probably quite sympathetic to the notion. I'm more concerned about how mega rich individuals can "DONATE" millions of pounds to Conservative Party accounts and of course hoping for favourable conditions for their businesses, because I perceive most people will struggle with how we have been conditioned and lied to since the modern discovery of weapons.

I'm now obliged to explain this and historically what it. I will just say this. The human being is only one organism. In a universe that carries endless possibilities. But we only seem to thrive when we are screwing everything up. Our fields are filled with the corpses of insane conflicts.

Where no political parties are allowed. Every decision is made online. The Houses of Parliament are opened as a tourist attraction. Umbrella authorities and watchdogs have total jurisdiction. Companies have tailored tax officials, about how to make change for the good of the population. Unfortunately, our less able or capable to normal folk. British parliamentary standards have been eroded.

It's got so desperate that today many voters don't even care. I've touched on a few mission objectives for being in power. The glaringly obvious one is to keep everyone safe. So, who thinks that this is the current state of our society? Citizens are so tolerant and passive. I think that even when the Chancellor is openly taking cash out of your pockets, it still won't be enough to create a reaction.

As a nation we have got dismissive, opting to prefer the brainwashing of our trusted executives and corporations. Almost to the point where politically controlled media companies, dictate a daily narrative. It's like the news has ceased to exist. Where polished frontmen and women sit proudly on the headline shows. Telling us how to think and how we should react. I would go as far as to say that without realising this. The modern world has become a mirror of George Orwell's 1984. Where Big Brother is being played out in our lives. All the players of the book are part of our routine. We are realising totalitarianism, mass surveillance of society, repressive regimentation of our interactions in life. In fact, we are living the matrix! There is one facet of modern Britain that is the foundations of everything evil in this country. I'm talking about the Financial Sector. It's not just the Banks. Although they are a massive part of the problem.

According to the history books we should be blaming the Egyptians for our woes. You see right up until around B.C. 2000. No-one used currency. Everything was traded in goods. People would work for grain or some other commodity. Now I am not by any stretch of the imagination advocating a return to those simplistic ways of trading and selling. But just observe where we are now. Some have every right to demand.

A right to good healthcare, Including dental. A right to a just society. When the rule of law is fit for purpose. A world leading transport system. Unlike the disaster currently being served up. You see I have barely touched the surface of the current failures. Interestingly though there is a very clear and obvious problem. I'm of an age to remember some of the British parliament's major erroneous decisions. I can't blame the usual protagonists, because they (the parties) are just followers! I would compare them all to a bunch of sheep. Blindly following the policy makers. children have a right to know who is who?

I would even go so far as to say that the backbone, of a successful family, is to have total trust in the family fabric and all the surrounding components. The "Raison D'Etre," to being part of a successful British family, has always been sharing. Whether that means the joint efforts of home making. Or the joy of others getting married or passing exams. The old cliches like sportsmanship or fairness have always been passed down as ideals to live by. So, it struck me like a thunderbolt that essentially, it was just a lie!

This feeling of betrayal and deception started jumping out at me. My mother's little white lies started adding up and making more sense than I could ever have imagined. I was taking the pill and entering "The Matrix." Waking up to forty years of cheating. I began doing all those basic mathematical calculations. Except that now for the first time I saw that 2 + 2 didn't equal 4!

I had always had suspicions about our family. How none of us resembled each other. I viewed my sister as Mediterranean now. My brother could have been living in Russia. But my bedrock, the one constant, was all at once gone. The year was 2005 and after the recent necessities of having to once again change jobs I began to analyse my life and start asking and answering some of those difficult conundrums I began wondering about.

I have a theory about life, the planet and everything that constitutes being a human being, but in the interests of my study into the world of deception post 05. I will keep things simple. I'm going to highlight the first major eye-opening moment in this post father universe. Well, the real Eureka moment occurred on the 07/07/05, when a group of radicalised maniacs targeted and created mayhem and carnage on the streets of London.

I decided there and then that I was wasting my life in self-imposed exile. I watched the events of 9/11 unfold and decided to begin making moves to return to the UK. I was concerned about my parents, and I was also aware that certain things were happening in my body that I needed to address. I also want to make a whole plethora of observations about tangible things that I have been able to experience and judge. Hopefully in a positive manner, so that future generations can use my scribbles as a template for a workable solution to all the evils that we (humanity) are responsible for!

I remember the day I boarded the Intercity express train from Dortmund to Berlin. I was calm inside but focused on my mission. I had to use the train because my partner of 15 years had the family car. I had pre-booked a hotel in Schonefeld, literally a stone's throw away from the major airport in the Capital, I settled into my seat, and it was in between my reading the newspaper and watching the stations flying past my window that I began doing the difficult work of getting real about where I was, where I was going and most importantly, what was going right and wrong. I'm convinced it's only when you step back and take stock, that you realise what is working and what is not.

A little inner voice was shouting at me. I like to compare it to my own security blanket. The silent whisperer who occasionally makes an appearance. Advising when to fight and when to make flight. You see this journey began in 1990. Some fifteen years earlier. I was dating a girl who was living and working in Berlin. An incredibly crazy, long-distance relationship. Neither of us spoke each other's language. I would drive the two hundred and ninety-one miles from Nord Rhein Westfalia, glimpsing the remnants of the old East/West divide. A sinister watchtower here, or a Russian built helicopter there. But it was in the company of my girlfriend that things really got surreal. Our conversation was very limited. Lots of referrals to dictionaries.

Occasionally we would attempt whole sentences or try just translating newspaper articles. You see it's funny what you will do when you are chasing a nice girl's ass! The point is the love had been missing for about two or three years. The only person making any effort, was me and I was probably tired out. A combination of factors, I think. The complete absence of desire to improve or challenge was the most obvious. But that is the deadly consequence of complacency. I had changed careers twice. Learned two languages. Qualified myself for a German trade, and made attempts to ingratiate myself with her family, plus I had also made attempts to become more socially acceptable to my parents!

To what end? I'll tell you. It was another of those internal conversations I was having in train isolation. My first Berlin bound trip was literally just weeks after the fall of the "Wall," we travelled past some barracks that had been housed for Regiments of Russians. Along with those of the East German soldiers! Occasionally you would see freight trains in sidings carrying ten or fifteen main battle tanks. The odd military aircraft would fly over, or an occasional helicopter would buzz overhead. It was quite surreal.

Considering how we (the NATO alliance) had spent decades training to prevent such a confrontation. I can recollect my first impressions of the old DDR. With the run-down station in Magdeburg, or the sight of the grim, cold concrete blocks of flats. You could sense how much deprivation must have been visible in this part of the world. Something I had confirmed a few years later during a trip to the eastern border of the old DDR and the Czech Republic.

The only piece of normality on this train was arrival at Berlin Tiergarten the journeys end for Eastern bound transport. I disembarked from this arrival station heading to the underground. The strange thing about this, was how quickly I compared it to London. Now considering the fact that German society was only just beginning to realise the importance of reunification and that there was hope for the end of the Cold War. I'm always struck by how much utter incompetence was demonstrated by the UK and the US at this time.

Background:

This small introduction to me, my family, and my acquaintances is laid out chronologically to give you a flavour of what I am, have been, and what my roots are. I am from a small family group consisting of my mother and father, a younger sister and an older brother.

We are a unique family for lots of reasons. I'm drawn immediately to my childhood spent mostly with travelling from location to location. I'm told it was always to facilitate my father's work. He was a Geordie by birth, Gateshead I'm informed, and he became a financial consultant for Shell, the oil company, based in London somewhere near Waterloo station.

Consequently, both he and my mother, a proud Londoner from Purley, South of the Thames, trawled through the available properties around the Sutton area and eventually settled on the town of Cheam. My memories of this place are vague to say the least. What I can remember is meeting the World Cup winning footballer Martin Peters, playing lots of marbles and conkers, plus drinking bottles of disgusting milk. This is the reason I think, why I can't stand the stuff, is because of all the drugs that veterinary experts give to cows?

We then moved as a family to Hastings on the south coast. So that mum was close to her parents in Eastbourne. Great people. Nan was the cake baker, and my granddad was a veteran of both World Wars. The first in the REME, the second in the Navy. I think I loved Hastings with its pebble beach and wooden divider wind and wave breaks. I remember fishing for crabs here and catching lots of them. Until one day we took them back to our seafront facing flat and they all escaped. Fun fact, did you know that crabs can climb walls?

After a short period of time there we transitioned again. My father got a job selling cars for an Austin/Morris garage located in suburban London. From memory just outside of Carshalton. An area very dear to me for lots of reasons. My brother eventually moved there after a long time in Wimbledon, I went to his wedding there and after many years of Army service, I finished a charity run/cycle marathon at the Royal Marsden Hospital which is incredibly close to there! Unfortunately, it is also where we had my mum cremated. Funerals are normally very sombre and sobering affairs but the one thing that I will take to the grave with me was an insanely funny advertisement in the entranceway to the crematorium.

I looked across to my sister and pointed to it. The mood lifted quickly because we just couldn't stop laughing after seeing what was written. It said something like Bishop's Funeral Home, the leading place for all your needs! Rated highest by trip advisor. "You've got to be kidding, right."

But my mother wanted to be as close to her parents as possible. So, my father compromised and settled us in Epsom at Tattenham way. It was literally yards away from the home of the Derby. I have good memories of here with an allotment at the back of the house and a lovely neighbour, who was a captain in the Army Medical Corps. She was the first person to teach me about the value of so many things. Including my siblings. Something I never really understood until years later.

I think we stayed here for two years until we moved to Abinger Hammer. The most amazing place for young children, with low traffic, high nature and great locals. I believe my sister is still friends with our Spanish single-parent neighbour. We used to go rambling in the acorn littered woods and even climbing up the rocky embankments. I even got hooked on catching the wildlife like newts and frogs, but my fondest memory of them all was when I discovered what was hidden in the woodshed. A classic set of cricket balls and bats. There was even the pads and gloves which was my first introduction to sports.

I remember picking and eating the wild growing strawberries then running inside to watch the test matches with dad. Happy days. We only stayed here for about a year and a half and then moved to Godalming in Surrey. Now obviously I can't prove anything, but it seems logical that the day we had our collision with a motorcycle whilst returning from Guildford, was when things went pear-shaped!

For the sake of this introduction, I'll skip those details until a bit later, because in Godalming, I did pretty much all my studying, first junior school and then secondary, and I also found the usual adolescent distractions, until in 1982 I crashed out of everything to do with education. I jumped into lots of work experience jobs including lifeguard for two pools and one leisure centre, until, after failing another re-sit for exams I joined the Army aged 17.

I served twelve years and left to work for my would-be father-in-law as a cabinet maker, taking all the exams in a foreign language, and then working in a small business selling sports equipment, mainly Nike and Adidas, until I joined the airline in 2005, before illness enforced my long-term sickness absence in 2013. I was then dismissed in the pandemic, and I've been researching and writing this book since.

Putting things in perspective:

The title "finger on the trigger" is loosely based on my previous existence as a serving soldier in the British Army. But the trigger section is not a direct reference to the firearms that we carry.
It's actually a direct link to living with MS and the fact that you are constantly looking for reactions to all manner of different circumstances.

I know lots of individuals both male and female, young and old, whose journeys are the entire spectrum of auto immune disorders. From Parkinson's to Alzheimer's, MND to MS, but here's the thing, I have many conversations with MS sufferers who are pretty much as varied as the ice-cream selection at an Italian gelato restaurant.

Whereas the other conditions are mostly similar and have a devastating profile. Some of my recent friendships have involved people with Alzheimer's and Parkinson's. Some are what I will describe as "wanderers," the others, frequent memory issues. A very dangerous combination when they don't remember turning on the oven, or where they live.

The saddest cases I have seen are MND, afflicted. Just ask Rob Burrow and Kevin Sinfield, or Doddy Weir, if you're a Union fan. A colleague from my first Army unit called Johnno, became the first poster boy for MND but sadly he only lasted a year until his illness ended the game

Which brings me back to MS, a condition that is not considered a death sentence, something I truly believe, by the way. The triggers are different for each person, but they can usually pass after a certain amount of time. But the trick is to find the triggers that are applicable to you.

Get skilled at lying about what is going on. Most importantly don't put yourself and your squad in danger. I personally handed back my driver's licence the first day I had an episode of optic neuritis. The other point to make is any money this story makes will go to *Emms Wiltshire MS, support group.*

Prologue:

I want to add a final tribute to my late mother and father who battled the illness and a multitude of other problems during their last fifty years.

They taught me patience and understanding, however, and although my parents never managed to enjoy a cruise, or anything even remotely wild and adventurous,

I can now accept and acknowledge, that mum could at times appear very vindictive, which I can put down to decades of failure and long periods of ill-health.

And, as previously mentioned within this book, I want to highlight certain key points, and for people to fully understand, that just because someone has a medical qualification, it doesn't mean they are competent, and additionally, just because someone might hold an important position, it doesn't mean they are qualified!

Most telling of all, is that just because someone is unlucky enough to have become unwell or disabled, it doesn't mean they are any less qualified, or competent than the next person.

My family have been failed in so many ways, and over so many years by "the system," including the basic fact that our car seatbelts failed to operate properly during our serious accident.
And perhaps it should also be accepted and understood, that current medical procedures and advice can now only be considered as "unfit for purpose!"

There is also a concern that combined with the regulators – the very people who are supposed to ensure we are all protected against unsafe practices – that this is no longer the case, as they now seem unable to fulfil their duties, and simply add to the expense and confusion of a badly broken system, no longer capable of offering any essential or reliable support.

The other threads I have posted in this book highlight just how broken this country is, and indeed the world really is, but the good news is, we have still got each other, so good luck to you all!
Ross Bowran.

The Point of my ramblings:

I have written this book with the intention of highlighting the inequalities that we are faced with on a daily basis. If you are unlucky enough to be presented with a neurological diagnosis or disability you will have to learn to adjust.

Something I have been doing since childhood. You would hope and trust that the gatekeepers of your society would be working to ensure that your safety is always the highest priority.

Simultaneously you should expect that you are protected against the consequences of failures and incompetence. Where the policy makers and leaders are held responsible and accountable for their actions. This means if you draw a six-figure remuneration then you had bloody well better be qualified and proficient at meeting your obligations and responsibilities.

I have left many open-ended discussions or topics for you the reader to decide what is right and wrong. I have also drawn a few controversial conclusions, but that's okay, because as we have seen in the 2025 realities of daily living. Truth is a difficult game to grasp.

Just remember the people that sit in positions of authority and control are not the definitive answer to every question. The church and countless other miscreants have a mouthpiece and authority to make decisions in the House of Lords?

The government has been allowed to sell off the country's utilities and infrastructure. The health industry is completely overwhelmed by years of mismanagement and incompetence. A little wonder then, when I began my journey back in 2012.

The figure of ex-pats who have fled from these islands now stands at 300 million worldwide. So, for anyone who still needs to understand why this country wants cheap labour. The answer is in this paragraph.

I briefly alluded to the situation I faced with the regulatory bodies. Well guess what! Right on cue, I have noticed today that the C.A.A. has virtually never passed a decision against one of the largest carriers in the U.K. instead leaving passengers and employees to fight "tooth and nail," for redress, but I can almost guarantee that this state of affairs is repeated throughout "Britain."

Originally, I took my grievance to the local MP Rees Mogg. I then tried for legal representation. But the only episode the lawyers were interested in was against the NHS, so, as you can see the difference between me and say Trump or Musk, is my pockets are not deep enough.

I am actually quite relaxed about all the noise that occasionally comes out the cupboards. Yes, I have taken a massive amount of hardship with navigating the health system. You are only interesting to the quacks as long as you take their medicine!

Whatever level of MS You are assigned ALWAYS challenge. The doctors love to say that your symptoms can be totally different from the next person, to which I say "Waargh! "This is a lie and a deflection tool that doctors use to prevent people from getting to the truth about their complete illnesses.

Which for me I truly believe is a co-morbidity called Epstein-Barr virus. Funny how we have a global health system that can produce a vaccine for Covid in weeks and yet for existing conditions or ailments we are no closer 50 years later. Anyway, you have to decide!

Today's date is Wed 26th Feb 2025, it's time to be honest and say what needs to be said. I am a great believer in advancement through meritocracy. I have also seen three different things this morning which gave me a renewed resolve to complete my work.

The i newspaper today had a newly published finding of a study into the benefits of eating Omega 3 rich foods for anybody with MS. A quite surreal revelation, but also something I have known about since childhood.

I'm convinced that the body is the best provider of tips and tricks to combat illness. I was given the option of taking a whole range of different types of food from a very early age. I immediately started to eat salad and veggies in preference over meat. I remember having massive arguments with my parents about their diet choices. I eventually got an apology from my dad for probably preventing them from getting BSE, due to the fact they were eating beef every Sunday.

The point is, listen to your body, and adapt your diet to as healthy as you can. I also take B12, vit D supplements and CBD OIL, which I find helpful. But you have to work out what works best for you.

The second thing which caught my attention, was a BBC news report. That detailed the story of the wife of Rob Burrow. The woman who stood by her husband and became her primary caregiver. Something that my father had done for my mother! I suddenly realised I needed to raise my glass and give all my carers a big shout of thanks...SO THANK YOU!

I expect that everyone who is dealing with a neurological problem who ends up with caregivers sometimes Forgets to show the right level of appreciation. You are sometimes dealing with daily, even hourly situations that require your total concentration. I know my mother was on occasion a real bitch. I'm never going to stoop that low. But I also know I can be very picky, for which I now apologize for unreservedly.

The third thing I was made aware of today was the findings of the Grenfell Tower report, blaming lots of individual failure. A flawed evacuation strategy and then lots of blame aimed at a massive mixture of groups and companies. The council and finally the watchdog. All of which were partly responsible for allowing the cladding to be used in the construction process.

The similarities between these actors' failures and what happened to me are tenuous at best. But the problem is that they exist, and I am now in a wheelchair because of it.

The regulators in Britain are deliberately toothless and favour large corporations and industries. I mean how else is it possible that OFWAT, OFGEM and any other utility regulator can favour a large price increase during a cost-of-living crisis, or in my case with the airline.

How come my flight hours data can be adjusted by the airlines own crewing department, or the amount of assistance offered to crew members affected by serious incidents on board, or even the amount of follow ups of crew members affected by heavy landings, turbulence and air quality issues that have occurred on board?

I am a huge glass half full kind of guy. The day after the accident I was in with my mother, I was just happy that I walked away. I watched mum deteriorate over the years and I was determined to be her explorer and consequently I would bring back memories from all the places I visited. Something that I recommend to all MS sufferers to experience for themselves. As my old bunkmate Keith once said to my mum. "You don't use it, you lose it "

Finally, to all MS sufferers be brave and patient. "Don't take shit from anyone," just look at Cadeena Cox. Paralympic cyclist and runner!

Relevance and Choices:

The reason for writing this book is to place lessons from my experiences with MS and explain the choices facing everyone who harbours a neurological condition!

Shortly after my initial period of sickness and enforced absence from my workplace. I began a much-travelled journey. Undoubtedly replicated a thousand-fold. By anyone who has to navigate the surreal world of mystery Illness and diagnosis. Mine is bizarre story of trial-and-error incompetence and utter ignorance and arrogance.

I recall a conversation I had with the manager of the Brightwell centre. Formally the MS therapy centre for the West of England, Doro Passantes. She informed me of how reticent and secretive some MS sufferers behave, not wanting to expose their own experiences or feelings. Probably to better to slip under the radar than to broadcast their own unique stories and difficulties.

It's something I didn't really want to accept or appreciate until one day during the pandemic when I began piecing together my own history and slowly putting the jigsaw puzzle together and then realising a truth that I had known about for decades but had hidden deep down inside my subconscious.

I had seen the route my mother had taken, giving up at the earliest opportunity, probably because of inadequate communication and condition knowledge. She also had my father as a rock, driving around for her and making sure she got her medication and therapies, and also accompanying her to her countless hospital appointments. Fetching the latest news about the progression of medical care and the MS Support groups.

But what has struck me the 50-years since those days and years, is how little we've progressed. I have listened to my body and adjusted things in my life that I have made to work for myself. Knowing what weather conditions are going to affect me. Dressing accordingly. Knowing what food, a trigger is and either avoiding or being very cautious!

The crazy thing about all these variables, is how much you listen to the warnings and how you react, but perhaps the one thing that makes the most difference is how much you accept them as an inevitability. I have no doubt that if I had succumbed to the restrictions my illness triggered, I would have died years ago. I wouldn't have travelled the world and made loads of friendships. And I definitely wouldn't have been accepted into the forces, or the airline and I would never have been able to expand my horizons!

I am also quite clear about the elephant in the room. When it comes to modern medicine? I mean think about it. During Covid we are able to produce a vaccine in the space of a few months. Whereas the neurological conditions like MS or MND are fifty years and counting!

I truly believe that the best defence against these conditions is physical fitness and diet. I also believe that the conclusions of the doctors are flawed. Thinking the sclerosis of the brain is the primary cause for concern. I think it is a bipolar disorder. Where the signals being transmitted up and down the spine (including the brain stem) is where the problems lie. I also think that there is a lot of benefit to be had with natural growing anti-inflammatory treatments like curcumin and ginger to name just a few, I also think CBD oil is beneficial for anyone who has to deal with spasticity. The best thing I can do for you is recommend a few basic remedies. Cut out processed foods. Drink lots of water and don't smoke!

I remember the dance played out by my mother with all her appointments and referrals. The catalogue of drug prescriptions or scans. Each one never providing a golden ticket for repair.

But here I note that at no point during those early years of uncertainty in my mother's illness and subsequent onset, did anyone ever think to ask her about her recent trauma of events! Something that was severely lacking in my own journey too.

I highlighted way back in 2012 at the start of the triage, the unusual events of medical relevance. None of which were met with any enthusiasm. I was actually surprised by the lack of follow up, or scanning, giving the possibility of a secondary infection or injury which could at least be treated? But you see, this was 2012 and the NHS, for all the years of research and testing, we are no further along than when my mum got her first spinal tap in the 1980's.

Or when Bill Johnson was told his MND diagnosis in 1985. Indeed, it's true for every serious illness that comes under the neurological umbrella. I'm inclined to believe that part of it is financial, but I also think it's money-go-round. The pharmaceutical companies have cornered the market. They can pretty much name their prices. NHS will pay and you can't argue against them!

Nobody in our world is healing, like say, a patient with a broken leg, or someone recovering from a heart attack. The areas where the medical staff are doing really good things is minuscule when in the round. Let me spell it out for you. Breathing, Bleeding, Brakes and Burns, are what they are really good at!

You'll probably notice that the other conditions and complaints are rarely mentioned, and are no doubt considered as a difficult area, and one that GPs are reluctant to even discuss. Wanting instead to pass the baton upstairs to, 'qualified neurologists,' a practice incidentally I find utterly unacceptable and useless. You see it's the spinning wheel syndrome all over again.

I mean, sure these people may have studied the brain and have a working knowledge of what a condition like MS looks like on scans, but actually, having the tools and equipment to get a new way of treating the infection is sadly woeful. In many ways I'm reminded of the Covid lockdown and how, during the investigative phase of the pandemic we suddenly started repurposing old drugs?

You all have to use your own brains and instincts. But my tips are the following: - Ascertain what any doctor who wants to examine you has for credentials. Also find out if they treat other MS patients. You will find that you might be asked to take part in testing. These muppets have over 50 years of data to fall back on. So, my reaction would be a simple, 'WHY?' But then it comes down to you. Listen to your gut and try to go all special forces, but most importantly. NEVER SURRENDER!

Something that I know and visually recall affecting my mother but has now irreversibly changed my life is the drifting apart from friendships. An unavoidable consequence of the restrictions found in the battle for independence and self-determination. In many ways I know that I have neglected opportunities and olive branches.

Probably a throwback to the parent's financial meltdown of 1986. I really struggled to find empathy for anybody who abandoned our family during the years I was in Canada. I mean just imagine the anger I felt towards my siblings when I discovered how heartless they had behaved towards mum and dad. I forgave my sister, but in my opinion, my brother is just a sad excuse for a human being.

He proved me correct years later when I was back in Britain trying to find a way to get a well-paid job and bring my family from Germany over. But typical of his narrow mindedness he insisted I return my late father's car because, "he said so." Brother, just so that you know. Your actions resulted in the breakdown of my long-term relationship putting additional strain on my family and causing the start of my mental health issues.

My partner for 16-years was entering remission for breast cancer. I literally just had to move EasyJet bases from Dortmund in Germany to Bristol in the West of England. Despite the fact we were promised as a base that we were doing a marvellous job. "They lied," and as their Union representative, I was told that we would all be offered an alternative. A classic example of corporate power and greed.

However, this story still has a few more twists and turns:

Whenever I watch the Paralympic Games, I'm always fascinated by the ability of injured athletes and competitors to shrug off their shortcomings. Putting on their colours and trying to keep going to show that the spirit is always there. One of the competitors I have watched out for, is Kadeena Cox. An MS sufferer and a pretty good athlete too. I always think, "What happens if you get (IT)! You know the feeling you get when the body starts shutting down?" I then realise IT DOESN'T MATTER!

So, let's have a little moment of reflection and appraisal. Which is actually quite poignant and relevant when we discuss the options and treatments available for the "also rans?" I personally have dealt with lots of those situations during my years on the airline. Epilepsy to allergic reactions, or diabetics to the classic self-inflicted wounds, like drug abuse or alcoholic meltdown. But when it comes to complicated neurological and other disorders. There are no band aids. It is something the white coats love to remind us of.

You are pretty much reliant on the patient's own personal experience and instruction. Or the travelling knowledge of support staff and family members who might have been instructed what to do if an emergency happens. I've been witnessed to varying degrees of medical competence on flights. When professional doctors and nurses offer their services during a difficult situation. I'm ever grateful for most of those occasions!

But I have also experienced the worst level of intervention and co-operation. On a few occasions we have taken the initiative back from helpers. Feeling uncomfortable with the competence displayed. Which brings me nicely onto a very important and interesting point. The entire story of my life is littered with the incompetence and failings of the "so called leaders!"

We are constantly and continuously asked to place trust in individuals and organisations who have the responsibility and supposedly the experience and knowledge to make decisions based on a raft of qualifications and recommendations that "should" provide answers and guidance, to be the proverbial Buddha in unusual or challenging circumstances. But bottom line...THEY SHOULD KEEP YOU SAFE?

Notice I used the word "should" something that the OED describes as verb.
1) Used to indicate obligation, duty and correctness when criticising someone's actions.
2) Used to indicate what is probable.
3) Formal (expressing the conditional mood) referring to a possible event or situation.
4) Used in a clause with "that" after a main clause describing feelings.

But as we all know in the modern world and especially in 21st century Britain. The "should" fix disappeared post war. The mainstay of society now is driven by successive generations of upper-class idiots. Qualification waving mediocrity. Or overwhelmed and sideways promoted boardroom staff. Who preach the market speak of productivity and key economic indicators, without the need to worry about safety factors or providing a worthwhile remuneration package. Only worried about the dividends and benefits associated with themselves and the shareholders!

In fact, I would go as far as to say that in my humble opinion, "WITHOUT EXCEPTION' the entire country is being run by a bunch of greedy apes. Siphoning off money to place into offshore tax havens and power to be shared with the other elitist oligarchs and executive club members, believing confidentiality that their policies or decision-making is of very little consequence, knowing that their club will never be challenged.

Even on the rare occasions when they are exposed as being utterly incompetent or corrupt. The people who have to take responsibility are always the ones in minor positions.

Just look back at some of my disclosures. The nepotism and sideways promotions in the Armed Forces, Government, and the mainstream financial institutions.

Where even being bankrupt on the Monday means nothing because the old school tie will get you financial support and comfort by Friday. Or, if you are demoted and disgraced on Wednesday, you can always sign up for the Church and be a Captain by next week!

Another alleged classic is of course British politicians. Forever, and seemingly, being caught with their hands in the till, or fiddling expense accounts, cash for questions, inappropriate and unacceptable behaviour. I could of course go on, but it wouldn't make any difference to the fundamental failings of our society.

I personally blame everybody who has been part of the country's facade since the 1960's, controlling the narrative and reminding us of all about the greatness of our nation? Where going to Church is good? Despite knowing full well that we live in a culture of deviant and perverse chancers.

Where every branch of the democratic system we are subscribed to is flawed. This belief that first past the post is the fairest system. A system that has only one purpose! I'm talking about the inevitability of a two-horse race. A country where we are spoken to for the majority of the time by complete tossers! In a society that likes to portray itself as first world and progressive! We rant on about the fairness and value of the "RULE OF LAW," but simultaneously and continually proving that it only applies to a very specific demographic.

We are constantly reminded of how great the NHS is. But don't have the finances in place to make it work. Overpaying mediocrity and failure while penalising the staff who actually make it work. Mr. Wes Streeting wants to make a positive impact and change. Well, let's be clear. Unless you employ people who actually can make a difference. Take away the dependency of pharmaceutical companies and start with basic services that "serve" local communities you are barking up the wrong tree! AND FOR THE RECORD. I SUPPORT THE PAY DEMANDS OF THE NURSES BUT NOT THE DOCTORS.

The Real Reason:

Convention dictates that we should behave in a certain way. For informal occasions we follow a dress code, speak in polite paraphrase, and nonsensical small talk. With the desire to be as inoffensive as possible! "The

Norm," in Western privileged society gatherings is to pick a safe subject, and far away from the questionable antics of the establishment.

My father who was managing director of a car firm in South-East England, had three go-to subjects. So, during these soirées you would here the latest progress of the A-road leading to London, how terrible the latest global tragedy sounded, and which airlines served the best in-flight cuisine. Which is just about as safe and uncontroversial as it was possible to get!

What I feel most sad about is not, how insincere everyone behaved back then. This would have been the nineteen seventies, but moreover how things have not improved. Whenever I watch the news. It's like Groundhog Day. The list of injustice is not even hidden nowadays. The select group of entitled and titled are so blatant it should make countries rise-up. But it never happens because the world instruments of conformity and status quo are so entrenched in society, that people are quickly persuaded to challenge is to lose!

Until Today:

You see today is probably the only day in our lives, maybe even ever, when it's a good thing to challenge. So, every instrument of normality, each countries web of administration is obsolete. Likewise, every framework of society is disappearing to the history pages. The recent world virus, indeed, every species threatening disease demands immediate combative solutions. So, let's list the most pressing potential, death causing, diseases.

It's one of those multiple-choice questions and the scope of potential answers is quite staggering. We all know of the worldwide illnesses which kill on a regular indiscriminate basis. Things like malaria, cancer or more recently covid, monkey pox, or Ebola. But when you delve past the obvious you soon discover that it's not the headline making illnesses which are the most dangerous. It's things which we tend not to give a dangerous value to. Because we are part of the divide and conquer elitist scum.

We inoculate against stuff which seem to exclusively affect African countries. Like yellow fever or, trypanosomiasis (sleeping sickness), but worldwide, more people die from pneumonia, heart disease or things like HIV. Outside of medical emergency people are dying from the effects of conflict, climate emergency or even just bad driving! But let's just backtrack slightly and talk about climate change. Because if you still don't believe how serious this is, let me paint a picture.

When I was stationed in Canada, I was young naïve and very easily persuaded about things, which I should have questioned more vociferously, but I was not strong enough or convinced enough to speak out about. Until that day I drove along the Trans-Canadian Highway to Vancouver. You see there is a section of road along this route which offers unparalleled access to the Athabaskan glacier. But the only problem was, when we got here, it had moved!

The only exceptions must be the police, but only for balance, to stop uncontrolled anarchy and violence. The world's financial system must be dismantled and the responsible CEO's, COO's, stock market brokers, and backers, and in fact every single individual who has got involved in this closed market system, should be made to repay every single profit gained, towards a world fund for a fairer wealth distribution system.

When I look at the nouveau rich. With the second homes, or the three cars parked on the drive. I often wonder how it can be in 2022, there is such a gulf between people and places. But it's irrelevant. You see there is only one disparity. There are those who make a difference and those who mark time. Let me explain. I am a trained soldier, cabinet maker, air crewmen (both civilian and military), I have been working as boat crew, leisure centre lifeguard, I also dabbled in the theatre, playing music for pantomime, I have climbed mountains, abseiled out of helicopters, and. But what I've learnt from thirty-years of graft is. It doesn't matter. Because none of the work has had any meaning.

Elephant in the paper:

Let me start by painting a picture. In 2003, I was treading water, both figuratively and literally. My triathlon training involved many components for each discipline, one of these was the dreaded swimming float. A test designed to strengthen arm strength and improve endurance in water. You basically swam for a given time without using legs to propel you.

Touching the poolside was only permitted on turning. Our trainer never tested on anything less than one hour. Difficult is an understatement. The second treading water (figuratively) was my reappraisal of my situation.

I had never been good at accepting mediocrity. You probably all know the symptoms. Wake up with no desire to embrace the new day. Because for me, this is mankind's biggest challenge and probably our greatest failure. We as a species have successfully negotiated the error strewn recent history. We have shrugged off the feudal system, we have rejected fascism and communism, most people even agree what we have today Is ok.

This is where I pull the emergency chord, "are you kidding!"

At what point do normal people look around and view the modern world as a success?
Let's do a constructive criticism. Gross food inequality (including access to clean water), corporate vandalism (this is where the big and powerful under-cut the small guy), asset stripping (this includes mining of minerals and chemical elements), planetary environmental destruction, but perhaps the worst of all is over population.

Especially now, shortly after Brexit, the pandemic, war in Europe and a looming economic catastrophe. I mean just over the horizon there's an environmental disaster lurking in the shadows. So, where in the world do we start?

Well for starters let us pull the plug! My entire life I've had to listen to, watch and in a few cases participate in the insanity of the human race. So firstly, on behalf of the youth across the entire planet, I am ashamed to have left this mess for you to sort out.

I actually think the right time to make the required changes was 1945. The conclusion to the Second World War. The majority of humanity wanted to Ctrl+Alt+Delete. In other words, restart from point zero. I believe normal thinking people would probably choose right now. The Eleventh of June 2022. Across ninety percent of the globe people want a new start. The ones against this way of thinking are obviously the key holders. Or people so far away from our 21st century lifestyle that we have no bearing on them, and they have nothing on us.

You all know them, the position holders. You see, in a normal group structure the ones calling the shots would be the alpha male/female. Look at Mother Nature, you have on one side the silverback gorilla (m) or on the other side is the prey mantis (f). Well, we have evolved now to such an extent that the leaders are mostly not fit for office.

We should start by looking at a cross section of the world's top politicians.
Britain P.M. Boris Johnston, latest popularity ratings 34 %
Joe Biden U.S. President, 41 %. (Gallup)
Emanuel Macron, French Premier, 35 % (Elabe)
Olaf Schulz Bundes chancellor, 36 %

I could of course go on linking up country after country, if wouldn't be any different no matter where I looked. The point is that the figureheads of any country are ultimately only sacrificial lambs. They serve no other purpose than distractions from the real policy makers. Until that all defining moment when they must fall on their sword and do the accountability dance.

I mean think about it. Do you really believe any of these comedians could come up with those policies? Of course not, the legwork will always be done by various think tanks and advisors. The incorporation into practice is achieved by civil servants and various departmental budget co-operations. Which is then signed off by the treasury etc. etc.

So, let's rewind a bit:

The total for all these departments and specialists in every topic for every nation worldwide is astronomical! So why do we need them? It all comes down to "Divide and Conquer." Imagine what would happen if your countries brightest scholars left their decade long study to discover that there were no well-paid jobs left? So, imagine a law student. leadership? We will discuss this a little later.

So, let's think globally. The greatest man I ever knew was Captain Hawthorn. He was a decent guy who gave me the best advice I ever had. He said, "think outside the box." Everyone always follows, regardless of whether they are going the right way or not. People are also very predictable and mostly for the wrong reasons.

Let me give a few examples from my life, but also a couple of international screw ups, to highlight what I am getting at. To undertake any military operation successfully you need to provide certain strengths, whether they are required or not is entirely dependent on the duration and severity of the task at hand, or, if there are specific skill sets called for, then it is a requirement to ensure these eventualities are factored into the mission planning.

For example, I remember during Gulf War Mk1. We packed off everything and believed it would perform perfectly. However, and quite luckily, once we had unpacked in Saudi, it suddenly dawned on the technician's and pilots, because of the desert climate our helicopters were about as useful as a chocolate teapot. It hadn't occurred to anyone that this sandy climate would block the engines filters.

So, you see how blind people can be, the crazy truth was. Companies like Aerospatiel (French) had previously sold helicopters to the Iraqis included with special air-filters! The lesson here is mission planning. It's a very British thing this, it'll be alright on the night, kind of mentality. But the truth is that this inexcusable laziness costs lives. Just look no farther than soft top Land Rover's during Afghanistan.

The next one is Nigel Broadband (name changed to protect the innocent) another great guy whose hobby was scuba diving. But more importantly he held a coastal skipper yacht licence. I sailed many times with "Nige" he was always fantastic to be around. I remember one occasion when we did two weeks in the Baltic Sea having started in Kiel Germany.

We put into lots of fun town's harbours but only one really stands out. A place in Denmark named Aarhus. Or as we nicknamed it, "our house." I am certain I was only selected as an after-thought, you know to make up the numbers, but I think this gave me the hunger for adventure which has defined my life. I'm sure it's what started the inquisitive part of my brain, but whatever it was, I was hooked. From helping to secure the fenders to hoisting sail's, steering a heading to cooking a meal. Everyone took a turn to ruin a few rations.

The crazy thing was, you were permanently full steam ahead, (not under sail) but it never felt like work. I can also say it was here when I first understood the meaning of teamwork. We got the chance to learn every aspect. I became a pretty good navigator and within the shortest time I could plot the best route following the charts watching the weather and mapping our progress.

The search for the truth:

It's difficult when you put pen to paper, or in modern language put finger to touch screen, because you must choose something which people might want to read. So, I'll begin with the incredible story of the boy who disappeared!

My parents had driven us to Bognor-Regis, a sleepy seaside town on the English south coast midway between Brighton and Portsmouth. A dreary pebble beach with those ghastly wooden sleepers which serve as dividers. I remember the trip, a mixture of pointless parlour games. You know the type of thing, eye spy, or I went to market, even registration plate number climb.

This chaos was interrupted probably halfway down. I'm unable to exactly pick out what it was, but I do remember my dad picking sides, pulling over and throwing me out. I still get flashbacks of the British Leyland maxi driving over the hill. With me feeling bloody angry at the injustice of the whole process. I even remember us stopping after they had collected me. It was a pub with a crap beer garden. I was still seething with hatred and had gone into "shutdown mode." You all might know the self-preservation strategy. "Say nothing," and whatever happens, "do not forgive!" Don't forget either. Anyway, after that short break with my mum trying to diffuse the tense stand-off, the journey continued with more pointless memory-based insanity.

But it was here where my real life began. I spent the rest of the drive staring out of the window, and getting a real kick out of watching the scenery change, whilst simultaneously and surreptitiously listening to, but deliberately not engaging above the bare minimum.

I was becoming a massive journeyman. Not the dictionary definition. But more in my own interpretation. There is nothing quite as satisfying and beautiful as "going on a journey." After probably an hour or so we arrived at Bognor. My dearest disembarked, and we then dragged ourselves onto one of the segments of the beach.

My brother and sister then played at organising. Draping a towel on the pebbles, quite close to a wooden partition as I recall. This snapshot is quite revealing, going a long way to show how things would turn out in their adult lives. They then divided up the plates and plastic cups in preparation for a picnic. I had found some inner peace with my own company. Just nothing to compare to your own thoughts and the seaside. I went swimming but then came the craziest two hours of my life, so far.

Those greedy bastards had used my dip to behave like a cross between Monty Python's gluten Mr Creosote, and the students of Hogwarts, during a feasting session. I came out of the water and got the devastating news that the food had virtually all gone. I remember drying off and taking the last drops of orange squash out of the thermos flask.

It then dawned on me. REVENGE, oh yeah, in any form possible! I must have been about 10 or 11 at the time, and I wanted to leave a statement. "Fuck with me at your own peril!" So, I did what every parent probably has sleepless nights worrying about. I got dressed and excused myself by going to look for crabs. I then went in the words of Crocodile Dundee, "walkabout."

I am reliably informed by my granddad that I was missing for hours, that the local police became involved, and when they found me, I had walked two miles. The only thing I can recall is, it was getting dark when we were reunited. I had tasted freedom, and it felt good. I became a serial offender, with sociopathic flight risk. It's like a calling card. Because if like me you're small and grown-ups don't take you seriously you use all the methods to get your voice heard.

So, there you are! Any reports of missing children, the likelihood is not always the severe, things like abduction, enslavement, paedophilia, or prostitution, I know do go on. But most cases are more likely to be from communication breakdown within the family, or possibly eloping teenagers.

It's Nostalgia! Trouble at Mill!

There is something poetic about somebody as illiterate as me trying to understand the concept of English language terms and phrases. For example, despite my curriculum vitae, I don't possess a language qualification to support claims of me being a well-educated and competent native speaker of the mother tongue. This has been my life since my ninth birthday. Caught up in a web of lies and deception. Carefully crafted to help hide the reality of someone who's forced to navigate life with a hidden disability! In some ways I'm blessed to have avoided the trauma and pain that my mother was forced to endure in the name of medical progress.

Something which I have no sympathy of, or even belief in! It's something I will refer to as "the lie," a process of deceit and manipulation of such staggering proportions that nobody will ever understand, unless like my family and hundreds, if not thousands of similarly affected individuals and groups, we can come together and share our experiences in the hope that a dramatic change can be infused into healthcare systems and plans for the treatment of individuals and affected patients.

You see as with of all procedures that the white coats like to endorse, the modern remedies that we are being recommended are highly invasive and for the most part utterly ineffective.

So even with our recent experiences during the pandemic we are like sheep, blindly following the herd. Seemingly incapable of understanding what is going on and trusting mediocrity and failure. A sub-heading to describe how highly qualified, overpaid and for the most part underperforming professional snake oil salesmen/women are playing out their duplicitous dance with the devil.

It's important to know and understand that the doctors in this country, no longer have to swear the Hippocratic oath, which means a solemn undertaking not to ever conscientiously put their patients at risk. Just don't let them peddle "the lie and get away with it," always question, "what are the potential side effects, and where is the proof that this actually works?"

On the one hand pandering to the pharmaceutical industry and corporations. Prescribing unethical medicines and treatments. Knowing full well what potential risks and side effects are involved. On the other hand, what if they are our only options? Which BTW they are not! I think I would blame it on laziness and a mindset which is programmed to follow the directions of the media and our politicians. But just stop for a second and consider what I have just written. I mean who should you trust?

Not the politicians! After the pandemic, definitely not the doctors! After Brexit, and definitely not your fellow citizens! With all the parts of society that have recently failed or have been caught out. Definitely, not the civil service, or indeed any umbrella organisation purporting to be a neutral watchdog! Just look at the water or energy sectors!

It's what I like to refer to as Monty Python's "Trouble at Mill," moment. I defy any sane person to watch this sketch and not be drawn to the comparisons with the current situation we find ourselves in. It also helps with how the "Trouble at Mill" comedy theme soon fades, and incidentally in my opinion it was the funniest comedy sketch ever created, "The Spanish Inquisition," joke, with Irony and classic double entendres, overflowing at all levels!

It starts off with a metaphor for being a true Red, White and Blue native. A cloth capped 1912 resident of "The North" makes a symbolic "Knock, Knock, Knock, Knock, Knock," which is met with a sheepish "Come In." He bursts into the room and utters in a thick Yorkshire accent "Trouble at Mill," to which a young southern sounding woman responds, "Oh No, what sort of trouble?"

He then replies, "One of beams gone out of skew on treadle!"

The lady answers, "Pardon!"

The Yorkshireman then very quickly rattles off an immediate copy of the original statement.

Which is then met with a, "I don't understand what you are saying!"

He then speaks slowly and more clearly "One of the cross beams, has gone out of skew on the treadle!"

She then looks him up and down and says, "Well, what does that mean?

To which he answers, "I don't know Mr Wentworth, just said, I was told to come in here and say, "Trouble at Mill," I didn't expect to be treated like - The Spanish Inquisition?"

It's just the beginning of lots of fun and simultaneously silly exchanges where a great level of misunderstanding and confusion can be extracted from a supposedly innocent person's ambiguous relationship with the language and British culture or humour!

This sketch then goes on to introduce us to Michael Palin, Terry Jones, and Terry Gilliam, all dressed up in red as three period Bishops representing Catholic Spain during the religious revolution of late expansion around the time of the 16th century.

They manage to incorporate their trademark humour and style into a very serious piece of historical lunacy. It all lasts about 3 or 4 paragraphs long. But every single sentence has great wit, pathos, surrealism, and translates seamlessly into today's world. It attacks the gatekeepers of supposed standards and morality.

It also highlights how much we have been getting wrong. For example, the ease with which Michael Palin makes his entrance is peppered with metaphors. Lines are crossed at every step. You are thrown into the reality of an absolute power. Where one leading voice (in this case the Church) can literally behave with idiotic lunacy and get away with it.

I'm sure you can draw your own parallels, but when Palin bursts into view and shouts, "Nobody expects the Spanish Inquisition!" Followed by the qualifying statement. "Our chief weapon is surprise! Surprise and fear," Our two main weapons are fear, surprise, and a ruthless efficiency. "Oh no, our three main weapons are fear, surprise a ruthless efficiency and an almost fanatical devotion to the Pope..." there follows a slight pause. "Amongst our weapons are surprise, fear a ruthless efficiency, and an almost fanatical devotion to the Pope - and nice red uniforms!

No wait I'll go out and come in again. I'll let you the reader decide if this little skit is a classic or not. What is really important is how little idiosyncrasies and accents demonstrated in this clip. And then reflect as to how we, as a nation, are constantly changing, navigating a minefield of differing abilities of spoken English. It also demonstrates the failings of a diverse and totally dysfunctional society.

Let me give you the heads up here. We are lumped together under one flag and supposedly have all got the same goals in life. But post the fall of the Iron Curtain in 1988/9 this island has been slowly becoming a symbol of utter chaos and failure. The biggest clue is in the word we utter as our badge of honour and freedom! ENGLISH!

The giveaway is in the suffix, 'ISH!'

Or to be more precise and specific, let's give the definition of the whole thing... "Ish," is added to nouns and names to form adjectives which indicate that someone or something is like a particular kind of person or thing. For example, "childish" indicates of, like or appropriate to a certain youthful person.

It's the same kind of behaviour when you interpret numbers, times and quantities. For example, when determining how old somebody's child might be. "I think he's twelve-ish" could possibly be used during an informal discussion! Which brings us nicely onto the nationality question. What is the definition of the dictionary for "English." Strangely the word is broken into two parts. Eng, referring to being relevant or related to England. Plus "Lish."

So, you see where somebody identifies themselves as being a proud patriot of their chosen country, in some ways they are demonstrating absolute ignorance of the fact that somewhere in their family's history they are related to African heritage. The latest evidence hints strongly towards Ethiopian origins. But heaven forbid you speak too loudly about the facts, because it goes against the narrative that has been followed by countries for centuries.

METAPHOR ONE:

This takes us onto the two definitive metaphors that I love to use when discussing the subject of our lives and origins! Trust your doctor....... You see most people are so focused on their lives and survival that they don't really want to spend time analysing their own experiences and family history.

Something which I think is really important and valuable when determining a person's health and well-being! Something that doctors are totally indifferent to. I am the product of a failed healthcare system. Both of my parents were killed by NHS failures, and I've spent a lifetime working out exactly what is going wrong with me!

The qualifications displayed, advice you receive, or can even expect from a professional in the medical field is. For want of a better answer: - a two-horse race, where one of the horses has been exposed to performance enhancing substances.

I don't want to be unfair or disproportionate in my experience of the white coats, but I'm going to be blunt. Aside from the surgeons and doctors who are responsible for certain aspects of my family's health. They are a bunch of snake oil salesmen. Touting preparations and therapies designed only for one purpose. To get Pharma companies richer and simultaneously make themselves a nice healthy profit and lifestyle.

METAPHOR TWO:

Listen to your body! ...You see I have lived with a condition for fifty years give or take. I have been forced to work out triggers in my own circumstances which can affect my ability to function. I am also very sensitive to dietary requirements and weather conditions that can have a detrimental impact on my health and well-being. But perhaps most importantly, I figured out from a really young age how important being fit and active was.

My body was also telling me by unconventional means that certain exercises, experiences like swimming, running, and travelling, were best placed to offer the kinds of opportunities without any risks. My entire youth was spent travelling on the trains and knowing that I was never very far from cover or protection. You see it's something that links everybody who lives with a disability. "What is my exit strategy!"

It's something that links every single one of us. This naturally includes the roughly ten-million wheelchair users in the UK, but also the thousands of people who live with hidden illnesses. Strangely enough my mother who was diagnosed with the same condition as me, never had to be placed in a rolling battle bus, because she had a husband who helped her with her mobility issues. Let me put that into perspective. If equates to one fifth of the population. Which when compared to Europe is a massive failing of internal governance within our society.

The average comparison between European countries is woeful. Where the average is only about one in four. Something that brings us nicely onto a country's primary obligations towards its citizens. The largest duty for a country is to provide protection for its people. I am not singling out the obvious areas like national security or the daily patrolling of the borders or the streets.

I will talk about the fire, ambulance, and police services a bit later. No what I'm focusing on is the obvious areas within society, where we should expect a ring of protection. You know what I mean, I am talking about things that are governed and monitored by umbrella organisations, beginning with...NATIONAL OFFICE FOR... etc, etc.

For example, we expect our tap water should be SAFE and CLEAN, which currently are not:
*We expect our Utility prices to be fair and affordable! Which most of the time aren't!
*We expect our roads to be in a good condition. Which they are not!
*We expect our flats and houses, or public buildings to be safe! Which they are not!
*We expect our transportation systems to be safe! Which they are not!

In the US constitution, it states what their government have an obligation to protect and enforce. So why does nobody here ever protest demand a better standard of service, and a legally binding obligation for regulators to enforce refunds to bill payers, who don't get the services they deserve?

Having the conversation 2:

I have just been assaulted by the television describing things with ridiculous exaggeration. The subject was a soon to be released feature film that was set in a fictional fantasy future universe. The offensive line that I heard was "visually stunning!" Which when you think about it for a second means nothing more than "something to look at." All this commotion got me thinking about every aspect of human existence! I mean how often do you see or feel something that is stunning?

We are all of us born into a social soap opera. The first goal is to reach the end of infancy, which nowadays means negotiating a mind-blowing amount of medical interference and local council administrative form filling and nose poking.

The worst of which is the mental role playing of the nanny state. A myriad of appointments and obstacles that must be completed or overcome. For example, periodic intrusive and unapologetic health checks. Weights compared. Bodily functions tested, even down to checking out the ambiance and suitability of living arrangements for the children.

Unless you are wealthy or are a position holder. Which is a metaphor for everything that is nonsensical in Britain. Just look at the hours invested in completing all these things. You have the GP appointments followed by the specialist task specific scanning and monitoring services. All of which are time draining and remind me of the 'needle in a haystack' analogy.

It's nothing more than scaremongering. I mean OK once in a blue moon something untoward might be detected. But doesn't this reek of self-promotion. It's job justification insanity and it's only something you find in our Western healthcare systems.

Which I can imagine offends most mothers and families. But let's not pretend because this is reality in 21st century Britain. Never mind that the basics like the health and cleanliness of the health visitors is never questioned. Or that we as parents are expected to be conformist's and allow our children to be vaccinated, because they say it's safe! Or the state can remove kids when "they think" they are in an imperfect situation. How am I able to cast doubt on all these inconsistencies?

So anyway, just imagine you get to kindergarten. Well irrespective how much emphasis is placed on the fun side of that endeavour you will realise very quickly how trapped you are. The word I'm drawn to here is routine! Because even this early in life, you are expected to be tested, challenged, or have values installed, like downloading the latest operating system for the computer. It's the beginning of the pass/fail nightmare which is modern life. Oh yeah, they vaccinate you here too! Then providing you meet the required test scores, next comes first/second school, and then probably more school, but here's the snag, irrespective of what we have ever learnt in the classroom, it doesn't really matter.

Bible chapter:

The scriptures describe turning water to blood, a plague of frogs, pestilence, etc... All these tragedies are described in Exodus, a part of the Bible, which is one of those untouchable works of literature. A modern-day divisive quandary, placing interpretation and belief against a multitude of positions. On the one hand it can fuel hatred or distrust. In some circles it can breed disgust even disbelief, but the truth is irrespective of what side of the fence you are sitting on; in the grand scheme of things, it can only be viewed one way!

It's an irrelevance. Our planet has existed with the latest scientific evidence and discoveries for 4.5 billion years. It has evolved and transformed throughout its life from a bubbling molten mass of elements and materials, into the blue dot that we first discovered and appreciated with the photograph taken by Apollo 8 on rounding the Moon.

I think that this was the single most important achievement made by humanity. Showing how small and insignificant we are against the beauty and complexity of this world.

But like anything that humans get their hands on we have endeavoured to destroy it. The point is, we find ourselves currently living in the modern-day equivalent of a world disaster movie. Not a very comforting position to begin writing this book. But I'm certain there is hope, an overwhelming desire to correct the failures of our ancestors and a sense of bringing the average mentality from corrupt narcissistic destroyers to a team who want to be part of project globe.

Well guess what ...Forget the unknown! ...The events I am going to list only cover two years, from late 2019 to July 2021, are also painfully real!

We start with when Covid was first detected.... back of the sofa!

One of Britain's self-indulgent excesses is to be found throughout the Home Counties, where nestled between the built-up towns and cities lies a whole host of imposing, braggart behaviour. Protectively placed mansions and gardens, built to articulate power, position and most importantly wealth. It's like a who's-who of the neighbourhood. A palace here or a stately home there. It even extends in some cases to castles.

Just imagine if you will the jaw dropping sums of money, labour and influence that must have been used to not only finance such vanity projects. But additionally supported the maintenance, and the improvements required to enhance the ambiance of such architectural dreams. This for me is an example of what I call the "Rocky" syndrome, a R.E.M.E. (Army) air-tech colleague of mine in Germany, who laughingly joked how all the senior ranks in the British Army, acted like children playing with their train sets. You might understand this comparison if you've ever seen boys being selfish with model railways. Deciding what goes where and how quickly! But most tellingly who is in charge.

I have visited a few of these sumptuous, opulent countryside retreats, most of which are national trust, but all of them pretentious eyesores and they have always left me with one overwhelming impression. A feeling of sadness and embarrassment, where life for the privileged was placed in unimaginable surfeit. Knowing how the poor domestics lived in squalor. Two stately homes which I have visited that come to mind are Blenheim Palace and the house and grounds of Longleat in Wiltshire.

The reason I have started off highlighting this anomaly is because it is something which recent world events have polarised to reflect how utterly ridiculous, mean and unnecessary humans really is! I mean look around and what do you notice? I'm finding increasingly that everywhere I look, I see waste. Either objects engineered to excess or the manufactured creations of man disappearing into our water supplies.

High-rise monolithic monstrosities like the Burj-Khalifa, the Dubai islands built to mimic the continents, or stadiums built in the Qatari desert nation, with air conditioning to provide comfortable viewing at the football World Cup! Water pollution like sewage, agricultural waste and fertilisers full of phosphates and goodness only knows what other chemicals or washed-out plastic bags and micro plastic polluting our rivers and oceans.

It's something which I think people in Britain are more interested in today than ever before, but why haven't we bothered to address these problems before? It's like everything that Britain has ever had its grubby little hands on across the whole of history!

During this story. I'll address the elephants in the room like the slave trade, human rights abuses of Empire and occupation. Curious how this never gets mentioned during schooling years. It was all about heroes and military success stories, or as I prefer to describe it.

Denial: A very British disease! It's the old argument, where history is only written by the victors.

But why now? what has happened that we have to reappraise the story on how we've influenced this planet. Once again as it has always been throughout history it comes down to haves and have nots. The reason why we allow pollution, like the water supply, is because utility companies that should be responsible are publicly listed, stock market participants, and periodically making dividend payments to their shareholders, instead of reinvesting profits into a cleaner service, It's the money-go-round gone bad!

Dividends fuel the insurance industry, the banks and finally the shareholding pensioners and millionaires. I'm not a Mensa prodigy but even the amoeba know that this is wrong. Rewarding the tosspots at the expense of the planet. Which is why I want the next virus to do a better job!

Let me make something crystal clear, this book is not about politics or national identity or prejudice, look at it as a type of Haynes manual. The engineering guide to your average car or van. This, however, is not by any stretch of the imagination about motor vehicles. It's about my life, a fifty something year old's navigation of the modern world and his attempts at making it all make sense. So, apologies for the first few paragraphs because I have to set the scene for this spaghetti western of insanity and stupidity which is what living on this planet means!

Everybody is aware of the craziness that's dominated the last few decades. Unfortunately, no matter what circumstances we are facing we always have this tendency to bury our heads in the sand and hope that things will get better. Or that the consequences won't affect us! Which is interesting isn't it.

I'm not saying that our current leadership is bad. But just glimpse around the globe and search for that someone who's a standout visionary who inspires and builds hope and confidence in these troublesome days. Do you know someone? Or are you like me, a disenchanted doubter who wants to get off the rollercoaster. You see the statistics don't lie.

We have managed to get through five prime ministers in six years, ever since David Cameron bowed to pressure from his backbenchers demanding a referendum on the European Union. The only good thing to say is our muppets are not the only idiots, even toothless organisations like the UN are effectively a laughingstock, where pariah states like Iran, Syria or most recently Russia can pick and choose which resolutions apply to them, and disregard anything that they find uncomfortable!

I think the best way to address the issues of the day, is to do something Pythonesque, criticising normal world behaviour for what it isn't! Which means acting like the Monty Python "upper class twit of the year," contestants, a Python-Cleese spoof of what happens when you allow the entitled moronic off-spring of the rich and brainless minority to rule or shape policies in a country or organisation.

Which is quite ironic considering it's exactly this set of circumstances that have allowed Britain to be forced to leave Europe or have overseen the banking sector meltdown of 2008. Or oversaw the financial assistance during the covid pandemic, without any checks and balances. Just on PPE alone during the lockdown our government handed over £8.7 billion.

Something made me immediately compare the BBC with the government of today. It's all about image not substance. It's something which goes back to the Conservative/Saatchi & Saatchi election campaigns, when they used the slogan "Labour is not working."

The key was not the narrative itself. It was how the party was perceived. The same noises which have been coming out of the BBC for years. The difference between back then and now is, they have installed party friendly sympathisers onto the board and select the Director General, which means as an impartial and independent organisation it cannot be trusted. But by the same token, neither can the Conservative Government!

Oh, hang on, who are the financial backers of the BBC. Are they aligned to political parties? Of course not, it's the license fee. A tax on the public which raised nearly £3.8 billion pre-pandemic. It also means that we are the employer. So, what infuriates me the most is why during recent monumental events the headlines have become doctored.

I think the average license fee contributor has little or no understanding of how much under the counter dealing goes on with their national broadcaster. Just for example a successful program like Top Gear is sold worldwide, it even has its own branding, but does any revenue go towards making a decent morning news program?

I'm obviously not privy to the answers to these and hundreds of other questions, but what I do know is that this broadcaster is nothing more than a public relations service. Broadcast throughout the world and attempting to promote us as a progressive and inclusive nation. What a lot of bullshit!

I returned to the UK in 2008 and couldn't understand how the BBC was even allowed to continue broadcasting. Especially after scandals like Saville and other implicated presenters. Even A-list talk show host Noel Edmonds made a comeback after his Mr Blobby house party disaster. It just goes to show how every cloud has a silver protective lining!

But the worse thing is how terrible the modern programs are! The BBC news is dumbed down and patronising, it's so awful it reminds me of the old Soviet era national broadcaster Tass! Everything is on a loop, with virtually no substance or content. Which is interesting as BBC World News. The programme which is screened worldwide is a very fair, balanced and informative station. Let's do a comparison. During breakfast television in Britain the weather is broadcast for hours and all the presenters on both television and radio are clones, with zero personality, every topic is airbrushed, and bleached, down to the minimum level of entertainment.

With everything seemingly designed to prevent criticism, or cause offence. Which is quite ironic because It's offences that caused the Yew tree investigation. I'm actually lucky that I didn't get chosen to go on Jim'll Fix It.

The presenters also appear to be working to a directive. For example, the lady who does "Question Time," seems to be continually steering the debate to a favourable position for the Government, and fending off critical opinions of audience members.

Something about these Conservatives which confounds me, was how they recovered post Thatcher! Until one day around 2008, I finally found the missing jigsaw piece. It was just after David Cameron had been elected. I was working for EasyJet then and had just done a Glasgow and back. The return to Bristol was quite full and I knew we had a VIP on board. Because there was a close protection officer packing a weapon. What then was so special about this? Turns out it was Liam Fox, the Tory MP for Somerset. Let me remind you of a few things that are related to this story. At this time, he was the Shadow Defence Secretary, so he and all the other cronies were just trying to make their case to becoming the next governing party.

Labour's Gordon Brown was Prime Minister, but he was falling behind in the polls, then fast forward to the 09 expenses scandal, in which Mr Fox, was asked to pay back some money allegedly over-claimed, yet incredibly he maintained his role in the Shadow Cabinet!

This was followed by the election victory of 2010, and he was made Defence Secretary under Cameron until he was allegedly forced out for allegedly granting access to a close friend and lobbyist. But he wasn't sacked! He resigned. Meaning he kept his benefits, influence, and most importantly his Parliamentary powers.

Answers on a postcard: But that is just my point, who do you write to or contact that you think might make a difference. I personally would elect someone like Stephen Fry or Frankie Boyle, because (a) they would have the common sense to make intelligent choices. (b) they would not waste time calling a spade a spade! It would be extremely presumptuous of me to list the areas that have been failing in world affairs. But I find it unavoidable to say what I fear is just over the horizon. It's like the old mission impossible episodes where the operation tape will sell destruct in a matter of seconds. The trouble is, it's not a matter of IF anymore. It's about WHEN, we are still navigating the challenges of Brexit, energy and the cost-of-living crisis (thanks to the war in Ukraine), and a multitude of different issues created by the lockdowns around the globe during Covid.

What have we learned? Personally, I have discovered that every facet of normality in not just Britain, but also the whole world is screwed up. For starters let's look at education! We are taught how valuable a sound knowledge is. In fact, people are cajoled into thinking that qualifications are the ultimate measure of success, but what did Covid demonstrate? It taught us that the World Wide Web is more than a school substitute. Students were pretty much left to the internet and computer learning.

Now I can't dispute that the overall quality of their study can be compared favourably to a classroom or university lectures per say, but one thing I gleaned from this unusual experimental set of circumstances was that the overall results and performance seemed to indicate that schools are essentially obsolete.

So why don't we all just take that leap of faith and focus on remote learning? During the lockdown I've learnt by watching web tutorials, how to cook and paint, I'm now a wannabe chef and artist. Not bad for a disabled beginner! My bread is amazing (thanks to Jamie Oliver!)

Why does this matter. As anybody who knows me can testify, I am Apolitical. It's one of those things which really pisses me off. We (as in everybody on the planet) have got to make systemic changes. Which means we need to ditch this perpetual charade of voting every few years for carbon copies of the failing predecessors, there is always a big sales pitch which ultimately leads to a two-horse race. With the establishment on one side and the left on the other.

During an election campaign, the public are reminded that going to the polling stations is essential or a duty in fact. Because their vote counts. It's supposed to be a statement of conformity, hope and optimism, a confirmation that our democratic system is the fairest system which honours the sacrifice of millions of people, either those who died in the world wars or by the losses suffered by civilians who were killed as "collateral damage"

But here's the catch. It doesn't matter if you live in Bristol or Kuala Lumpur. Just putting a tick in a box is not going to make a blind bit of difference. In many ways it's comparable to the examination classrooms of your schools. You might have a good day and collect the necessary marks to achieve certification, but in the grand scheme of things, what are you qualified to do?

What is your accomplishment?

It's the hamster on the wheel syndrome! What goes around comes around! The next set of politicians will eventually ball's things up again, like the last lot. The students with their new certificates and degrees can occupy meaningless positions of administrative authority. It's a continuous and repetitive cycle. Where one bunch of egotistical power mad despots and autocrats get to play with their train sets all over again. What I suggest everyone does, is to pull up on YouTube the twelve tasks of Asterisk. A 1976 animation spoof of the twelve tasks of Hercules.

It's a light-hearted look at how unimaginative and deranged the ancient world must have seemed, giving Hobson's choice missions to unwittingly hoodwinked participants. The only thing I want to highlight however is task 8, getting a form A38 from the Roman administration offices. An impossible process which has all the similarities of navigating modern day administrative centres like the local council or government departments. The only way to achieve this goal was to confound by using confusion tactics. Thus, satisfying Caius Tiddlus!

Time for another elephant in the room comment:

Why is it possible for someone like me to navigate my way through all the disinformation and smokescreens of this societal problem and yet the mainstream media totally bought into the narrative? It's strange isn't it, whether it's print media, radio and television they always seem to stick to the official propaganda. Supporting the democratic and academic process, despite knowing how flawed the system is! Just look back recently to Liz Truss and Kwartang to see how that panned out!

Because I no longer live abroad it's hard to gauge the impact of things like Brexit, Covid, or the other major changes to relationships with our neighbours in Europe. What I do know is how much stupidity has been demonstrated by the UK population and the Conservatives. But hey it's what you must expect from a dysfunctional political dinosaur of a parliament. The one thing I do know about our European neighbours is they think that we are barking!

I mean how many nations do you know that are governed by antiquated laws and protocol, where a minority vote share decides who governs? Quick question where was Boris Johnson when Covid broke? The reason I know this is because it was a warning sign, but it wasn't enough for the public to query!

Yet, moving on from this tangent, what is the best solution to this dilemma? Move away from all obsolete study. Focus attention to learning twenty first century technology and ring fence everything to do with green compatible industry. The most obvious of which is power generation from renewables and green championing programs.

Things like massive scale solar and wind farms or offshore tidal power plants. I'm impatient to find out why this changeover of technologies took until the Ukrainian crisis to expedite the transition! There are also many savings to be made, by scrapping traditional professions and jumping into the twenty-first century?

Scrap all of the old post-graduate professions. Slim down on the ancient subjects studied and for goodness' sake for once and for all, discontinue and ban anything to do with archaeology, or am I the only one who gets offended by reading about or watching some wasteful research projects on ancient history? It was a long time ago, lots of people died! Do we really need to dig up the bodies? "Utter bullshit!'

I'm going to divulge the secret for life's advancement now. It's not about how many qualifications you have. To which I say to all the professors and life students. "Your free lunch is over!" It's actually about who you know. I've been privy to business lunches!

An old BBC sitcom called "The Young One's," has a classic argument about the exam system in the UK. In the sketch one of the leading characters called Neil declares, "verbatim regurgitation is against my principles," or (word for word repetition without comprehension), is against my beliefs. To which Rick replied, "I wanted you to test me, not throw up on me." (Joke).

It seems silly now, forty years after watching this as an impressionable youngster in the final year of secondary school, but it got me thinking.

Yeah, what a ridiculous set of compulsory tests these exams are. It doesn't prove anything other than the recollection of random facts. At the time I was dealing with complicated home issues, so I literally gave up on the whole thing. Do I regret it? No not one bit. You see, I truly believe some people thrive in dusty, stuffy rooms, with chalk-stained blackboards and teachers. NOT ME!

It turns out that I was right all along. It's all about positions of authority, control and influence. A classic example is King Charles who took history as a topic at university. Q. Is history actually a thing? It's the ultimate level of nepotism. Being spoiled in the Palaces on the one hand and being gifted a qualification on the other. Because everyone in a family knows their own story! You can draw comparisons with people who major in geography, or any other soft fields. As opposed to the sciences and mathematics. These subjects scarily enough are often deciders in future career paths. Even though they are about as relevant to modern life as "Thomas the Tank Engine, or Peppa the Pig!"

I recently watched Fry & Laurie in a sketch where the merits of democracy are highlighted. It makes quite compulsive viewing in today's world. With Stephen Fry defending our system to a busker, stating it champions freedom of belief, thought, and speech.

He rants about how Communism is the enemy to our democratic process, something quite topical and tragic especially in the current state of world affairs. But for me the key point of this joke is how programmed we are to think that we live in a fairer society, where the organs of the state are not controlling or prejudiced, and the police or military are not used for personal gain. Military YES, Police NO!

Just think back to recent history. Black Lives Matter protests or the environmental movement with our citizens glueing themselves to transport hotspots or Sarah Everard marches in solidarity with the behaviour of some of the Metropolitan Police. And didn't it escape people's attention how the reporting of these events was dumbed down by the media? Other examples are the marchers against vaccination or lockdown, it's a massive list, but I'm sure you get the point. It's like the film "The Matrix!" But the difference is, this isn't fantasy or fictional it's actually happening, right now. "SCARED!"

When you consider that we live on an island. All I'm going to say is xenophobia, asylum seekers, queuing trucks, massive economic losses. It's one of those scratched vinyl records that keeps going on and on and on! And then of course the Queen dies, and Russia invades Ukraine!

Every single time a new suit is invited to the Palace it starts a whole chain of events, culminating in the swearing in of the new ministers and more importantly their civil servants. It's like the faceless board of a university, or the non-executive directors of a FTSE-100 company. They're all swimming in the same resort spa, all making the same pop-star wages. Here's the deal! No one is willing to challenge the status quo!

WHY? Because it's easy money... and you are too cowardly!

It all revolves around the education process. I personally don't give a toss if you think you are Liberal or Green, Conservative or Labour, Social Democrat or Communist, because those party representatives are just like the students who want to wave their qualifications post-exam. Except students do the waving in front of potential employers whereas politicians do the waving at election time, in front of the general population.

But my point comes down to, who is really better qualified? Do you honestly believe that all students have to wave their bits of paper at employers? Or every parliamentary seat will be equally contested? Our whole system sucks!

During the recent post-Brexit years, I was reminded of a very poignant speech given by (Thatcherite), Conservative, Lord Tebbit on15th October 1981, telling unemployed people to, "get on their bikes." It showed how irreconcilably flawed our system was then and still is today.

Deliberately motivating people of working age to migrate in order to escape the cost-of-living crisis, combined with the record high unemployment figures and a whole host of other mitigating factors. One of which (the financial crash) caused my father to lose his business, our home and all his possessions.

This throwback to the mass exodus of the 1980's is shout to the "Aufwiedersehen Pet," television series. Which is quite an accurate representation of the times, thousands leaving Britain en-mass. Mostly to English speaking nations, but also to other countries with sunnier weather. With two key differences in their motivations.

You see up to this point British people were relatively reluctant to travel abroad. Favouring very little change to their lifestyles, then suddenly there was an explosion of new destinations. But the problem with this massive shift in attitudes created a three-tiered system.

The first tier was for the rich and entitled who had always had foreign holidays. In fact, most of them were already owners of foreign properties, companies or both. They favoured a more culturally beautiful lifestyle, choosing the less trodden and more expensive exclusivity, things like New Zealand, the Caribbean. Indian Ocean islands or maybe tours of ancient civilizations like Machu Pichu, temple ruins in Vietnam and India or the history and food of Italy.

The second tier could afford places like the U.S. (Disney & Hollywood), or Spain and Greece for the sun and the booze. At a push you may have seen them on wine trips to France or beer tours to Germany.

The third level was cheap package holidaymakers, with zero tolerance for foreign customs and traditions A large slice were 18-30 holidays, with very bad manners, excessive drinking and eating only British food was standard and no effort made to learn the language and culture!

It's something that has been increasing steadily since population density began to rise. or even those who sought employment overseas. This was the moment two splinter groups departed from Britain for good. Lots of people saw how they couldn't afford the UK anymore and bought property abroad.

A large portion of these migrants unbelievably were coal miners and council house dwellers, who had been gifted their properties by Thatcher as a buy-off to compensate the closure of the mines! Also, pensioners who had lots of savings and a healthy monthly income from their pots, who bought holiday homes and indulged in a double lifestyle. Occasionally sunshine, or family when it suited. Unbelievably lots of these muppets voted for Brexit! Probably the ones that bought Cornish fishermen's cottages.

Right quick question. How do you evaluate a person's achievement in study and the actual usefulness of whatever job they perform. I have a theory surrounding this very contentious subject. So, with the recent world events in hidden focus, let's take this subject head on. There are three crucial criteria to consider in this direct comparison.
1). Does the profession or qualification show itself to be of irreplaceable importance during a pandemic like covid (health emergency), natural disasters like the climate crisis, including earthquake, floods, wildfires and catastrophic weather. Or the everyday services and support agencies which provide essential help in national operational/security needs.
2). Does the profession or qualification have high potential importance, for example am I going to make a breakthrough discovery or has my job the potential to become of international importance or significance?
3). Would you like fries with that?

You see just by placing these three critical areas of focus, we can see how many professions are surplus to requirements. What about you. Did you do anything meaningful in this period?

I was reminded today that there is a classic measuring instrument when you classify employment. Its job over calling syndrome. Because apparently people with a calling are much more committed to their profession! To which I replied, have you seen how post-Brexit and post-covid our government treats doctors and nurses? (May make people who have a calling, get themselves MRI or CAT scans!)

The problem is something that commentators tend to oversimplify. But like a chessboard with just a few pieces still in play. It's cat and mouse trying to dot the eyes and cross the tee's, the pyramid scheme is failing, and no one wants to take up the slack. The wealthy and powerful have got their money, yachts, or property. They've also crucially got passports their second country and residency! If you take away one thing from this paragraph, think migration!

I'm sure many of you have seen this brewing from the late 80's, the ironic situation where every year tens of thousands have been emigrating. Or at least laying down the foundations by purchasing the foreign property or buying time share options.

I once had a chat with a soldier from the Duke of Wellington Regiment. The majority of whom were Yorkshire based. He was one of those people looking to go, because as he put it. "My area is overrun by foreigners!" I had left in the early 90's, so I dug a bit deeper.

"What makes you say that?" I asked. He just grinned and said, "It's a result of our sodding Government's foreign policies since 1991." I knew exactly where he was coming from, the moment I got home to visit my folks. But hold on a second who thinks that being English born somehow places you at the front of the queue, for anything?

Because I can assure you it doesn't. We are a nation of immigrants. Granted some of us can trace family roots back generations. The truth is that the employers here always called the shots. If you look back through history it was firstly Knight's then the duke's and landed gentry until finally today, we have ended up with a strange combination of parliamentarians, CEO's, rock stars, and footballers!

It's always been about the race to the bottom, "What's the least I can pay you!" Trouble is nowadays the people have got higher expectations. They want XYZ! Which is something our leaders have always been foolishly promising. But they can't even provide basic healthcare!

The keyword here is growth, but ask yourself this, can our planet really oblige? If it was down to the human race, we would drain the earth of everything, killing everything including ourselves and in a few years, we would leave behind a sewer. Oh no correction, we have already created the sewer. Do you feel embarrassed yet? I don't know about you, but I'm convinced that we (humans) have to change and bloody quickly.

We have all got expectations and hopes and dreams, however I think that March 2023 will go down as <u>the</u> one that broke the camel's back. It has become the levelling jewel in the crown of not just royalty and privilege but most tellingly the entire worldwide community of disenfranchised or asylum seekers. Everything surrounding normality, conformity, and good citizenship has been seen as the lie it really is. People are caught in a shit storm of increasing interest rates, mortgage rises, sky-rocketing energy costs.

The so called "cost of living crisis."

In Britain, June 2022 there were 230,000 no fault evictions, and homeless and street sleeping has increased to unprecedented levels. Everyone has a scapegoat, suspicion or theory, but the truth is painfully obvious. Just look at the set-up of our democracy. I've always viewed it as a failed system.

British people have been sold a dream. Own house, create family, get good job and build a lifestyle. If you have faith and belief everything will work itself out. You don't have to be a rocket scientist to know that this is bullshit.

I've seen the dreamers, taking their two children on foreign holidays twice a year. Leaving the pet dog or cat in the kennels. Parents live in the south of Spain because of the weather and their pensions cover the expenses whilst their two homes are converted into polite conversation pieces for dinner parties. Or they are using the additional income from Air B & B to fund the next cruise. Ring any bells? Because believe me when I say I've witnessed this.

The majority of these aging slipper-wearers have been mollycoddled their entire lives. It's all about perception. Because people throughout the world are driven to one key objective. Get me to the next level, but here in the UK, its support you old farts!

Bold Statement:

Here's a truth many of the world populations are unaware of, but I want you all to read, George Orwell's 1984, at the end of the story you can draw your own conclusions. There is however one especially telling giveaway. "Big Brother" is always watching!

Let me explain. Because it doesn't matter if you are in Britain the U.S, China, or Russia. Every state intentionally or inadvertently wants to have control. I began writing this story about three years ago. Switching from humble recollections about my past, to the comedy and insanity of everyday life, the state of the planet and unprecedented events over the last 4 decades. But what made me think uncharacteristically radically was a science program on the BBC. It was with Professor Brian Cox, postulating about the state of the world. Advocating democracy and also contemplating what if questions!

He hypothesized the, for some, ultimate tests. Are we the only intelligent species in the universe. Should we be trying to play the Star Trek game. "Five-year mission to explore," etc, etc. encouraging the development of future missions to the Moons' of neighbouring planets. Should Musk or Bezos be allowed to explore and inhabit Mars? But he then struck a chord.

A simple but staggeringly important disclosure. Every country has a seed bank! Something I was unaware of. But possibly more importantly there is also a seed vault at Svalbard in Norway on Spitsbergen. Which keeps duplicate seeds from the entire world nations.

It's the ultimate backup plan, against asteroid impact or every other possible disaster scenario. It's been quite daunting choosing a subject to appeal to the mainstream and at the same time be inclusive to everyone, hoping for and encouraging a future world of potential.

I have read a lot of books, newspapers and articles. The truth is we are not the superior species on earth. But even Cox admits it is likely that at some point this Earth will become uninhabitable, and we (if we survive) will have to start from scratch.

I watched another program on TV about the latest scientific discoveries and research. It turns out Einstein and Stephen Hawking were right, black holes are the key to everything. We are in a perpetual rotation. Alive, Dead, Alive etc.

We have all heard of the event Horizon, haven't we? Well just imagine that whatever happens to fall in, doesn't just disappear. Because the older theories hypothesized that not even light could escape. Suppose it is transported through space/time and arrives in an alternative reality! So, use a little imagination and put that into Orwellian context. Makes you think differently doesn't it! This is not an episode of the Big Bang theory.

The next section of the book is a nod to philosophy. Or the nature of knowledge, reality and existence. I don't want to cast nasturtiums about the value of knowledge per say, but. I really do think that we (the people) have been the victims of the biggest heist since Oceans 11 or the Italian job, since we allowed the pharmaceutical companies to make bucket loads (billions) of profit, by essentially becoming the legitimate arm of drug pushing! The modern-day snake oil salesmen!

It's one of those tragic stories that resonates with everyone when a young man or woman is unexpectedly diagnosed with a dreadful illness, but what I find fascinating is how companies like Bayer or Pfizer are championed, with the medical community rallying around them and even politicians jumping on the bandwagon, singing their praises.

Because the patients are rarely at the heart of any medical breakthrough. Big Pharma is very deliberate in this strategy, they also control the narrative circulating along non-invasive procedures and treatments. Well, let me throw a spanner into the works.

You see my mother contracted a nasty illness in her early forties in 1979. It was one of those unknown diseases that the world of medicine had no real answers to, but instead of investing in a supportive therapy programme she was pushed into the hands of the drug dealers!

Anyone nowadays who has been through a neurological disorder knows, that the priority must be an accurate diagnosis and a proper understanding of how the patient is affected with symptoms and triggers. But back in the early 1980's there were no cat scans, or MRI's, it was very much a case mystery.

Where the doctors used people like my mother as a testing platform for goodness only knows what kinds of drugs. My memory for this period is fragmented but I remember her taking drawers full of medications, one of which were opiates. It was like living with and looking at a zombie!

Why tell this? I'm telling this because in 2002 she changed her GP, who stopped all the pills except one. Makes you wonder, doesn't it! Twenty years of bashing in the dark. The only pill she kept was paracetamol!

Q. So why is it that our so-called Health Service has learned nothing for fifty years?

A. It's all about competence. I'm sorry but you are all a waste of rations.

Let's move on with the doctors. Did they prove themselves to be invaluable in lockdown? I don't think they did. I don't want to rubbish their contributions, I dare say they all did the best job they could, but until the vaccine was released, they were going nowhere! The nurses on the other hand were really involved in ensuring the patients were getting one to one care.

So, without wanting to put all doctors in one boat. Let's be honest and fair. I completely understand that doing a doctors training can be fraught with challenges and it also demands a massive amount of commitment to the cause. But apart from the nuts and bolts of emergency medicine or the stress and safety aspects of surgery, what branches of healthcare have a proven track record? Well obviously, as someone who's an interested observer I can give my unbiased perspective of the recent developments in the NHS.

I'm going to start with my personal run ins in the British health service, starting with a NHS dentist, aged 8. I was dispatched to hospital for a tooth extraction. I had a gas anaesthetic, and when I came to, my gums were bleeding like crazy. I can distinctly remember rinsing my mouth for weeks afterwards. It's probably this episode which gave me a wary predisposition towards the scrubs. This soon developed into a distrust as every dentist visit predominately revolved around another tooth extraction. I can even picture an old git deliberately being rough during one exchange, resting his weight on my chest!

My first experience in an actual hospital happened around 79/80 with mum's investigative procedure. It took weeks to get the disinfectant smell out of my nostrils! Now I'm not going to blanket slag off the NHS, because that would be unfair. BUT it hasn't escaped just me, but also the majority of people I've engaged with how incredibly inconsistent, overwhelmed, in some cases incompetent and worst of all unsafe the healthcare NHS is! I'm obviously unable to provide any black and white damning evidence. But what I can do is recount my family's experiences since the late 1970's.

Obviously, it started with mum around 79, but then 82 was granddad's going. I waved him goodbye in Polegate, Sussex for a routine procedure. But he didn't wake up from the anaesthetic! My father's mother was next. Routine varicose vein surgery. Or rather not so routine! Then thankfully we had a break from death. Sounds positive doesn't it. But the problem was both my parents were constantly in and out of hospitals.

Mum got two new hips and dad fought off unusual growths. This was then topped off in 2002, dad was by this time constantly undergoing dialysis and had a fall. He was assessed for underlying injuries or infection, but the doctors missed a head injury sustained in the fall! Then finally 2012 mum went into hospital with a suspected acute bronchitis, contracted MRSA and came out in a box!

I have tried to add my own experiences later in the story, of relevance are my exchanges with Jacob Rees-Mogg my parliamentary Member of Parliament, who I shared my experiences, dissatisfaction and frustration with in 2012. I won't spoil it for you, but sometimes you have just got to be prepared for what I can only describe as a cluster fuck!

The point is when you read about Harold Shipman or Lucy Letby, you kind of get an understanding of how dysfunctional the system in the UK is. It's not a unique or unusual situation either because in different parts of British society you will inevitably come across different failings, some police officers for example, and in my opinion, are a bunch of misogynistic, bent sex offender's, whereas some politicians are expense fiddling fiddlers, television is rife with wrong uns, (Jimmy Saville), but surprisingly the area where I think we are let down most is the public sector. Or to give them a more appropriate moniker, "the state sector."

It's what I see more as the "jobs for the boy's sector," where the higher positions tend to be filled by public school second team players. These tend to be over educated and overqualified Eton, Charterhouse, and Harrow graduates, who benefited from family connections, friends of friends, or the lower talent pool. Whereas the first team are the over-qualified, over educated rich offspring, who know how to hold a pen!

You'll recognise these groups by the giveaway dress code. Lots of tweed and Harrington jackets, drive Range Rovers, and have a giveaway speech impediment, where they substitute sentences for the "yeah," or Boris Johnson style bluster and bluff. Not bright enough for the banking sector or the exchange, but easy to hide away in a continuous schooling position, or research project. The real dropouts tend to circumnavigate the racecourses, pretending to know about form by spending the family silver!

Let's talk about the deadwood floating around the public sector. Not just hospitals, like the managers or administrators? You see right across the "state sector," we have created cushy little hiding places! I don't think highlighting this anomaly is in any way groundbreaking or even remotely surprising, but what I hope is, it creates a new dialogue about who does a meaningful and useful job!

You see I think we (not just Britain) have allowed and encouraged this kind of meaningless employment. Certain groups are drawn into playing the "zero" game. Where accomplishments are scarce, administrative jobs are a cycle of duplication and unnecessary complications. With spurious management positions doing little of significance, except taking up unnecessary and unproductive positions.

People are funnelled into thinking that they are doing a worthwhile and fulfilling piece of work. Because when you think about it, we have just become worker bees in a hive. So, the next time someone asks if you are satisfied in your work. Think very carefully about what your answer really is.

Everyone spends hours devising the best strategy to advance! A situation which can only take one direction. The death of the planet. Just think about it for a moment. We are all desperate for a slice of the pie. (The pie being a little house in the country! Or for those with bigger pockets a Caribbean island), it is a physical impossibility to continually expand, but our governments and perhaps even scarier our parents are all desperate for us to grow. They constantly talk about building more homes and facilities hopefully enticing the younger generations into marriage and family growth. Or is it just me that thinks that this whole conversation is as perverted as the worst porn movie ever made?

Crazy really how certain behaviours or acts are immediately labelled as being disgusting or depraved, if you just glance around anybody who tries to wear the moral superiority look, you'll see very quickly how absurd the whole supposed differences are.

For starters just because you slap on a ring and recite some unbinding words doesn't make you special! If anything it makes you conceited, duplicitous and very much in denial. When I used to take my children to the zoo, one of the animals I was always drawn towards were the wolves. A beautiful creature that was very aware of where it stood on the wild pecking order, an animal with a sense of family and teamwork.

I've seen their cousins in the wild in Canada (coyotes) and they have got a presence. They are also very different from say the gibbon or chimpanzees.

I dare say that you are thinking, where are you going with this? It's simple really isn't it. Human beings, chimpanzees and other ape species will fornicate, copulate and masturbate anywhere and everywhere. Wolves on the other hand won't. So, does that make them better than us? I put it to you that different beings have different behaviours and habits.

For example, wolves and coyotes make monogamous friendships and they keep them for life. Whereas the ape species (including humans) are very rarely faithfully together. Oh, sure they can do the grooming and occasionally fight off a predator or rival, but essentially, it's each man for himself!

Think that we were special?

So, bearing those revelations in mind let's just have a conversation about the inconsistencies within our pair bonding! There are so many different intricacies to do with partnerships it can become difficult to know what is acceptable, what is unacceptable and what is downright inappropriate and potentially dangerous!

I remember my first kiss. It was with a girl called Theresa at Busbridge primary school in Godalming. It was one of those stolen moments of innocence, it was also quite an achievement for me. Because I was not a big mixer in strange company. But here's the deal! This one moment of indiscretion is one of the defining episodes in my life. It wasn't a dare or a bet I was just interested in what the fuss was all about. I think the rock band Pulp have the song I most associate with it, "something changed." Actually, as I write this, I'm reminded that I even composed my first song in memory of it. I like to compare it with taking the first cigarette or a glass of whiskey.

In my eyes it showed a little step towards adulthood! But despite me not sharing the experience with my parents, it was not a gratifying event or fulfilling moment. I had already figured out that winning a sport race or going to London with my bike were by far more satisfying and enjoyable. This all sounds very revelatory or deep and meaningful. But the problem was and still is that society is in this shit hole that's democracy and is very unforgiving and opinionated.

If I had been given a pound (£) every time someone in my presence started spouting about relationships. Marriage and sex. I think I would have become a millionaire! It was literally everywhere, family, friends, work colleagues even during earlier pre-teenage periods of my life, in school playgrounds, sport clubs and the major influence of my younger years. The media.

I used to deliver newspapers from quite a young age, about thirteen. I would get up early and try to read the interesting bits of a morning. Usually the back pages first, hoping Arsenal had won! Which in those days they did quite frequently. But what fascinated me was how my older brother would drag out a copy of "The Sun," an infantile read, which focused on gossip and gutter politics. I used to think "why would you want to see pictures of girls with no tops on?"

It's this little truth that makes me proud of where I was, aged thirteen. However, oh dear, wind the clock forward a year and I was thrust into the world of dating, with all the complications and challenges of the opposite sex. It's something I'm not proud of, but it was the hormones, peer pressure and an inevitability because, every conversation, every television show and every girl I fancied ultimately became a mission impossible episode, with me playing Tom Cruise.

It's only when I look back now that I'm embarrassed and incensed by this national drifting of standards, because what it demonstrates is a blatant disregard for child safety. Where the potential hazards of sexual contact without proper education and understanding of the dangers posed by different infections can be life changing. However, what I find the most demeaning is how our culture has manipulated consent, where "grey areas," have prevailed in the whole suffocating cesspool of society, and we are First World!

Which brings me nicely onto the next point of contention. As I'm writing this today the Metropolitan Police behaviour and culture has become irreparably damaged. A former Prime Minister has been accused of misleading Parliament and the country is flailing around in a pit of misogynistic, scandalous and immoral conduct and behaviours! Well guess what. It's same old, same old, as far as I can see, because during all the time I've been on this planet, British people can't keep their hands to themselves. I guarantee that if you trawl around the Internet, you will find indiscretion after indiscretion. That then throws up two very challenging questions!

Why do we (everyone) tolerate bad and immoral behaviour? Are our girls EASY? Why do we allow our peers (key holders) to police, govern, try and sentence? Are we STUPID?

Surely even the obviously idiotic amongst you must want a fairer system. I've made it clear where I stand on the political section. The police and legal establishment are in league with each other. Which means that you (we) can only force change by adopting a different approach. I recommend the modern-day equivalent of a silent revolution. We have to start by dismantling the "grey area," as it breeds discontentment.

Put the brains in charge. Not the banks, corporations and multinationals. Definitely, not the politicians. Close all official assemblies and adopt a zero-tolerance approach. No three strikes and you're out policy. Let's have a one strike and you're fuel stance. Just add serious offenders to the national grid. No ceremony is required, just the knowledge for those who have been wronged against, that the offence was dealt with fairly and quickly! Oh no hang on! We can't do that because the establishment have put protocols in place to protect against miscarriage of justices.

Which is basically code-speak, for I might be unquestionably guilty, but I have the "get out of jail free card!" What we need is a system that is not like a leaking watering can. Full of holes and subsequently open to abuse by the rich and powerful. Just look at everything that has been thrown up during the last fifty years. Irreconcilable family destruction (of which I am a part.) Forced adoption!

Market manipulation, unimaginable wealth exchanging hands on stock exchange casino culture trading. Which is interesting when you consider who took the hit of the 2008 financial crash! FTSE 100 companies paying eye watering bonuses and rewarding mediocrity with massive dividend payments. (Which is insane when you consider that this includes utility companies, during a pandemic/cost of living crisis!)

Military deployments of a questionable and damaging nature. The first Gulf War was justified, but everything else was not. The London bombings and terror attacks have been caused by political irresponsibility by fighting in an unjustified manner. Oh, and Yes of course BREXIT and COVID!

So where are we with the legal system? I put it to you that what we need is a Citizen Court. Disband the legislature in full and have a jury system that is based on local elections. The foreman substitutes any judges and decisions are all majority verdicts! Because what do we have now. NFFP! (Not fit for purpose)

At least this system would cut corners, at present any obvious situation where guilt is unquestionable, requires a very expensive and deliberately time consuming, verdict delaying public enquiry. A favourite of our democratic system. (Just look at the Grenfell Tower tragedy), dampening down anger, if the enquiry lasts long enough several people affected will have died, it is also a good employment tool for the entitled and privileged. A chance to be a leader and pass judgement. Most enquiry authors are plucked straight out of the pool for "upper class twit of the year." N'uff said!

It can't have escaped the average person that the scales of justice are tilted inexorably towards entitled and privileged. Where friendships and connections between power, finance and position make it difficult for there to ever be any kind of normality. If I swing the clock back towards my childhood, look at what the British establishment were tolerant of.

On the BBC you had perverts like Jimmy Saville, and any people investigated during Operation Yew Tree. Children's television shows like captain Pugwash, which were constantly filled with innuendo and inappropriate activities. There were also programs like "Top of the Pops," which we now know harboured other predators!

The newspapers I read in the mornings were a litany of extra marital affairs, politicians being forced to admit wrongdoing and all manner of uncomfortable and embarrassing revelations, but the one thing that I had faith in was our armed forces.

We had recently during my schooldays witnessed the Iranian Embassy siege conclusion. To plaudits and fanfare, with no glory hunting headline grabbing. Then there was the task force dispatched to the Falkland Islands by our evil Bond villain, Margaret Thatcher! Where despite the inadequacies of their equipment, our military showed why they had our total trust and support. Which is precisely why now, I look back on the 1980's and think. "We saw it then, but we did nothing!" It was a marriage of all kinds of vices back then.

When I took the dog for a walk, I was constantly avoiding pornographic imagery, hidden in the woods or tiny tins of illicit drugs like cannabis and heroin, which deniers placed in tree trunk crevices. My eyes were constantly looking up at the telephone lines and wondering what idiots had thrown their shoes onto these cables, my sister then pointed out to me that this was code for, "drug dealers work here"! You couldn't make it up, could you?

People from countries other than the UK should take this as a warning, it must revolve around, clearly defined boundaries with clearly defined penalties. No exceptions or grey areas! I'm convinced that this is why democracy in Britain is not fit for purpose.

The airline I used to fly for did drug testing one day in the aircraft toilets and found cocaine, I've also spoken to stewardesses whose drinks have been spiked. Now I'd never been offended by or been set against recreational substance abuse. But this all changed one day in Germany in 1989. A very stupid young technician decided that he was going to drink and drive.

I was party to the whole arrest, there was a post-mortem, and a group of senior ranking line managers were tasked to discover if there was systemic drug abuse in the Regiment. So, I spent the next two weeks listening and observing. I'm not going to lie. It was really bad. Which you probably would think, cleaned itself up once and addressed!

But that was just it, it wasn't dealt with properly. The only way I can describe it, is to say it was dealt with the British way. In other words, not at all! Just contemplate what is going on today. Smack heads doing horse tranquillizer, uppers, downers, even iron filings. I'm looking in a fifty-year old reflection. Which my friends are, and why I have no hope for the children. Not in this country anyway. I actually think the kindergarten should take charge! It can't do any more harm.

I'm not intentionally trying to make this story something resembling a first-year philosophy students torment with moral and honour, perhaps because it will never resonate with me, but I think most likely it's primarily the fact that wasting words on pointless discussion is like listening to a gossip exchange between neighbours. I remember housebound moments of that nonsensical drivel and me thumping the family piano, desperate for a pause in the talking.

It's something my old friend Basil Fawlty summed up brilliantly on the series Fawlty Towers when his wife Sybille speaks to a neighbour on the telephone. Women like to call this behaviour, making small talk! Whereas men and in particular Basil would say, "did you get nail varnish on the neighbour's cat!" When situations change dramatically, women are impervious, and they won't be rushed.

I now need to address the rise in violence and crime generally in the UK. I am used to watching and reading about incidents in the media. But when I think back to my last tour of duty, in Northern Ireland I am certain that even there, we had less incidence of this type of brutality. I'm going to make a few uncomfortable disclosures about this, so listen carefully...Back in 1990 there were guns around, but it was minimal. I remember however going back and forth to Berlin to see my girlfriend. You could have picked up anything. The Berlin Wall had just fallen, and the streets were filled with Russian soldiers and East German black-market traders. I went to watch the Russian stall holders.

You want AK47, two hundred marks! (old German currency) it was everywhere. It was literally like watching the fall of Rome. In some ways it reminded me of a game of ice-hockey I watched in Medicine Hat in 1985, that was USSR v Canada, and at full time the Soviets were trading Olympic medals for Levi jeans.

We then have to factor in the Kuwaiti/Iraq Gulf War trophies and the Afghanistan deployment post 9/11. All of which greatly expanded the floating weapons in civilian hands! This is obviously not even newsworthy, because it is so well documented. But I think I have put my finger on why the frequency and hostility of attacks rose so dramatically. It wasn't just these historical world events, or the desperation of isolated populations, nor was it as a direct result of radicalisation of the Arab community because of the illegal Gulf War 2 in March 2003.

What was changing was people's sensibilities, don't forget that film and television for many countries was playing catch-up. So going from Bambi and Snow White to the seismic waves of modern programming was a massive shock for many cultures.

I'm not alone in thinking this either, it's something that was in no way pernicious, it's literally being struck like a runaway train. The whole concept of a gradual progression in material was non-existent. If you analyse popular television series, that were sold globally, even police crime stories were full of violence. God only knows what effect films like Platoon or The Matrix would have. But it also doesn't take into consideration the inherent dangers of the internet, something which has an unlimited number of potential dark spots. There are multi-player shoot-em-up computer programs and live chat rooms with all kinds of violent content. The U.S. has been struggling with this since the 1980's, just look how many schools have been attacked?

People who are living with conditions like MS are not immune to the news... but sometimes we are thrown into the story. Happily, I was never placed into a Gulf War setting. I did, however, know lots of people who were sent, and I recall many conversations about guys who returned with weapons. I think I was that event, and the fall of Communism that has put so much death on the streets. Oh yeah, and combined with digital video games, the film and TV industries, we all see it, but people with neurological disorders don't have the time to get angry.

What does this mean? I'm afraid it's too late to close the stable door. The horse is long gone! The rise of terrorism in the world can be seen as a direct consequence of the failings of the U.S. and its coalition partners. Including the U.K. We had the moral high ground in 1990. But the truth is, no we didn't. Don't forget in 1990 the coalition forces were in Arab territory under invitation. The mission objective was achieved, but like a clique of gossiping housewives we couldn't leave it. Like a dog with a bone, we wouldn't let go. That is a big part of why New York was attacked!

In case you're wondering where this is going. I'm about to explain. Post-war Britain was in shit state. No money, no jobs, no clear plans. Germany was also in a bad way. Completely bombed into submission. With pretty much the same outlook as us. Now bearing in mind that we both participated in the two World Wars, it kind of feels wrong that our royals have kept any public support, especially when you consider that they are in fact a German family!

They changed their name in 1917 (during the First World War) purely as a public relations exercise. Would have been King Edward VIII was a known Nazi sympathizer, but even that wasn't enough for us to get rid of them. Just look now at Prince Andrew and his alleged misdemeanours, or the way Harry and Meghan were allegedly treated. I'm sorry all you royalists. The Queen is now gone, and so must the rest of them!

I'm English born and raised in various parts of the country, but I've also been lucky enough to live and work in many different countries around the world. Which means I'm very fortunate to have seen the beauty of many different countries, and the stupidity in many others.

The crazy thing is, especially now after the public voted for Brexit, we're starting to understand why we must cooperate and work together. It's not rocket science because thousands of asylum seekers are making life threatening journeys to cross the English Channel. I appreciate that this is quite a divisive issue. Point is that even if some are economic migrants they are still looking for a safe place.

We sold our rights to live free of any immigration when Rifkind made his comments or even when the average Joe voted Brexit. But most tellingly when Bush & Blair decided to fight Gulf War 2. Makes you realise how important putting a tick in the right box is, doesn't it!

I am convinced that if a survey was conducted around Britain today, the vast majority of people wouldn't know how to vote ......THE SYSTEM IS BUSTED! No one political group has any concept or convincing argument for the way forward. It's all about sticking plasters, with no one wanting to upset the apple cart. What is needed is drastic change and reforms! So, let's GO!

My entire life has been poisoned with this acceptance of conformity and capitalism. It was started by our grandparents and great-great grandparents, the post war generation, in which the nation's leaders and global organisations strived to create a new normal. But all they created was this modern day "Pyramid Scheme!"

I can understand why people around the globe would look upon the Western countries with disdain and suspicion. On one hand we are championing the behaviour, policies and actions that we want addressed and adopted, whilst in the same breath throwing obstacles and conditions that we want implemented. Put it this way. I don't think anyone should be expected to follow anything that first world countries ask, ever. I'm also sure that this is why large parts of the global community are about to boycott our terms & conditions!

Playing with marbles:

The only reason I have got round to writing these recollections is for me to put my truth out there. I don't think it's unfair for me to criticise the way I have been handled this last ten years, but it is more important for me to make as detailed and reflective an account as I possibly can so lessons might be learnt hopefully reducing any repetition of the mistakes made!

I'm going to begin with a sobering thought I picked up from an industrialist guest who I recently watched deconstruct the last 50-years of failed British politics and economic policies. The hardest part of that little taster was how blindingly obvious it all was.

The gentleman described how one of the biggest challenges of this country was to try and achieve a balanced and healthier economy. One where the average citizen was able to afford a decent living standard. Where wage growth reflected a better representation of hours worked and the social benefits and opportunities that this unlocked. As opposed to the current dysfunctional system of society. Where certain professions and occupations are disproportionately rewarded for just being present or "in post!"

You see I feel disenfranchised, incredibly frustrated with my current situation and I have absolutely no faith in anyone or anything in Britain anymore. I hope daily for the dawn of a radical exchange of power, politics and mentality which forces dramatic changes across our islands. But it won't happen because everything which make up the pillars of society are intrinsically linked to the capitalism which we subscribe to. the corrupt political landscape, monopolies like the banking sector, or indeed every financial system/institution.

I am currently enjoying watching the imploding status quo of the last 75-years. Funnily enough it ties into the death throes of Britain's late Queen. I often wonder if the private conversation of royalty during private audiences have also created the circumstances required to perpetuate the current cluster fuck.

Most important questions in politics:

How are we governed, by whom and from where! It's got so interconnected that everyone is playing a real-life adventure which can only go one of two ways, we either survive and prosper or we sink into the abyss. I have got to the point where I hope that humanity becomes the latest life force that dies out. Extinction is the logical solution. Or am I missing something?

You see we live in such a screwed-up world nothing makes sense anymore. I will try to give my reasoning for this assertion and like any scientific paper I invite everyone to review my findings and claims to establish whether I am indeed making valid arguments or if I am wrong to the point of bordering on insanity!

I will begin with a sporting analogy. I have tried to get my head round the problems we face, and it turns out the answers are always staring us in the face. I have read the hitchhikers guide to the galaxy and my resolution is slightly different from the number 42. It's because in my twisted grasp of reality the actual ultimate question of life, the universe and everything is not the ultimate question at all.

The conversation we have ducked out of for the past half century is so overdue, it's a bit like the utility bills which arrive now like Texas hold-em poker hands where you know you are going to get cleaned out. An attack on morality something which risks undermining the institution of marriage.

Right then, let's kick-off with education. It's one of the pillars of society. Even in the furthest, remotest corners of the globe a level of comprehension dictates your social standing.

So why then does a certificate make a person better able to pass judgment or give the best advice? I'm of the minority opinion that gifted do not always have to be the most qualified. Let me explain an interesting conversation I recently witnessed on the television. It was an attempt to get people talking about philosophy and philosophical thinking. The grounds or subject of the discussion was the following poser. Is water wet? Or does it make things wet?

Which is a typical, intellectual experience. The deliberate over complication of a relatively easy to solve puzzle. I dare say they are naturally predisposed to things which I would appreciate the most and where I would spend the longest in quiet contemplation. I love the creepy crawlies, and I have finally discovered why I identified so much with them. So, imagine if you will, a young boy who was always second best, yeah, that's right, I had an older brother and a younger sister it's life, Jim!

There is something quite poetic about this travelling from place to place by train. In fact, it happens to have been a recurring experience in my lifetime. From those early years chasing after my brother and his fanatical train-spotting hobby. With some of his friends, we used to travel around for miles. I would pretend to be an enthusiastic "gricer" but in reality, I was more interested in the journey and the discovery of places and scenery.

I'm convinced it was this time, which programmed me for my entire life. You see it's not about the destination. It's more about the journey! My greatest trips for the record were. Taking the London sleeper to do the Highlands of Scotland, A fishing weekend in Torquay with a mate from the post office and then a long weekend trip from Germany/Copenhagen to visit a girlfriend, (Tina), but the greatest buzz that I ever had, were two unexpected moments courtesy of the train spotting habit.

One weekend we went to Stratford locomotive depot. It was where the London Olympics were held in 2012, but in my youth, it was a dirty oily bunch of buildings that housed lots of locomotives. On that occasion I had the opportunity to drive a train from out of the shed and park it. Another incredible journey happened one weekend when I got the driver of a train to let me sit in the cab of a journey from Redhill to Hayward's Heath.

For everyone who has always looked sideways on their train travel. I can honestly say that you are missing something. It's the same on an airplane. That's the thing post 9/11, it probably won't ever be allowed to happen again. So at least I can claim that one! Some of the amazing trips I have made are of great relevance to this story. Like doing my ticket recycling. Not dissimilar to the modern-day waste recycling. Whereby I would cycle from school to Milford train station and hunt for discarded pink cardboard train travel tickets. If I found ones to London or Portsmouth, I would board the next service and then go with my bike to have a little adventure.

On one occasion I went to Waterloo and visited the tourist attractions of an evening. Eventually getting home at half ten. Which my parents didn't have any idea about. I was always outside. Either playing sport or watching. I used to go to Godalming cricket club in the summer evenings to watch and occasionally get a pint of shandy. I think it was another of those times where I would do things just to be active. I knew I wasn't like other children, for starters. I was having severe issues with studying.

At the time it was always put down to being a difficult child. But in hindsight and knowing now what I have always suspected. It's obvious I was using all my knowledge to distract from my hidden illness. Welcome to MS, "just hide it!" The first tool.

Whenever I think about Berlin, I always recall that first visit. I'm certain it was six months after the wall was torn down. The city had a buzz. When the whole of the Eastern side of Europe was flooding across borders. On my first day to the centre, I saw some amazing sights. Through the Brandenburg gate I saw the poignant graffiti on the remaining pieces of wall. I saw a single Russian soldier who had the job of guarding a special monument to honour the war dead; just outside of this there was the German Bundestag (Parliament), I viewed the East German buildings with their mirror glass facade.

Obviously, these were some remnants of the old Eastern Bloc. At the local weekend market people were trying to sell you things like commemorative objects from the recent past. Old Soviet hats and uniforms. Copies of soviet propaganda, there was nothing from the old era that you couldn't find. But the big draw was pieces of the wall. I wonder what happened to that stuff. I mean who really wants a random piece of concrete? Just imagine if somebody had died up against that piece of the oppressive regime. Anyway, irrespective of the circumstances that greeted people flooding into the west, there was a lot of hidden historical gems that littered the streets of the now soon to become German capital.

For example, in Spandau the last remaining prisoner from the Second World War, Rudolf Hess, was still locked up. The street where my new friend lived, had an unforgettable name too "Fehlerstrasse," which translates to "Mistake-street!" Something that always makes me laugh, even all these years later. I have lots of great memories from that place. I used to go running whenever I visited. On my initial visit I arrived by car. Navigating the old Berlin corridor with guards still manning the watchtowers and checkpoints. I found the experience fascinating, just picturing how it must have been during periods of tension. But on most of my subsequent trips I would catch the train. A great journey, with just one transfer in Hanover, although it was very relaxing compared with the autobahn!

Also, a clean and comfortable journey when taken against travelling on British Rail. It was during one of my flying visits to my friend that I started to realise just how shit Britain was in comparison, I also began documenting the disparity. During this first tourist visit I started a hobby. Which unfortunately came to an end after I was taken ill.

I decided to go for a little jog. Something I have tried to do in all the European capitals. I ran through the Grunewald Forest and nature reserve one day and finished at the Berlin Olympia Stadium. The iconic symbol of the Olympic Games of 1936. Or as some people like to call it. "Jesse Owens," Games. Imagining the inner fury of the Fuhrer watching a black man beat his Aryan race!! During that run, I began thinking how to make a comparison, life on the continent and the average person in the UK.

Before I expand on this theme I'll give a summary of my travels to this point. Summer vacations to Holland, Switzerland and Denmark during my childhood. School exchange to the south of France to practice language skills and play sport, rugby, and football. We as a family were very private and I suppose in a way privileged. I don't recall any of the other kids being able to detail their foreign experiences. I think most of them would turn their noses up at the thought of eating food from another country!

To get started, let me give you an idea of my travelling up to this point. During my childhood my parents would always take an occasional foreign holiday. The first one I recall, was a camper van trek through France and Holland. I was about 8 or 9 and at primary school. During the entire holiday I was tasked with keeping a journal. Writing about where we were, or any useful

language titbits I picked up. I must have loved the Dutch accent, because everywhere else we went I would do the rolling accent, all the while smiling.

We then went to Switzerland where I found it quite creepy. It got me thinking back then, how many Germans have overcome their prejudice? I can report that they are much better now. It's still a massive problem worldwide. On one piece of protest, I did the unthinkable in my little town. I got a Caribbean friend from St Vincent to run in the Silvester Lauf. Hoping he would win the top prize. Unfortunately, he came about fifth, so no point made.

Now don't forget this was1990 the fall of the Berlin Wall was a millennial event. Incidentally, one which I was happy to be part of. But aside from learning the language and buying my first new car. I was struggling to find a good reason to continue with the military thing. My travelling to the East, provided this timely diversion. That sense of being part of history got my juices flowing again, Nevertheless I began doing the calculation thing. You see, I'd observed the decline of Great Britain If I'm honest, every time I drove off the ferry at Dover.

But realistically it was something I had chosen to ignore and disregard, even as a schoolboy. I experienced my first doubts way back in the 1980's. Curiously enough, around the time Thatcher was at the height of her powers. She'd grabbed headlines in a few high-profile events. The Falkland Islands and the destruction of the Union workforce, but what I focused in on, was the state of the two countries. Germany seemed to be functioning wonderfully. It's manufacturing industries were booming. The likes of Volkswagen, BMW and Mercedes were advancing. Indeed, every consumable you could imagine was being produced.

Every piece in the "white goods" market stood out in the department stores. They also had one obvious advantage over everything British. They were reliable and good value for money. I remember some of the things that my parents were making do with. Everything mechanical was prone to failure. And I recall how Christmas presents every year would normally break down before the holidays were over. It was something that had always puzzled me.

How could it be possible that the country who won the World War, was performing worse than the Germans? My father took me one year to the Farnborough Airshow. Supposedly to show how superior our industry was compared to the rest of the world!

Now I understand how the Cold War, focused everyone's attention. But "REALLY'I mean, C'MON. The more I researched, the more obvious it became. it has all been typical Conservatism's, playing people off against each other. An example of this was the coal miners' struggle. Dividing families to push through their agenda. In my family's case she killed the British car industry and my father's business with it. The same is true of many other industries too. Just look at our train building sector, or the steel industry.

The wealthy and anybody with any influence was collected, pretty much in the same way that the Bork, assimilate influencers and workers into their collective. A reference to Star Trek, the next generation. But the key to this whole real-life drama, is how they have managed to get away with it for so long. It's easy really, when you think about it "an open secret" whereby key players are used in a covert or clandestine manner. Sharing information and knowledge with one ultimate intention. To make money. Allowing the participants within this arrangement to be overpaid and rewarded beyond their ability.

I'm talking about the stock market! It's the world's cash cow. People are selected to occupy boardrooms and management. Not based on ability, but purely to ensure the stock market keeps ticking along. The rewards are obvious, if you look for them. Dividend payments. Or additional share options. I once knew a friend of my brother's, who was made bankrupt one afternoon. The guy was a merchant banker, dealing on the exchange. Well guess what. He wasn't broke for very long, because literally within weeks, after he lost everything, he turned up just north of Barcelona, in Spain. You see it's not what you know, it's who you know!

But against this backdrop a Conservative approach was never challenged? Why. Because the Tories had essentially bought out the Army and Police. Something that I was becoming more aware of, also something which was making me more uncomfortable with every passing day.

I was continually doing short term detachments, one of which saw me thrown in as an auxiliary military policeman. Another was to cover for a small VIP Flight. This was in Holland. Another was helping to organise adventure training in Chiemsee, a resort on the border with Austria. Doing my climbing thing and taking people hiking in Switzerland and Bavaria.

Finally, I got tasted with crewing on board various yachts sailing around Denmark and for two weeks going over to Canada sailing Lake Huron, Lake Ontario and Lake Eerie. My favourite little excursion however was when I got to go climbing and hiking in Morocco. A three-week adventure driving down from Germany through France and Spain and then crossing by ferry into North Africa. I loved that trip for so many reasons. The one I always find myself using as an anecdote is the "Bob" story! Or for want of a more accurate description. One for the ladies?

You see we were using two civilianized Land Rovers. I was driving the lead vehicle in an extremely busy motorway through Lyon, in Southern France, I was surprised to find a French driver suddenly pull over to my side and started making faces at me. After a few seconds I decided to pull over to the hard shoulder and wait for him to come over. To all wannabe dictators that being caught is a life sentence, which I found a very disturbing lesson from our past. It wasn't the fact that he'd flown to Scotland to search of a peace deal, or that he was unmistakably a key contributor to the Nazi regime.

No, what I struggled with most, was the way that participants were treated differently depending on rank. It is something I think, that goes to the heart of every episode of murder. From the beginning of time. So, here's a thought; You kill, or even try to kill, "you die," I mean if a 5-year-old kindergartener can work this out then why can't we?

This is the point where I start my case for treason by the likes of the banking sector, the political parties, the corporate elite and the upper-class families and their supporters and services that basically cover up their crimes and tracks. Ensuring that the myth which everyone inexplicably buys into called "capitalism," is a noble dream worth buying into!

Ticking the box:

The usual suspects have all been wheeled out and interviewed. Now obviously I'm not talking about criminals or deviants, although for what it's worth I might as well be! No, I'm actually in the process of identifying the people in my lifetime who should have been in prison! Some for utter stupidity, others for being a danger to society and in some cases themselves, others committing a dereliction of duty and finally a small contingent of very powerful individuals. Most of whom are rich, and entitled sons and daughters of? You know the sort of people who I'm referring to.

Do you remember those times when you started to write an essay or story? It's difficult, isn't it? Well, this is my contribution to literary history. The big difference with my work compared with everything that went before is I want to do the right thing! I want every man/woman/child to read this and then act accordingly. Either take one for the team, or prove you are worthy to live a useful existence. So, what do I mean by a "useful" existence? Well to understand this we must journey way back in human history.

I remember a project I was once set during a school class. I think the subject was chemistry. We were asked to select the most world changing person or event in world history. I remember lots of the suggestions too. One person tried to convince us the wheel. I supported the idea of the computer.

A suggestion which twenty-five years later I disowned having seen the potential for destruction. I also recognised way back in the 80's the possibility for both good and evil.

In my childhood I used to spend enormous amounts of time travelling on the railway network. Unlike my brother and his friends, I didn't see it as an exercise in collecting numbers, and I fully embraced the idea that I was living a life of privilege. In fact, we as a class chose about ten different answers. The discovery of electricity. Isaac Newton, the internal combustion engine, atomic energy, Albert Einstein, the power of flight, Darwin's theory of evolution, the creation of metal tools.

As I'm sure you'll agree these are all valid choices. I could of course add a large amount of contemporary worthy suggestions. For example, the double helix DNA or maybe Alan Turing or any number of medical discoveries and procedures which have added to the life expectancy of fellow citizens. But what is missing? The answer is the age-old conundrum, "what is the meaning of life?" To which I have the answer.

Because anybody who has the luxury and time to contemplate such riddles is unworthy of the gift they have been afforded! Just allow yourselves the next hour to break down your existence. What have you and your family achieved. Think about it as one of Einstein's thought experiments, and I'm not just talking about your immediate family either. I mean the whole family tree. Who in your family has contributed to human progress?

So, for all the children who are currently walking the walk, I mean of course trudging backwards and forwards to school, I give you the reality check. Because throughout the world hundreds of thousands of ducklings are quacking along to the demand to learn arithmetic and language. Of which I suspect the majority will be in total agreement of and wholeheartedly support. But what about the other nuisances and labours you are also subjected to?

I estimate every youngster is given eighty percent irrelevant teaching and non-factual drivel to distract and frustrate. The goal is always sold as an example of a mixture of higher education required qualifications and the opportunity to join an elitist brotherhood. Just look at waste time to. Just think about how much of the curriculum in any country has been doctored to reflect the propaganda of the ruling class. I could give loads of examples throughout the continent or even the world, but I will start with Britain. Why? Because it's my land, therefore I have experienced it first-hand.

Drinking a potion:

Something unforgivable is happening in the normality we call modern life! I think it's fair to say that we are living in a shit storm. It revolves around the standards and pressures which we have imposed on ourselves due to twenty first century dynamics.

The key change in thinking has been our dance with economics, where growth is everything. We are constantly judged by affluence. The properties we own, the car we drive, the type of holidays we go on etc. That type of thinking is unsustainable. Unfortunately, it's this overindulgent culture and climate that rules Western societies today. I'm talking about the insatiable desire for more.

Obvious club members are the nouveau riche, a tiny fraction of the population who are cash cows. Oligarchs, entrepreneurs or even lottery winners. But this is no blip or unseen behaviour. I, unlike most, know this exists because it's a true reflection of my youth. Members of my extended family were well off. Where home dining was an occasion.

Gatherings like Christmas were championed like the celebration for a prize-winning thoroughbred. No meal trimming was spared. Right down to lavish excess in cutlery or tableware. Even the quality of individual ingredients became talking points, because my folks lived in the old school mentality of "show and tell "image meant everything.

Bragging rights always featured utmost in their faces. Which is probably why I always wanted to have nothing to do with them. So, for me from a young age I have always frowned upon the capitalist mindset.

Our parents and grandparents were probably beneficiaries of Britain's Empirical past. The image I remember quite vividly from my childhood, was visiting a museum in London and marvelling at the beautiful artwork and historical artefacts on display. I'm not sure when I realised how wrong this was. I can tell you the moment that it first affected me. I was in Canada on a military attachment when I spoke to a member of the Black Foot Indian community, who quite graphically described how British occupation had changed their lives and culture. What struck me way back then 1986, was how recently British colonialism was affecting peoples and countries around the globe.

I had many bar conversations about the history of our ancestors. In most we agreed how utterly deplorable our leaders behaved. One term I recall often used by the Cannuks was pirate mentality robberies. To describe how native communities were essentially priced out of their territory. I'm embarrassed how many old families of Britain have profited from the misfortunes and suffering of thousands of communities worldwide.

So, anyone who tries to justify this past, should first research what their parents and grandparents did during those empire and commonwealth periods. Don't forget, the only commonwealth was the "common man's" wealth stolen by Britian's wealthy!

Usually when anybody bad-mouths British history and wealth attainment, they are immediately castigated and dismissed as being "unpatriotic" or "disrespectful" despite the evidence obviously pointing against the defenders of our "little lie." What I find inexcusable however is how the truth has been hidden all these decades.

It's common knowledge in today's world that well placed individuals in the old-world order were to a large degree responsible for the processing and investment of the lion's share of treasure gathered by our forces and companies. I mean just the fortune's gifted by the exploitation of the African slave trade would comfortably fund entire countries in today's market. I don't know for certain my real family estate or whether they are embroiled in this or other financial dealings. Like the theft of land from indigenous peoples. Theft of tribal jewellery and historical artwork. I could go on, but I'm going to leave that up to you. The point is that all those historical fortunes are now gone. It's not that someone who inherited has been careless. Oh no. The wealth still exists, but you can't see it for the trees! It's all spread out over countries and families. I dare say it is also tied up in many a corporation or even a country's transport system.

So why does this matter? In fact, why is it even relevant? I'm inclined to give the abridged version or not answer at all. Allowing you the reader to figure things out, but curiously I don't think you the average lowlife, have the mental dexterity and imagination to do just that! You see my suspicions began in the 1980's when Thatcher had just been helped by the SAS in the Iranian Embassy and the stock markets were loving her ideas for accelerating wealth redistribution!

The problem was not rooted in political ideology and ambitions, although I did find her quite repulsive. It revolved around a quite innocent conversation I overheard at the townhouse of one of my brother's rich friends. They were discussing how his job as a merchant banker in the city was bringing massive amounts of upheaval to everyone in the banking sector!

Unwittingly she had opened Pandora's Box. Playing the stock markets in the UK was relatively new for private investors. It was seen as the domain of pension fund managers or the main high street banks. What the Conservative Party did was to make investment opportunities available to every person. Presumably fearing a backlash from voters because of years of industrial action by the unions, the Tories made a series of concessions to business and opened public utilities to bidding. placing all strategy into the hands of a very limited number of financial institutions.

For the average hand to mouth workers this meant a huge change in cash flow. Everybody was effectively forced into opening-up bank accounts. Which essentially meant the banks and the government could follow debt and fraud simultaneously! I think in hindsight we now realise how bad the decision was. She had given the banking sector "Carte Blanche," to self-regulate, set charges, rates and to prosecute debtors.

Unfortunately for my family it proved to be a two-tiered system. We lost our house, whilst as I previously mentioned, the brother's friend's family, (the merchant banker), went bankrupt on the Friday, followed by a stock market win on the Monday, and then moved to Spain on Tuesday. "As millionaires," no less!

His friend still lives in Godalming, Surrey, so never really got the chance to jump ship! Which is what it all boils down to really. I knew this exit strategy was underway during the 80's but it has been gradually increasing year on year. I'm convinced in the beginning many emigrants were convicts heading for the sun, or countries without extradition treaties. I firmly believe that nowadays it's mostly just individuals and families who have a nice little nest egg. Probably achieved by working in lucrative industries or perhaps wanting to find a better climate for retirement.

Whatever the reason. I think it's essentially just a true reflection on how shit living in Britain has become. But this isn't new or recent. I'm sure it goes back to the Thatcher era. Her governments were ramping up the anti-union rhetoric. In the coal miners' strikes they employed the old favourite tactics, of divide and conquer. In London, the capital was absolutely thriving on the mad dash to privatisation. A legacy of which is still killing the poorest and our nature. Prime example for this were the water companies. A self-propelling cash cow. Doing next to nothing for long term improvement to the drainage, sewerage and river or sea protection. Instead, they have taken the monthly direct debits, paid six figure remuneration packages to CEO's and given shareholders a lovely yearly dividend payment?

The sad consequence of this period in British history is that a vast number of nationals have emigrated from our divisive islands. I'm one of them. But I can honestly tell you that the people who live here now are very different to the ones I grew up with. The quick correlation with present to past is demonstrated incredibly simply by taking a tour of the country. Something I have tried to do as a gauge for my own personal understanding of where the country is positioned. I would occasionally visit my old town and public houses.

A good a place as any to rekindle old acquaintances and friendships. To my surprise there is a massive north-south divide. I visited an old school friend who spent his income trying to get a foot on the property ladder. Which reminded me of the days where noblemen were rulers of mediocrity.

Allowing people just enough to keep them from starving, but in return expecting them to fulfil the menial tasks and demands placed on them without any prospect of advancement. Only in today's world the nobility has been replaced by the banks. It might be appropriate at this juncture to reveal how many expats currently are living abroad! The answer, believe it or not is circa 200 million. Something I can totally relate to. Especially knowing how many of my old colleagues and schoolmates are currently doing just that. But what this staggering statistic doesn't reveal is the WHY?

You only have to glance out of the window to answer this question. However, I'm more of the opinion that during the last 50-years we have experienced a transition. From world leader to the dustbin! It actually fits quite perfectly with British culture and the historic failings of virtually every aspect of our two-tiered system.

A classic example of the haves and the have nots. A sad future for frail and vulnerable groups, or the world's indigenous tribes and ethnic communities, but I recently stumbled across a very interesting discussion about the direction of human dominance. Unsurprisingly it highlighted the usual suspects in the global premiership table. It seemed a reflection of mindsets in the "First World Nations." Incidentally a term I find offensive.

It's a direct extension of previously tried and tested methods of "development," which, if you think about it. Is nothing more than feudal system 2.0. I doubt 10th or 11th century Kings and Nobility would have anticipated their power, wealth and influence could survive intact over a thousand years. Although the arrogance of royalty has always seen itself superior, so maybe that's exactly what they did think.

In England's historical past "Ye Olde Times" seems like a turn of the page. Where the ruling class' had serfs and peasants occupying the lower echelons of society. Today is the same, except we have Chav's and Dogger's. A blatantly rude and dysfunctional lower section of society, intentionally kept in low paid settings. Doing the country's dirty work! Nowadays however, it is immigrants who frequent the minimum wage kitchen.

Retrospectively the Britons helped discover, invent and developed the Industrial era. Accelerating past the stone age, to glimpse in wonder at the technological age, with aeroplanes, computers, high speed trains, but to what end? Another English-speaking nation used this era to become a world leader in forward thinking and innovation. So, you see already in the 19th or 20th century we lost the title of leader. I think the phrase they use for Britain now is noteworthy or admirable. Whatever the description used is, essentially, they mean "also ran" a term denoting a horse in a race that doesn't finish in the top three places!

Anyway, I have heard that the Americans, Chinese, and a very rich individual has decided to try and colonise the Moon. Probably one day hopeful of the red planet. What makes this incredibly interesting is it might signal the end of Nation states? I understand the adventurous nature of humans. I have climbed, sailed, driven and flown in various countries and cities. But apart from the actual thrill of the trip what is there to gain? Personally, I think it's the male egotistical mindset. It's the planting of the flag. Or for most men, it's the act of penetration. Another tick on a list of conquests. aren't we pathetic. Or it's the start of a new generation of exploration. I mean, who knows we might swap Europe or Africa with "Muskville," or "Bezosland," You heard it here first!

Isn't our culture's classification by class, insanity, just a metaphor for the human race? Compare us to creatures with hive mentality. Or perhaps the ants in a hill colony. Scurrying around. Serving only the Queen. Remind you of Britian's Royal Family?

An obvious comparison, but after watching highlights of the spectacle that accompanied the Queen's funeral or, the inauguration of the new King. Once again, I can honestly say how embarrassed I was to be witness to such an overindulgent ceremony. Of course, displayed on television with the pomp and fanfare that usually accompanies occasions like the opening ceremonies of the Olympic Games or the football World Cup.

But what people forget is, this is nothing other than a massive PR campaign. Now obviously we are selling this as a historic event. But actually, it has about the same draw factor as a new rollercoaster at Disneyland or the premiere of a movie! As an ex-serviceman, I know how much fucking about this causes for serving uniform wearers. It's the same for the Police and all emergency personnel. Every year we do it for remembrance, something I support BTW but the expense and the hassle for two people? During a cost-of-living crisis? Thousands using food banks and sleeping rough?

In many ways I'm reminded of that famous book by Lewis Carroll, where every little chapter or paragraph gives an insight into the crazy non-fictional world of being British. The Tea Party! The hookah smoking caterpillar junkie! An apparition of a talking cat! A rabbit with a time fixation! Tweedle Dumb and Tweedle Dumber!

Then of course a totally control obsessed queen, who runs around screaming, "off with his head" or using the heads of flamingos to hit croquet balls. The craziest part of this, is how much of it is true to life. But going back to my original point about our classification of class, the only other countries that adopt this fixation of a particular person or family is probably the Dutch, Belgium, Denmark or perhaps a dictatorship.

I was convinced that we were destined to continue this unfortunate trait. Until that was, I strained the grey, matter during the lockdown. Keeping occupied primarily like everyone else, bits of gardening or painting. Occasionally flicking through old photographs and albums. I turned to my Canadian memories and quite unexpectedly discovered a photograph taken in 1986. It showed the trans Canadian Highway at the Athabaskan Glacier.

For years that image came and went from my interest but on this occasion, I remembered what it was that made me take the picture. I'm pretty sure it was my first encounter with Global Warming. Lots of marking posts, showing how much the glacier was retreating. This might seem a little scary when you realise the amount of time it had taken to disappear, but confronted with the truth, we're forced to understand our planet's dynamics.

Our scientists have researched the origins of life. Occasionally revealing answers or possibilities. But the researchers studying ice ages around the Rocky Mountains found a significant tit-bit. They discovered the world has experienced five Ice Ages. So given this rock is 4,5 billion years old. That's every billion years or so! Sobering isn't it. But what this also tells us, is in the grand scheme of things "what goes around, comes around!" Which leads me nicely to the following point. When looking at the big picture, what does a long dominance of humans mean for the world? My initial impression was potentially a disastrous outcome. Don't forget you have to accept the consequences of Homo Sapiens on the world's ecological and environmental landscape to understand. But given how young a species we are and knowing how frequently the planet has changed from hot to cold.

I don't think it matters! I mean it could happen tonight, or because of the de-forestation, tomorrow. The increase in volcanic activity suggests that we might have an extinction level event sooner rather than later! I also believe a meteor shower is long overdue!

Now obviously I don't know long term. Quite frankly nobody can. But I think it's fair to say we dodged a bullet during the recent pandemic! I've been anticipating a mass dying event for a while. Especially when you consider how we treat it like a toilet. It's going to take a massive change of direction by everyone on the planet to become worthy of a second chance. Just become a neutral observer and decide yourselves. Is there any reason to believe humans are capable of being guardians?

I can almost guarantee somewhere tantalizingly close to you, there is currently an unusual crisis underway. Whether that's famine, conflict, global warming, natural disaster, even those unspoken unpleasantries like pollution, animal cruelty, mass poisoning by chemical firms, (pesticides, veterinary medications etc.) overfishing, over dependency on man-made products like fertilisers or farmyard chemicals. Inexcusable agricultural practices, plus the real elephant in the room. Human reproduction! I think that should be enough to get you thinking. 8.5 billion reasons in fact. I personally don't want the current status quo to continue, I mean what good have we ever done?

So, here's the off/switch and it's something we can all do! I'm talking about the solution that was offered in the film "Brewster's Millions." An act of dissatisfaction! In the film it involved voting "none of the above," a simple but clear message of unhappiness. Now obviously this alone would never translate into real change But, you never know, maybe somewhere out there is a visionary individual who believes he/she has the answers.

The supporters of some premier league clubs show their anger and frustration by turning their backs on the players. Another well intentioned, but ineffective protest attempt. I'm noticing a slight escalation recently in Britain with mass protests and marches by supporters of Black Lives Matter! Or a very well organised and supported rally against the Metropolitan Police, caused by the death of a girl by a serving policeman. Getting closer to civil disobedience though has been "EXTINCTION REBELLION.' Which goes to show how things are gaining momentum.

I predict the next few years will see a massive increase in violence and protests. Which is why all the big players have been systematically syphoning off their money and relocating to places like the Caribbean. To whom I wish to say, "you are going to die." It reminds me of the Great Train Robber, Ronnie Biggs, who absconded to Brazil, only to return home to jail.

Our problem is we are desperately looking for the comfort factor, by which I'm referring to the ladder syndrome. Most people I think, probably understand this principle. A very human process. It occurs throughout the world and affects every aspect of life. People are constantly collecting! I am reminded of my childhood when disproportionate amounts of my free time were spent looking for the next Shangri-La. I'm referring of course to the next trend or mania.

Which for me was train numbers, football stickers or photographs. Not the Tibetan Utopia, or some other earthly paradise! Although that's what people are collecting nowadays. It's this expansionist insanity, desperate for the best possible location, desperate for the most beautiful male or female. Desperate for the car, the jewellery, the clothes, the kitchen, the children. I'm referring to legacy building! But STOP Think about it. What is the point of all this narcissistic nonsense?

I have my suspicions on this, awkwardly I believe religion and the state have promoted consumerism a disease fuelled by one-upmanship, it's made us slaves to wealth. I'm not talking regional either, this has now become an international phenomenon. It's Want, Want, Want! Even the kids in Saharan Africa, pursue the latest football team shirt. A tragedy of biblical proportions. Part of me is desperate for a cure to illnesses and an end to poverty and hunger! However, the inner voices in my head are shouting. What's the fucking point! A classic upper or middle-class affliction. I'm going to be controversial now. Because I'm not sure anything would make a big difference anyway. Especially when you see the effect of global warming.

The area of the world that can sustain life grows rapidly smaller. In fact, I'm rightly concerned that helping these struggling nations will eventually make survival impossible. I mean, work it out for yourselves, today is 2024. Currently there is a massive amount of social wandering. Half of South America wants to get into North America. Half of Africa wants to get to Europe and the remainder of the population wants to get anywhere but the place they are currently in. What we understand from world history is the effect on life due to catastrophic climate events.

I have already mentioned the 5 previously unknown ice ages. But there is a lot more potential for destruction. A feasible possibility would be for a massive opening in the earth's crust. A cataclysmic volcanic eruption or perhaps even a ruptured atmosphere. The fact is human beings are not the indestructible beings we love to believe we are. Indeed, we are extremely susceptible to minuscule changes in atmospheric conditions. But you know, what the hell.

Earth is being systematically destroyed, partly by fatally flawed mining and extraction methods. Partly by environmental destruction like deforestation or pollution and obviously partly by climate change. So, when you think about the comfort factor, maybe think about the impact your short-term selfishness will do to the planet. In fact, here's a proposal. Anybody who wilfully causes destruction to the world should be executed by being nailed to an ant hill! Quite fitting don't you think.

Joined-up writing:

Which leads me nicely onto the act of joined up writing. I dare say a vast proportion of our fellow men and women are quite skilled at the writing of essays or stories. My old English teacher loved setting us homework to improve those talents! Which is perhaps why I am now questioning the purpose and importance of everything? I want you all to have a long think and work out when you last composed a letter or something where you physically put pen to paper? The answer of course is it doesn't happen.

The internet has become so powerful and addictive that people are simply spending copious sums on gaming, technical gadgets and applications. With the exception perhaps of birthdays and Christmas. All wonderful advancements in technology and yet they have produced a new threat. Which is apathy! Something truly visible during the pandemic lockdown. With fewer individuals able or wanting to work! Which invites the next question. What is it about this particular generation that changed attitudes and abilities? Intriguing, isn't it? The easiest answer of course is laziness.

Something by the way I reject. You see it's what I want to call the death spiral. I'm talking about exactly the kind of Conservative fuelled nonsense that they have been using all my life. Division and control! I'm not even just talking about British politics either. It's something mirrored throughout the world. Ensuring the pie is divided exactly how they want it to be. But guess what? The youngsters have finally figured it out! Because now with the access to unlimited knowledge and wisdom, they don't need to go through a rigorous examination and studying process. The information is readily available and accessible to all.

For example, anyone with access to the web can cook. I recently downloaded a vegetarian recipe tutorial, which was brilliant! I am getting efficient at this gardening malarkey. I've got cauliflower, broccoli and leaks growing in my backyard. I have also mastered water colours. Painting three classic Italian landscapes.

There is however one distinctly troublesome piece of contemporary computing which our children have got to navigate! The difficulty is going to be channelling it for good or for the right reasons. I predicted all of these possibilities way back in my childhood. When we used to travel to St Pancras station to visit the T.O.P.S. computer system. That was in 1979, the opportunity for immediate access to train information was staggering! We used to get the operator to search the network for certain locomotives or occasionally find out what rolling stock was at which location. I remember on one occasion posing a very innocent question and getting a very sinister response.

I asked "do you think the technology will eventually become an all-knowing thing, unfamiliarity with this particular skill set would probably make you uncomfortable with offering a reasonable answer. But I can offer you an irrefutable solution. Technology that your government has installed across society is currently monitoring your every move. By utilising facial recognition software, they can track you practically instantly. Voice recognition software can pick you out from the crowd, also any vehicle that you climb aboard has 24/7 total surveillance. I'm told it's something introduced after 7/7 in London. Are you worried yet? I'm concerned it is these intruders who silently observe, and I believe may now be responsible for causing a recent escalation of mental health problems with our youngsters.

The other obvious difficulties, with integrating the youth is directly related to qualification hunting! Placed under immense pressure to get outstanding grades in their examinations. Only then to realise that doesn't mean you are top of the tree. Because the West uses other promotional methods. Obviously, it could be attainment of qualifications, but most people have success thrust upon them, or revolves around nepotism, being a club member or something equally distasteful but more commonplace than we care to acknowledge. i.e., the conformity club!

I'm pretty sure you know what I'm referring to. You see human beings tend to play with childhood stories or fairytales. Aspirational metaphors, for a lifetime of plundering or winning. Incidentally literature with introduction to religious symbols and teachings, reinforcing the direction of thinking. Do you really think that giants live on clouds. Trolls are real, or perhaps witches and sorcerers, dragons and fairies exist?

I'm convinced it's our gullibility to the distracting nature of mind control and the way statesmanship has given people the false impression that nothing is impossible! Focus if you will for a moment on the global cinema industry. A multi-billion-pound enterprise. A trade most directed and fashioned by multinationals, the majority of which are Jewish led. Whose mission seems to me to be, distorting reality and encouraging people to believe in fantasies.

Government and Royalty love all that stupidity, a distraction is always seen as a positive. I noticed recently the blockbusters seem to have outer space, aliens or super-humans in their narratives, with concentrated resources spent on comic book heroes!

Well, hello you little muppets. Once again proving that humanity should never be entrusted with leadership. I personally cannot believe that you are that petty and unsophisticated. Guess what! You are? Let's start to destroy the myths and distractions. Almost the entire world population is reliant on the key targets and aspirations our societies have deemed irreplaceable. They form a decisive percentage of performance in our economies. Keeping the motor ticking over.

Most citizens don't realise how dangerous and manipulated this system is until, like right now, when the cracks start to appear in the plaster. Whilst writing this I always find myself side tracked or repeating myself and my thoughts. Here is the more concise version, showing our pitfalls. Let's talk about our financial model, a totally corrupt and ethically bankrupt system. Which even when facing an implosion, or massively questionable decisions, still manages to secure a financial bailout. Protecting all the wrong kinds of institutions and individuals. Surely now is the time to implement a safer and more efficient approach to wealth distribution.

We have played the pyramid scheme for a century too long; the medieval method of barter is outdated and unrealistic. If our fellow man has indeed evolved as we are constantly trying to convince ourselves. Then let's become service focused. Whereby the only currency is somebody's time? It's these conundrums that desperately need solving. Perhaps starting with the banks is a bad idea. It would however be a start. Our political umbrella is broken, so that too would be high on the list. The justice system is obsolete and toothless and needs a rewrite. Healthcare services are unfit for purpose. With so much deadwood you could start a bonfire.

Only a complete idiot would move towards integration into any number of societies or quirky institutions. But this is exactly the type of insanity that is driving the human race. For example, marriage. Home ownership. Civil responsibility. I look at governments and nations globally, with their so-called spiritual leaders. Hiding a culture of misinformation and mind games. Making so called rules and regulations that law can interpret and enforce! Which reeks of marking your own homework? I honestly get genuinely angry at the hypocrisy with all these institutions. Where every failure or problem is resolved by hiding the truth, then instigating lengthy inquiries and court proceedings! Ultimately this never produces justice, and the responsible governments are never held to account. But hey welcome to British justice... "little secret, there is none!"

I have put together a philosophical guide, that might actually work for us all as a starting point. It's all about interpretation. Our higher educational standards should translate into a better moral understanding and practices. Unfortunately, wherever you look, there are chasms in behaviours. People are just plain stupid! There is incidentally a plethora of evidence to support that last claim. Most common demonstration is the internet. Websites like TikTok and YouTube are the perfect example. It's like a perfect advertisement and champion of pro-euthanasia values. Alternatively go back into recent historical events to see how vindictive and nefarious we are as a species!

So, who actually believes that they are worthy? What type of person can put their hands up and claim to be living a worthwhile existence. I'm not going to offer you any insight into how I feel concerning this problem. But what I do know is 99% of humanity are a bunch of wasters. Living purposeless, meaningless lives. I mean who at the end of the day can actually claim to have achieved something worthwhile during their life!

Most people I believe are just grateful to be waking up the next morning. Large sections of society are acting out a real-life soap opera. Playing out mundane events and tasks. Desperately seeking approval and justification for having achieved mediocrity. I see marriage as being the first episode in this TV drama! I'm talking about the effort that goes into completing a series of prescribed and compulsory steps from first contact to death.

I could put my spin on this ludicrous time-wasting exercise. The excitement, the exchanging of vows, the joining of other families and extended families. Ceremonies, visiting friends, new-born, swapping presents, holidays, exchanging vows, flowers, gifts, celebrations. It extends right down to being present at every funeral, it goes on and on... etc.

It's all a bunch of institutional nonsense. It begins with religious doctrine. Circumstances dictate the outlay. But essentially every level of the operation requires a payout to all contributors. No salary can ever compensate for this kind of insanity. But that's ok because every connected family member and the guests of, are obligated to contribute? UNTIL... suddenly during the pandemic they began to understand this.

All these quirky behaviours became more pronounced, and you were able to see between the lines. I'm convinced that many male protagonists have seen through the facade for decades but were persecuted into conformity, wanting to jump overboard. But persuaded otherwise. I can't say I blame them. This is the point where I probably get accused of being a misogynist! Which I am not, but to the females out there, "WIND YOUR FUCKING NECKS IN!"

This got me thinking further, if we are such a waste of space. Which parts of our existential joke should we delete? Or at least have a rethink about. A quick glance at the internet and you find the image of progress. But our advancement is dependent on the acceptance that we all have to expire. I came to this conclusion during the first months of the pandemic.

I was watching television news reports and thinking, wow, what an amazing coincidence. In the initial stages of the virus spreading, I remember doing calculations and estimating how drastically different the planet would look afterwards! We obviously realise now, how far from the worst-case scenario we came. However, for a brief period it looked like our 8 billion, could have become 4 billion.

Just think how incredible that would have been! I began pondering all the unintended consequences of the disease, wondering what shortages would ensue. It then occurred to me that the current levels of stupidity would no longer exist. People would have to adapt to the new normal! If things got really complicated. Everyone would have to revert to what I call "plane crash mentality," each surviving group would have to start from scratch.

I remember reflecting on how we would react if a meteorite struck the earth. Now obviously these fantasies and assumptions have nothing to do with reality, but they did persuade me to reflect on the values that we have instilled into society as benchmarks. For example, why do we allow ourselves to be governed by dickheads?

Everybody who goes through life collecting badges and qualifications is complicit in this artificial conformity. It's an unspoken acceptance that anyone who holds a rank, certification or in some cases position is justifiably the authority for their chosen profession. Which I can tell you unreservedly and unapologetically. They are not.

What evidence they will all say? To which my response will be multi-layered. It will start with the teacher profession. We all have unending respect for those moulders of young minds, DON'T WE! To which I would like to respond with a firm NO!

Just think back to your schooldays and picture how frequently a lesson would become interrupted? My schooling finished in 1982, but I still recall how much of the time was wasted on accomplishing secondary lessons. The classic of course would be self-teaching. Either reading, writing or just staring at Jane Thornton's bra, and badges of honour, is deceiving themselves. I mean, To what end?

Does some certificate make them a better person? Does performing a task or job make them superior? What I would like you to do now, is stop and think. Who has a unique set of skills or can actually say with utter conviction that they perform a worthwhile existence? I'll give a quite poignant example, during the initial stages of the lockdown we were challenged to accept, unless we followed isolation rules, hospitals may have become overwhelmed, and we would reach a tipping point. We were essentially placed under rule 1 of our catastrophic disaster management plan. But when you look back at this time, how effective was the resultant separation? Countries like Sweden didn't even bother with anything other than focusing on the hygiene and sanitation? So, all those overpaid doctors who spent weeks organising a strategy that offered a solution were essentially just tapping into the dark like blind person crossing the street!

I mean think about it. Who is actually performing a meaningful role? During the pandemic it became clear very quickly who was an essential worker! It's something I often think about! Possibly because of how quickly the world was turned on its head. I'm one of those individuals who spent the majority of their time indoors, and in my garden.

Either adding chapters to this story, painting landscapes or pulling weeds up and helping cut the grass. Back to reflecting, those who performed the meaningful work in Britain, were the emergency services, the health and care sector plus transport industries and one or two agencies. I imagine people like the company executives and board directors were given a wide range of responsibilities and powers.

Also, some individuals in government and civil service were allowed access to essential services and information, but by and large the STOP button had been pushed. Occasionally you'd hear of groups that were working from home. Essential field operators went out to ensure the infrastructure remained intact and the rest as they say, is history!

We all, (most of us) respected the quarantine protocols and immersed ourselves in catch up television. and we twiddled our thumbs. It's why we lived through a positive and negative population jump. Individuals forced into shared accommodation in circumstances conducive for breeding, again proving how irresponsible and shallow a race we are.

One of the most important lessons of 2021/22 will be the different types of behaviour exhibited by normal people. Some showed empathy whilst others showed total disregard. Inevitably it all revolved around the decisions taken globally to protect each other. I don't know how you felt about this behaviour imposition I just think it was a lost year. Even if we had ended up with the possible worst case scenario deaths predicted. I don't think people would have been bothered. Eight billion strong and effectively killing our planet. So why the hell should we care? It was on one of those lockdown mornings when I started taking stock of the wealthy Western countries' politics and reactions towards their citizens.

I was embarrassed to see our "so-called leaders." I believe the British response was utterly ridiculous. Worrying insignificances were somehow placed above public safety. Pandering to businesses and multinationals when the focus should clearly have shifted immediately! Only changing course when it became obvious, they were killing off our elderly!

In actual fact, they were killing off Thatcher's capitalist social economy. To which I say, "good riddance!" So now let's take a moment to reflect and assess which segments of day-to-day society are robust enough to sustain another hit from the blue and survive.

Obviously the most vulnerable area of life that suffered from lockdown was the family. Children went months without school or purpose. Internal household ambience suffered through fighting and disagreements. For many groups, this close proximity to each other was an insurmountable hardship. Splitting some families and causing an exact reversal in others. Hence the spike in the birth rates?

Personally, I have been directly affected by this because my caregiver has given birth twice in as many years. It was obvious during this period that everyone who occupied a position of power was an absolute liar, failure, charlatan or just plain evil. Which got me backpedalling all the way back to my childhood. Thinking about those crazy periods of arguments surrounding qualifications and careers.

I actually have recollections of telling my father that my intuition and looks were my diploma's. I was always landing on my feet. Especially when the prospects and outlook was bleak. Whenever I got downbeat about life, I'm always reminded of Monty Python's Philosophy song.

Before continuing I ask you all to familiarise yourselves with It. I'm not particularly worried about the lyrics, but it's the subtext. Constantly comparing figures in the song to appalling drinking habits. Because my dear friends, it's essentially what being British is all about!

You see it consistently and I know it's not just our culture or nation. It's also not just alcohol. I could reel off a long list of vices. That ship has sailed though, so I'm going to spare you. Our juncture is clear, we are creatures of habit at analysing situations! What we are bad at is making the correct choices for the benefit of others. goes something like "Emanuel Kant, was a real pissant, who was very rarely stable.

People began asking questions, thinking for themselves. We've matured enough to forsake that sheep ritual. It's brought self-awareness and reflection. No longer willing to be slaves to our financial institutions and corporations. But of course. Whenever you venture into the streets, microchip intruders begin their devilish deeds. Using facial recognition technology to know exactly where everyone is! It's even recently become prime time television.

Some people might think this is violating human rights for privacy, to which the policymakers claim it's to protect and prevent criminals or terrorists. But only the exceptional minority worry about consent! And even my neighbour now owns one of those smart doorbells. An incredible observation and monitoring device more like.

I have observed this metamorphosis over the past few years, and I have to admit, I'm really worried for the future, or I was, until quite recently, when that sleeping Russian bear, began trying to throw a few spanners into the works of civilized society.

Shooting down an airplane from Amsterdam bound for Malaysia. Kuala Lumpur, somewhere over Ukrainian airspace. This after they illegally annexed a part of Crimea, which we now know was the forerunner for the war in Eastern Europe. They also have used proxy militias i.e. the Wagner group to project their diplomacy in lots of other international countries. Syria is one. Others are Mali, Libya, Mozambique, Sudan, Madagascar, Central African Republic. Most of these garrison stations have been set up to provide the government's security and protection. Reality however remains divided, Group leader Sergei Prigozhin, was known to have made millions in mineral mining contracts until his untimely death after he threatened to overthrow the Kremlin? Make of that, what you will!

Success is everything, producing nouveau riche, a hybrid of the established wealthy. A group of wannabes who have so much financial power and influence, that essentially, they are calling the shots. I'm reliably informed this new money consists of that entirely A table where oligarchs dance with Musk for example. instance who else other than over-indulgent Westerners would invent a greed focused purchasing philosophy. "Buy One Get One Free," displaying stopping the poor having the chance of a fair deal.

I think I'm quite well positioned to pass judgment too. My folks were suckered into that kind of mindset. Trying to demonstrate a higher level of sophistication. The way you dress, the way you speak, the manipulative way you try to demonstrate fair mindedness. So here is a thought. Ordering the Riesling with Fish at the restaurant doesn't make you a better person. Agreeing with your country and the media narrative that gets pedalled incessantly by your national media, doesn't mean you understand values or beliefs.

If anything, it proves how gullible you are. Knowing what plays were being performed at the theatre, but every half-intelligent wannabe understands that already. Perhaps this is what caused all the sensible money to begin leaving the shores of Western Democracies a whole generation ago. I'm not talking about a mass exodus fuelled by a brain drain.

This has been happening in plain sight since Thatcher, or the fall of the Soviet era. Every educated person understands this of course, when you start to see the collapse of internal systems, like the stock markets or the banks. Or perhaps much more vividly the collapse of whole political institutions, like the Soviets, or more poignantly the UK! And hundreds of thousands of people have marched to chase a dream.

So, what happened in Britain to propel our mass evacuation of decency? My theory goes right back to pre-Thatcher. It has its roots in the uncertainty that the oil crisis of the seventies provided. A strange part of my youth. It was a time of utter chaos. With OPEC nations turning off the supply of oil and gas. Our neighbourhood was continuously being thrown into power cuts.

I recall days where my mother was changing dressings of my spots by candlelight. A hazard of the times, a particularly awkward period to contract chickenpox. There was something about this period in history that makes me single it out as the tipping point for being proud to be from these islands. Don't forget how divided the country was anyway.

The working class was being squeezed at every level. With all the employers pushing down wages. Our nation's Government from every side, pursued a relief valve, but as we now understand. It was always shameful short-term thinking, favouring lifestyle choice over long term solutions. The Right increasingly followed toxic policies. Setting average household's, against each other. A tactic that was employed deliberately and callously. Sometimes pitching whole communities into conflict. This is an easily explained phenomenon.

Just look at how much emphasis is currently placed on the Home Nations individual status. When derogatory language and comments are the default position used when referring to another country's rugby or football team. It's the same situation where politicians make comparisons to the devolved national governments.

I'm an ex-military veteran, and I can tell you, this country is nothing without the good people of the other nations. But let's not kid ourselves. There was a time when the world was evolving from wartime. Everyone wanted to live in a different world. Democracy, it seemed was confirmed as a positive solution to completing a transition from nothing into prosperity.

Even the appointment of a left-wing parliament further strengthened the impression that our system worked. I don't want to dwell too long on this circumstance. The fact is the majority of our population had access to healthcare with the creation of the NHS. Our education system was performing fairly well, and even the poorest families were protected by the social security system, "From the Cradle to the Grave?"

Unfortunately, this battle slogan of compassion. An invention of the socialist has shown itself to be a Red Herring. Essentially making people lazy. Productivity fell and workers' demands exceeded their worth. Here is where we are today. Essentially completing a full circle of the economic cycle. A sequence of fifty years of failure. A litany of utter incompetence, interspersed with intentional economic suicide. Placing the wealth of the country in the hands of stock market bookmakers.

You see I am privileged to have seen this insanity from all sides. with the right balance between hope and expectation! My family fortunately were somewhere in the middle. I think an honest person would describe us eventually Forcing low to medium income households into making impossible choices. With disposable income forcing sacrifices. The Left on the other hand were not more prudent, squandering any prosperity by intuitively making handouts the default go-to setting. Even when they have been handed the Downing Street keys. I'm afraid they are famous for pandering to lepers. Whereby I mean every freeloader in the country.

Suddenly has a mandate. Chucking cash in every direction. Promising to support "The Good Causes!" Swapping countries and hoping for a more prosperous future. Some have already made their nest egg and quite frankly want to enjoy it in a more pleasant climate and environment. Some though, who have always had the money have the influence and probably most importantly have the key friendships are mindful of the paradigm shift currently underway in every corner of the world. A massive population explosion is currently happening and even the recent pandemic and global events like war in Ukraine or catastrophic natural disasters have made a dent in the overall density of people. Refugee numbers are becoming increasingly problematic, and countries are under pressure to accommodate.

In retrospect I predicted this forty years ago, shortly after leaving home. I also firmly believe that the rest of Western society did too, but I realise that forty-years ago, we were living in a very different world to the one we have now.

The West was bracing itself for nuclear Armageddon, we were drifting in and out of crises from energy to war, eighties Britain was a mess. Strikes, cost of living, declining productivity and then to put a cherry on top failing everything. Now bearing these facts in mind and knowing what has transpired since Thatcher, let's sit down and have a grown-up conversation about how we can achieve a sustainable, fairer world!

Because it's no longer good enough to rely on national values, where populations are hoodwinked into propaganda fuelled, media circuses. Where faith is placed (or more accurately misplaced) in divisive institutions, whose control and guidance is supported and funded by the shadowy, opaque and least transparent families and organisations, which leads me onto a key piece of advice I was offered aged about twenty.

My commanding officer concerned about me not integrating said, "always try to see the big picture (or world view)," something I have always found really useful, it definitely makes you more rounded and less likely to misinterpret a situation.

Which is why I have found it incredibly difficult these last few years trying to navigate a serious passage away from all mankind's problems. Paragraph after paragraph I have typed in the hope of resolving the human crisis. You can always do what the privileged and entitled minority do. Buy your way out of responsibility and threat, but even for this part of a Venn diagram it is crystal clear now that the mathematical outcomes are drastically poor.

I have toyed with looking at extreme values and resolutions, but these offer a similar outcome to the end game of a chess match. Fewer and fewer pieces remain on the board and the inevitable looks a foregone conclusion. Except for us with eight billion pieces backed into a corner the potential for mass extinction and suffering looks kind of final.

It's during a break in writing that I quite accidentally stumbled onto the idea for the book. I think I would probably still be like the proverbial blind man, tapping in the dark now if I hadn't changed direction. We have become self-obsessed with the world's ills, and this is when I had the breakthrough. There are literally hundreds or even thousands of people desperately trying to find the solutions to our existential crisis. So how about evening the odds.

Let's put some context to the scale of mankind's problems and give out some points of action, things which are still possible for remedy of mankind's failures, plus how we can change our attitudes. My first suggestion is about population change and management.

If two becomes four, four becomes six etc, just like real life exponential growth. It doesn't take a Nobel prize winning economist long to figure out how damaging and dangerous for the world this is. Understand that it's not aimed at the delusional expansionists like religious groups, tribe mentality families (Royal Families are a prime example), women who have no care about their unchallenged fertility.

What it comes down to is balance. I'm of the generation when we were encouraged to utilise the family assets. Leaving home was not a challenge but more like a duty. So, let's pause here and reflect. I am from a family with a brother and sister, which means if we all were successful, my parents would have their house, my sister would have her house, and my brother would have his house, so now I would have four houses!

The rules and standards which supposedly differentiate us from the cats and dogs. Of course, what I'm intimating at are the behaviours and traits which express our species and therefore ultimately define us.

People go through evolution on a daily basis, and the biggest give away to support this theory is how language is constantly evolving. With new words developing on a yearly basis whilst others are consigned to the history books. Some leave dictionaries due to loss of usage or relevance, whilst others become outdated and replaced due to fashion!

Living in the past:

In the General Election year of 1992, the Sun newspaper wrote a headline that read something like - If Neil Kinnock wins today would the last person to leave Britain, please turn off the lights!

The implication being that if the country elected a socialist government the general population would suffer immeasurable consequences and years of misery and hardship. It was a copy of this paper that finally convinced me that being British was a recipe for disaster. Something which I am constantly reminded today of how far we have since fallen.

I'm not talking about the Sun seeking contingent of expats who have made the move to the Costa's or even taken on Chateau renovations in the French countryside. I am of course referring to the 300 million expats currently residing worldwide who sold up way before the 90's. Probably starting in the 70's.

Which brings me onto my first exertion. What exactly is the definition of being British? Indeed, the very introduction of the suffix "ish" is quite an eye-opening concept. The dictionary definition is, "to some extent," like in the adverb, "Bullish," So, whenever we refer to each other as Scottish or English, what we are essentially saying is, I am more or less comfortable with being described as a native. Whether or not the statement is accurate or not? Which is quite a poignant revelation when we talk about the history behind the disclosures of our collective ancestry. Because everyone knows that your passport is a statement document betraying your complicity in our Island's history!

I dare say if we rewound the clocks to the 18th and 19th centuries, we would see the ancestral lines of the Britain we like to deceive ourselves that we belong to. Two World Wars and countless political and financial scandals later, and I don't actually think that any single family or individual can even justifiably claim to have a connection with our nation.

Which is one of those:

This section I have dedicated to recent events, and I want to share my experiences and thoughts with you, after finally getting to speak to a private, professional neurologist to see what conclusions he may have. At this stage of my degenerative illness, I am looking for answers to various questions and I am going to record the entire conversation covertly using an app on my phone I'm doing this because I want to demonstrate how all the while lab jackets are in cahoots with each other.

My first question will be, what exactly are my injuries? The purpose for this is to see if the doctor follows a script that is an exact mirror of all my previous consultations, and I will then start throwing in the missing jigsaw puzzle pieces. Moving the conversation along to the irreconcilable differences I can produce.

I'm interested in what explanation is given to the areas that I currently have difficulty in managing and understanding, plus what the best-practice scenarios are for people with my injuries. For example, whether or not I should have been allowed to work/drive or flown.

Following on from this I would like to have cerebrospinal fluid explained. The reason being the dictionary definition describes it as (CSF), a clear, colourless bodily fluid found within the tissue that surrounds the brain and spinal cord of all vertebrates.

CSF is produced by specialised ependymal cells in the choroid plexus of the ventricles of the brain. It acts as a kind of buffer, shock absorber and cushion, providing basic mechanical and immunological protection to the brain inside the skull. The reason for my interest in this is, I want to know what would happen if there was leakage. More importantly is if it could be detected on scans.

Leading onto the most important part of this line of questioning is. Can a leak of spinal fluid be contained? If so, what would need to be done and tellingly, why was this never even mentioned before. Is it because throwing a MS diagnosis out there the simplest solution.

The interrogation is going to be fun I can assure you. I'm not optimistic about an honest conversation, or even the possibility of a debate about the rights and wrongs of continually trying to make me fly or do any of the things an able-bodied person can do. But I also want comments on potential causes of my illnesses and damaged areas. So that I can get closure.

The more I ponder the possibility of getting some sort of answers, the better it makes me feel about doing the "full circle thing," from insanity of my parent's thirst for a house that satisfied their needs and desires. With both driving hundreds of miles a week to accomplish whatever it was they wanted or needed. The various episodes surrounding mum/me becoming ill but my determination to prevent it dominating my own life.

The grateful acceptance of career opportunities and employment in cool places and the friendships and bonds I have made along the way. I'm always drawn back however to my present situation and reality. The message for anyone who is looking for advice on what to do after this diagnosis is simple.

Live every day like it's your last. Don't ever be scared about anything. If you're frozen or debilitated just accept it and let it pass over. Don't become a victim just view it as a challenge and try to make it work for you. I was forced into a wheelchair in 2014, but I'm still able to walk in the swimming pool. I can still go scuba diving with a good buddy.

In fact, I know I'm a lot better off than lots of veterans from Iraq or Afghanistan and you won't see them crying or feeling sorry for themselves. It's all about mentality!

For anyone who knows me, "I'm still smiling."

When I started to make sense of everything I looked around for a fitting metaphor and decided to make a comparison with technology and the advancements in our understanding of complexity in design. When I used to work with the helicopters, I remember seeing all the incorporation of modifications and this is probably one of the ways our injuries will be overcome. There is still hope out there!

The elephant in the room:

Right let's start talking about the cabin air quality on board modern jet aircraft. It is something which most people don't understand or probably even care about. Because the umbrella organisations responsible for ensuring passenger safety must surely be well drilled and in the modern era absolutely beyond reproach or collectively immune to any question of whether they allow any form of safety violations to enter any service of aircraft or their systems. It sounds unthinkable doesn't it. I mean in this, the 21st century, no one would try to put passengers' safety at risk, would they?

But you see there are a lot of very dangerous and greedy companies, investors and shareholders out there, who are totally impervious to the human aspects of flight safety. For them it's all about the bottom line. Bums on seats etc, etc!

Which is why I want to bring you back to (High Efficiency Particulate Air) filtration systems or HEPA filters. You see in the old days when the passengers of airlines were allowed to smoke on board. The cabin air was completely recycled about every 3 minutes.

But today we have been living and working in a lie. Which the airlines desperately don't want you to be aware of. The airlines no longer recycle the cabin air completely every three minutes, it's become more of a compromise situation between the individual carriers, the CEO's and boards and the expected fuel economy of individual flights.

It has been reported that an aircraft carrier can save up to 6% of its expected total fuel costs by using this operating method. Cutting out the use of fresh air and replacing it with recycled HEPA alternative. Which for passengers who are using a lifestyle which involves infrequent flying trips of limited endurance. Is probably of little or no consequence.

However, for someone like me, who has been illegally worked and flown excessively to above the maximum safe limits of hours, it's probably not too surprising that I have experienced incredible side effects of the increased CO2 exposure. I am a living model for a person who has been exposed to a Hypoxia inducing environment. Demonstrating classic symptoms. Which have unfortunately been mixed alongside a condition I have lived with and dealt with since I was eight-years old.

The most criminal element of this practice is how the airlines use less than half the fresh air required to ensure passengers are comfortable and simultaneously inducing conditions that are triggers for the appearance of some other well documented illnesses that occur during flight such as an increase in shortness of breath or even loss of consciousness. A situation which I dealt with on a regular basis. There was also an increase in air rage alongside many other medical emergencies which required the pilots to divert. But guess what! What extent did the umbrella safety agency decide to investigate?

The answer is...THEY NEVER HAVE AND NEVER WILL.

I'm paraphrasing here but this is what happens when you let ladder hungry, capitalist wankers at the controls of the safety systems! Here's a thought. What do you do before setting off on your daily journey? I would imagine a massive amount of you will switch on the television to get the latest headlines. Including the weather forecast.

Another group might switch on the car radio to do the same, modern thinking and acting technophiles will be ploughing around the webpages of their respective go-to groups. You know the kind of thing I'm talking about.

Instagram or Facebook for example. But essentially, they are all doing the same thing just using different mediums! So, my question is this. What happened to looking up at the sky and seeing the weather, before making choices about clothing or transport. It might not surprise you, but our incredibly wasteful and self-indulgent politicians think that it's ok to spend £1.2 billion for this luxury. Which considering how frequently we are given wrong information is frankly a disgrace. No correction to that, it's a very bad joke. Look around you.

Who has noticed how frequently climate change is affecting our lives. Not just in Britain but across the globe. Recently producing record extremes of all kinds of weather events. From the very hot to the very wet. With catastrophic storms and events usually occurring only in disaster movies or written about in stories from historical times.

Which now brings me onto an area where we can dot the eyes and cross the T's, because these seemingly remote and unconnected areas of life are linked more closely than you will ever believe. Way back in my Army days, in 1987 in fact, I was deployed on a small exercise to mobilize with my unit and transit to North Germany to practice the transportation of supplies and equipment for a full deployment of a regiment's worth of helicopters and support personnel and equipment in case we were required to deploy by sea, and only allowing the aircraft to be flown once a beachhead was established.

I remember the briefing in some Army barracks in Colchester and I can then picture the organised chaos that followed until we were finally secured and sailing from Harwich, Essex, and out into the North Sea. Now I don't know how many of you remember the15th of October 1987? But I do because it was this evening when we set sail from the coast of England and then spent the next 24hrs dodging all manner of low-pressure waves and getting buffered by extremely high winds.

A hurricane in fact, but the point is this. Yes, the aircraft were well secured to the deck and yes nothing serious happened to us, but I think it was more luck than anything else. Even during the deployment briefing there was no mention of unusual or severe weather conditions. Even Michael Fish, the weather presenter for the BBC denied any possibility of anything so serious happening.

I'm grateful for that experience though, because it taught me that people who should be watching and protecting are simply pawns in the game of life. You see it's all about best worst-case scenarios. There were massive amounts of damage done by the weather. Something which we experienced when we returned to Britain a couple of weeks later.

It also taught me something very important NEVER BELIEVE THE MESSENGER! Which is why I am a total outsider when it comes to believing the consensus. Unfortunately, because of my time in the military I got very spoiled by watching, living, and experiencing all of the positives of working within an aviation environment that followed wherever possible the highest standards both with regards to safety and standards. But equally importantly to the engineering and support departments that provided the framework for conducting a comprehensive kaleidoscopic almost living organism.

Which is why I think I have found out the home truths about commercial airlines the hard way. Oh boy they really have cheated all of us. Probably the most disgusting, amazing secrets are the ones that you will never hear about. Unless someone dies! But guess what, I am dying!

What I'm going to is describe to you is evidence of systems that are concocted to maximize profit. Where countless red flags are ignored, deliberately downplayed, or manipulated using intentional breaches of flight safety regulations and aviation rules and standards. The whole strategy is something where entire companies are complicit with their backers and shareholders pushing limits beyond everything that can be described as an acceptable level of operating. The first thing that needs to be addressed in this industry is to highlight the failing areas of our industry/business or the umbrella organisation that should be responsible for maintaining the integrity of security and safety of not just employees but also and perhaps most importantly the passengers.

We have as a society become increasingly accustomed to the race to the bottom. Where price and availability are king. Where umbrella safety watchdogs, the state and legal professionals are guided by big business, the capitalist system and protecting interests of the shareholders and public listed companies where any whiff of pandering towards passenger comfort and safety is placed as far away from the equation as possible. Instead, priority is given to financial concerns and the inevitable consequences of focusing on the bottom line.

But here's the dilemma. Everybody has accepted the status quo, either intentionally or because our society demands this conformity of circumstance. I can use my personal experiences, and those of my family as a measuring stick to try to make my point. The truth is though that every single member of the human race is faced daily with difficult choices. It's what I call the blackjack sweet analogy. You see in my childhood I have experienced many occasions where the rules have changed.

The biggest change I can remember was when money was altered on the advice of the government in the 1960's, culminating in adoption of decimalization of the currency in 1971. To this day I still remember the teething problems of the adoption of the new system. On one random day in about 74, I was in the local newsagents buying my favourite sweet. The Blackjack. Where you could buy 12 for a penny. I even remember the confusion I caused at the till, somehow coming away with more change than I expected.

But the point of explaining this slight diversion in my life is to highlight how sometimes seemingly insignificant and unrelated events can hold more relevance than they would ever be credited with. I can still picture the little paper bag that my sweets were placed in, or mention the confused expression shown by the grown-ups grappling with decimalisation. I have had this stain follow me around my entire life. The changeover of the weights and measures.

The changeover of exam qualifications from O and A levels to GCSE or contrived levels of nothingness. I recently read an article outlining the modern qualifications pyramid. It seems to revolve around the (RQF) Regulated Qualification Framework.

A frankly tampered and bastardised version of previous standards. Whose very existence serves only to justify the existence of the regulatory body OFQUAL and the existence of umbrella bodies who ensure that every awarded diploma or mark compares equally across the international standards!

So, there it is, an important admission by the study regulator. Even the higher education institutions and qualifications right down to the vocational level training and apprenticeship system. It's not about being competent or even a skilled operator within a certain field. It's about being the owner who flaunts a piece of paper declaring that they have passed an examination to demonstrate an aptitude and understanding of a particular subject. In my experience of people who occupy positions of authority and influence. I can tell you that in most cases I don't believe them.

Sure, the majority of individuals who sit in a chair and offer their wisdom are practised spouting the rhetoric of the dark arts. But when the push comes to shove the majority are about as helpful as the monkeys in the "see no evil, hear no evil,' triptych. I can demonstrate this by using two different examples.

Firstly, when I was rushed to the hospital for a suspected stroke I wasn't seen for three days because of a Bank Holiday weekend. On the Tuesday, when I was scheduled to get scanned, I went to talk to the duty ward doctor and discovered quite by chance that she had put my details and symptoms into a symptom checker website.

There is then a massive catalogue of missed opportunities to address my concerns, but unfortunately, when forced to whistle blow against a mighty and self-protecting industry, you notice pretty quickly whose interests are being guarded!

The second occasion where I experienced the nagging doubts over qualification against authority was practically everything to do with flying in the world of civilian aviation. Where the boundaries of safety and safe operating have become blurred by two very important factors.

The Airlines need the aircraft to be airborne and the levels of discretionary over-use of hours for crew must be maximised. Once again this raises many procedural concerns. Who in the airline industry is supposed to be ensuring safety standards are maintained for both passengers and crew? How is it possible that umbrella regulatory bodies are being misled by the false reporting of safety violations and why is nobody responsible for the failings demonstrated by firms acting with impunity against the state's claims of protecting public safety!

Which brings me onto the section of this thread which probably should be titled the reason why the British state is broken! I have looked at incredibly varied and detailed explanations as to why my situation is appalling, the one constant I have been forever referred back to is the regulatory body of the UK. If you type into a search engine on the internet, "List of Regulators in the United Kingdom," you will immediately be confronted by an extensive list of literally dozens, broken down by subgroups.

Charities, Education, Environment, Business and finance, Health, Housing, Law, Social care, Transport, Utilities, and Others...

In turn under these subsections with their regulators our Parliament divides the responsibilities and assigns a supposed watchdog to ensure compliance and fairness are placed highest on a long list of duties that should be undertaken within any given field. Now call me a doubting Thomas, but surely, I can't be the only person who can see through this deception. For example, anything to do with energy is farmed out to Ofgem. An acronym, or a dumbed down soundbite to explain what sector of society they are responsible for.

They like to be presented as the energy regulator. Responsible for safeguarding consumers and promoting fair market competition 'accurate?' I think if the truth was really known then there would be public hanging in London.

Just look at what happened to fuel prices during Covid and the war in Ukraine? I once had a work colleague whose son worked for ENRON, the US energy giant who worked worldwide but the young legal analyst who was related to my co-contractor was absolutely stunned when he discovered this global superpower had gone into administration overnight and all the thousands of workers were effectively unemployed.

That was 2001. Everyone who is old enough to remember that, probably also remembers the promises that came from it. A once in a lifetime event. It'll never happen again! Unfortunately, the reality of everything capitalist system is...It will always happen, and it will probably be you next!

Food for Thought:

It's like a very bad disaster movie, something like a tsunami or an earthquake. Whichever way you turn, you can see cracks in the buildings or watch the power of the water destroying everything in its path. Britain should be energy self-sufficient. With immense resources in the natural world. An unlimited amount of wind or tidal resource. With a growing amount of solar and nuclear options. But that is for another discussion.

The point of highlighting the various regulatory bodies and the industry's they represent is to show what is utterly wrong and unacceptable with British society. Every aspect of our culture has become swallowed up by the three evils. It begins with a total lack of transparency between our parliament and the civil servants. Incorporating regulatory, "get out of jail, "clauses. With the intention of protecting industries and businesses from any potential liability or harm. Putting the shareholders at the top of the table.

So, here's the thing:

Remember how I have written about joining the dots and crossing the T's? Well, here's the thing. In many ways, retrospectively, I am an enabler. So too were my father and probably millions of other citizens. Living with unwell or poorly family members. Continuously trying to navigate a series of hurdles and obstacles, put in place by a succession of different departments, governments and companies that have no intention or interest in finding a cure to the relevant illnesses, but instead, they all have a vested interest in perpetuating a policy of management.

A series of studies and actions that keep the money-go-round ticking over and simultaneously provide a glimpse of potential progress in the fight to find an achievable solution. When sufferers of these conditions can live a symptom free life with their families and coexist together with the rest of society.

What we are all guilty of, is listening to and trusting the so called, "gate keepers," of our world.

From my earliest experiences of being dragged out to the church every Sunday to listen to supposedly wise words of wisdom and enlightenment. Given by a figure in medieval dress and spouting the rhetoric of a bygone era.

Watching from distance, the politicians who contrived to manipulate the narrative to the general public. An exercise of such deception I find it staggering to think the population were so easily influenced. Or bought! (Think council house tenants who could buy their homes.) Never mind the political skulduggery that resulted in the collapse of health & Safety standards, where businesses and corporations were basically given a blank check. To dilute conditions as long as the profits were stable. Or where the only consideration was the share price and dividend yield.

I personally have experienced hundreds of different situations where I have seen wrongdoings of utterly incomprehensible size and nature. Where mediocrity and failure are undeservedly rewarded by throwing buckets of money at people. Where a person is given unwarranted praise and attention just because they are the holders of a particular qualification or rank irrespective of whether or not they are any good or not. It's the old school tie mentality. Something I can honestly say I have only seen in this country. But I dare say is replicated the world over.

So now, let's do the missed opportunities. For me it's the initial onset or (POMS) a failure of my parents to notify the doctors about the car accident that was probably what caused my mother's MS. Then were all those occasions when I showed unusual symptoms and peculiarities. Long periods of sleep and fatigue. Things that rapidly turned into the reverse. I would be an absolute action junkie and doing everything at 90 miles an hour until I just drifted off. (Something I still do now).

The Army medical, both on joining and leaving, where no unusual circumstances and symptoms were recorded, despite my conversations about my unusual experiences in the extremities. Both hot and cold. The occasional influence of eyesight issues. Something I now recognise as optic neuritis. Even my long-term partner who is an intensive care nurse didn't have any idea about, despite having to replace my driving duties on numerous occasions. Plus, one night guiding me home because I was literally, "blind drunk," and not recognizing that there was snow on the ground, and I was experiencing the temperature effects of the disease.

I've been prone to the effects of the heat side of the illness too. Twice on running in marathons and once on the cycling leg of a triathlon. But I always put it down to the effects of either a recent cold, or food poisoning. Talking about food. I am a really complicated eater. Preferring the easiest vegetarian diet or just chicken. Something all the army colleagues found a bit strange, but it was something I didn't really understand, until I met some sufferers at the MS therapy centre who all concurred that it was a symptom.

By the way I actually think my adoption of this diet not only helped me to combat my unusual condition. But it also probably saved my parents from having BSE. Because they stopped taking beef as their Sunday dinner! I didn't understand why working with the airline would be such fun for me. But I also didn't really understand why it would be a double-edged sword. But here goes I'll try to explain.

The reason I have dumped my feelings and prejudices on the regulatory system in the UK is complex and doubly fuelled but it started way back in my schoolboy years. When I got friends with a boy called Muttley. I'm not even sure how we got together but the point is he was a co-team member of 'Pepperharrow cricket club. We would travel together to the ground in Alex's Ford Capri. A car I have always loved because of the CI-5 links.

The point is, that I saw first-hand on one return journey how bribable some policemen can be! Especially if you've been drinking. A trait seemingly ingrained into British culture. Now you might think that I would be against this type of leniency, but you would be wrong. It taught me that the system isn't perfect. We can't be the conscience for every little misdemeanour.

Alex was a good bloke, and he was also from the lower earning bracket. I also being totally impressed by the letter he had framed on his wall from the FA. When he applied for the England job. However, what that little episode taught me was, it's all about who you get on any given day

A bit like Eric Sykes (school friend from Rodborough) also known as "psycho," who I got friends with and discovered he worked for Thames Water. The local authority that controlled the area water treatment plants and rivers and also ensured the quality of water our taps.

Now Eric was a good guy, but also a fan of "The Undertones," a rock band who had a good singer called Fergal Sharkey. A prominent activist who was on a mission to highlight the waste and mismanagement and corruption of the nation water companies. I'm talking about all the way back in 1985. He had already identified the failings of the regulator that was supposed to protect citizens. But we have seen how far it has been taken seriously. I could of course say the same about almost all the regulatory bodies in Britain but that's for you to investigate!

Because I want to stop on the CAA. The people who have the responsibility to protect and defend the civilian flying community. I have all the relevant documents and paperwork for my flying career with the airline, yet one of the most important aspects of civilian flying is to try to get the safety barometer at just the right temperature.

You are educated about the various factors involved in the daily, weekly, monthly and annually flying work. The various duties you are responsible for. The safe operating environment and equipment you are expected to be responsible for. With a plethora of duties that are expected to be completed to the highest possible standards, ensuring the safety is always prioritised, and the crew and passengers will have a positive experience.

Sounds good, right?

But here's the thing... the training tranche of the company provides the basic knowledge and skills needed to fulfil your side of the equation. Ensuring all safety equipment is present, and in good working order. Committing the necessary emergency drills to memory, get a sound understanding of on-board procedures including interacting with the flight deck, plus, a whole range of secondary operational actions. So quite a broad group Nest Pa! You are taught about the limitations of the flying hours system. The obligation of the airline, the pilots and THE CAA.

What they don't tell you is "It's Worth Jack Shit" On my first year of working, I was intentionally forced to work "OVER THE MAXIMUM" Despite my talking to base management and the duty base Captain? During the second year in Dortmund, I was told that the base was doing a fantastic job, and the company was incredibly pleased, and the future was looking good.

They closed us down eight months after the end of the football World Cup. (Btw this was the highlight of my time at easyJet)

Unfortunately, my hopes and expectations were never really met. My long-term partner was diagnosed with breast cancer and the company never gave me any special dispensation to help with my family duties. (Yes, I have 2 children). The announcement of the base closure happened literally only 6 months after I took up the chalice of Union representative. Initially for the T&GWU, but ultimately for UNITE the Union. Utterly toothless and spineless organisations that have been bullied to death by successive generations and governments.

Anyway, I digress. I then had to move back to the UK because my mom was poorly. Moving to Bristol to try and sort out my mother and figure out a family solution for the kids and my partner.

Alas, things got complicated back in the UK. I was forced into a rental situation that didn't allow me any opportunity to fix my family. But weirdly enough that wasn't the final nail in the coffin. It was the Base management of Bristol. Firstly, appointing me as the Union representative for the base, despite my protestations. But then I was sent around the houses on a flying duty from hell. I was awoken by a telephone call at 02:00 hrs. From an early morning home standby.

I was transferred to a local base airport standby which required me to be available until about early afternoon. The next duty change was a requirement for me to passenger to Charles De Gaul airport in Paris. Until I finally was placed on a flight to Marrakesh, Morrocco, and back to Paris. Eventually getting to bed at 03:00.

Which is completely incorrect, and I flagged it up on a few occasions during the day. The Bristol base management were totally indifferent to the idea that this was an illegal duty. By the time I got to Paris I had no choice but to agree to fly because if I had refused the duty, I could foresee a riot breaking out.

Here's the problem. The company "crewing" department were complicit in organising an illegal duty. Done I suspect, on the instructions from Bristol management, because I had had the audacity to question their naming and shaming policy at the office. Trying to find a new solution to the spend per head on flights. The crewing department in London Luton, had tampered with and adjusted my actual flight records. Thus, avoiding any scrutiny from a watchdog. Which begs the question: - If they can adjust the "set in stone" information and tamper with the records and data. What else can they do?

In my investigation into these examples of improper behaviour and conduct. I am sorry to say I have found many other instances where the gold standard has been replaced by an excrement coloured one. There is the changing of the aircraft cabin oxygen recycling system.

A manufacturer setting that controls the recycling and replacement of the on-board air conditioning. I am told by many sources including pilots and trainers that the company changed the % of exchange rates, from 100 to 50 %, in order to pacify the passengers, which I dare say would be fine for the passengers who only fly once in a day, yet the crew have been exposed to these conditions many times a week. Never mind what the monthly total could have been. Did the CAA know? Of course, but it was a money saving exercise so who cares.

Talking about the turbulence injuries of crew on approach to Venice, or the lady stewardess who damaged her hand on the galley fixtures. Louise M, who was badly injured in an RTA because she was sent home in the snow instead of providing proper overnight accommodation. The list of failures is staggering and I'm glad I no longer have to deal with them, but what is absolutely irrefutable is the lack of transparency and effectiveness of the watchdog.

What we see constantly is the lack of accountability and public protection from prosecution. The positions of responsibility are often held by inferiors and inadequates, with no regard for the implementations of their duties but the protection of companies and individuals who are in the card game, sitting pretty with a flush?

You see the difference between living (unknowingly) with an illness and the ability to function as a useful person in society is completely conditional on many factors working in your favour.

For example (unlike me) having someone who has the ability to correctly identify and understand the complexity and intricacies of a patient's injuries. Which sounds achievable doesn't it?

Unfortunately, this stallion was long gone before somebody decided to close the stable door.

And on closer inspection of my scans, the radiographer and doctor who decided that I was able to return to the workplace was... how can I put this politely...BARKING UP THE WRONG TREE!

And that is the conclusion of my journey:

Fortunately, I suffer from very little pain. I'm fortunate because I know lots of people who have come back from Afghanistan or Iraq, and they are facing a battle on a different level to me. I'm able to get into the garden or go swimming. Occasionally I can go further afield. I have been to the Wiltshire MS support group, and I am friends with some of the Brightwell centre. A therapy centre in Bristol for all manner of neurological disorders. But the point is you have to continue because somewhere out there, there is a fix. I BELIEVE THAT!

So, you see. It's swings and roundabouts. You know what my proudest moment was in the Army? It was walking into the classroom in Milford to say hello to my old chemistry teacher Mr Davies to be able to tell the kids, listen to what he had to say. It worked for me. I know what exothermic reactions look like!

The duty medical officer on my discharge from the forces could also have picked up on my injuries and deprived me of 15 years of swanning around Europe the period I'm going to call Ross's "red period." Sounds disgusting but it encompasses the madness of adapting to a different normal. Learning new skills and jobs. Having two children. Travelling around the continent and making lots of friends and enjoying being able to invite my parents to spend time with my family and even share a holiday in France with us.

The airline killed my family in so many ways it's frustrating. First of all, even before my application was accepted, I couldn't get a flight to be able to check on my father who had had a fall on the stairs at home. My sister phoned to reassure me he was fine. However, the next morning I was contacted, to tell me that he had died in the night. The doctors in Guildford had missed a serious bleed on the brain and he passed away! I remember thinking "What the F."

A few weeks later I joined the airline and began flying. However, once again the medical community completely missed my injuries, and I was deemed fit to fly, which went hunky-dory, until I did my early Amsterdam in February 2012, and the rest you can piece together in the book.

One of my favourite films of all time is the 1986 Heartbreak Ridge flick. Clint Eastwood is gunnery sergeant Thomas Highway, and he has the best line of any movie ever. Tasked with training up a bunch of Army slackers and whipping them into shape for operations he says...**WE IMPROVISE, WE ADAPT, WE OVERCOME!** Which essentially is what everyone with a degenerative disease needs to understand. It's the only way that you will rise to the challenge, but hey if it's good enough for Clint. It's good enough for me.

Now I'm not expecting the medical community to perform miracles, which I would expect the majority of public would agree on, but what I have difficulty with is the whole structure of the health system! I think I would use the expression as "top heavy!" I mean you only must go into any hospital in any country to understand what I'm talking about. I have seen other countries and got some interesting feedback from friends and acquaintances around the globe.

So let me tell it as I see it. First of all, there are the two tiers. Private and Public. The majority of people around the world use an insurance-based contribution scheme. Or what I would describe as a monthly/yearly payment that is socially based on your income. It's a very fair way of minimising cy when someone in the household has an illness.

Britain is slightly different with 24 billion £ raised by national insurance and 12 billion £ raised in taxes. All poured into the NHS and virtually no clearly identifiable logic or systems in place that could be quantified to justify its structure and efficacy. Which when you think about it is quite poetic. Whilst we were all talking about the pandemic and the efficacy of the vaccines. masks or gowns no one even talked about question of where the money went?

Then thirdly we have private health businesses. Advertising themselves as the apple on top of the tree. Offering a first-rate service and "better outcomes!" Which I find curious for a few reasons. I have been treated by private doctors in Canada and my first impression was. Competent and polite.

A work colleague was involved in a car accident in Hawaii in 2000 and it was in his words "RUTHLESS!" They weren't going to even extract him and his wife until they got clearance from the insurance company.

I have seen a French hospital when we had our little crash going to Morocco, our safety climber only had a dislocated shoulder which was brilliant because we were able to continue to do the climbing. The hospital was "CLEAN AND FUNCTIONAL." Ian who had been injured was glad to get out. He remarked how bad the food was.

Both of my children were born in Germany and my eldest even had the pleasure of being prematurely born. Spending the first week of his life in intensive care. Which incidentally where my long-term partner worked. Heaven only knows how she coped with the covid virus. We haven't spoken for 10 years. The airline was responsible for this, because I was only on a beginner's contract, I didn't qualify for any special allowance. I was picking the kids up, dropping off and then also doing a full day's flying. Which incidentally is the equivalent of 4 times the effort of normal persons hours. The German health care system is excellent and in fact the crew of different bases of the airline wanted desperately to get their teeth and surgery done!

Even Diyasuke, my Japanese Pen pal and fellow Arsenal fan told me how marvellous the Japanese healthcare was compared to Britain. He cut his leg when here for a match and said he waited 5 hours before someone came to see him. They were also astonished when he began speaking perfect English. A little trick I used to do on flights where I had a basic understanding.

A good friend of mine Peter Fletcher was on a London Underground train when two Danish guys (tourists) spoke in their language to each other about how crap London healthcare was. Peter leaned over and speaking Danish said, "the walls have ears" and got out leaving them astonished and embarrassed.

The next target group must be the political classes. Unlike most other people, the artists of parliament are nothing more than a distraction. It's not even a disguised dance anymore. With the red team displaying social empathy whilst the blue lean heavily towards contempt for policies to the left and favour a return to serfdom or even modern slavery. You see even well-educated people buy into the democratic process in the civilized world. But what you need to understand is it's all a lie. For a start any new government has by procedure, got to follow the internal monopoly of the civil service, which is an internally policed and structured safety system. They work hand in hand with the financial markets and banking world. It all gets checked by the major departments of the cabinet and if they give the green light, it will then surface in the upper-house, and I dare say briefings will tour places like Buckingham Palace.

Every professional, irrespective of area of knowledge or level of qualification is tied into perpetuating the myth that voting is a necessity. Some claim it is a dutiful undertaking to respect the sacrifices made during the wars, or even more of a fuss is made by women citing the suffragette movement. In fact, you can vote for who you like, because it doesn't make a blind bit of difference. There are three elephants in the room. Firstly, you can have no regard whatsoever for the House of Lords. This nasty stain on everything that stinks about English democracy is actually a reminder of how Britain forces everything to suit the English ruling class. I am familiar with nations who adopt this two-tier system, some of which are more successful than others, but they elect their upper house which by comparison shows they are still millions of miles better than the mother parliament, because our peerages are handed out like sweets. An archaic golden handshake moment, completely tainted by vested interest, lobbying partnerships and misguided favouritism. And the majority of appointments are political party centric. Just look at the school ties! And they still allow the remnants of the church to sit here for fucks sake! This elephant has an irreconcilable phrase, which accompanies every member of Britian's upper chamber. The word is "Peer."

It's a word closely associated with legal services and the law. So, what or who decides an ability to pass judgment? This upper hand is always something that doesn't represent expertise. Worth reflecting on when you consider the line in law, where you are "tried by a jury of your peers. "

Secondly, we are currently experiencing a cost-of-living crisis, the majority of people who are low paid and hold lower-level qualifications have found that even basic levels of existence are fast becoming unmanageable. So come on, let's do a little bit of maths. We'll start with the economic unrest from 1911-1913. It's the period when working class citizens started getting militant and unionized. Demanding fairness and improved conditions for health and safety, plus a larger disposable income and consequently more life opportunities. This ultimately led into a world war. Where improved remuneration and conditions created a sense of fairness and togetherness. Curiously the unions then acted as peacekeepers and placated most unrest of workforces until the energy crisis of the 70's. Thatcher and the miners and civil disobedience started to challenge the status quo next. Until the financial implosion of 2008 to the present day.

The painful truth doesn't require a precede history lesson of the failures and failings of successive governments since the First World War. You don't even need to read historical archives to try to establish cause and blame! I will lay it out for you here.

A select few with the backing of establishment figures like the university system, or industrial powerhouse's, even figureheads in politics. Emit irresistible qualities. They are of a good background, hunger for success and will literally walk over bodies to achieve goals. Alpha Male, I hear you say! Well now this is when I lose my patience. The thing is a lot of ladder climbers exudes this misplaced confidence. They are habitual failures but also know they are untouchable. We had this type frequently in the Army. "Chocolate teapots" they were known as. "No fucking use to anyone". Ultimately, they coasted through life and were so useless they would get a sideways promotion.

This is where Britain is right now. Just look at the surplus brigade! These are the position sitters. The majority of which are elevated management. They are the ones credited with policy making or implementing changes to procedures. But if you analyse this carefully you will quickly realise that these wasters are thieves of ideas! The workforce will have produced the eureka moment only to have it stolen by a bonus hungry muppet. I'll let you be the judge of that claim, I doubt you can find evidence to the contra, however.

Thirdly comes something which I have observed over the last 50 years. It's not a simple to define set of affairs, or even a phenomenon that is easily explained, but I will try, it's a bit like the school system, which divides potential wizards and practicers of spells into four separate categories of the dark arts. The t of which is named Slytherin! Now I'm not going to claim our political representatives are like a fictitious magic establishment, but I truly believe that J K Rowling understood how many comparisons would be drawn by this juxtaposition, it screamed awkwardness and unsavoury candour, politicians might on paper hold office and exercise their pledge to represent their constituents as fairly as possible. Now put yourself in that cesspool of dirty politics, pandering to party, lobbyists, personal sector, friends and you'll find out very quickly who is clean!

Whenever you get into any kind of understanding of our financial system you can quickly realise who has their fingers in the till. Just find out the non-executive directors on the boards of FT100 companies, or worse still who is a serving director of a company outside of the UK? It's going to stagger you when you see it with your own eyes, as any metaphors would be raised. They certainly raised the eyebrows in my household. Especially the way the ceremonial processes are explained and described in the Potter books draws you immediately towards the stupidity and childishness of our own Houses of Parliament.

The third elephant is the democratic process. I have lived and worked in a few different places, I've also through travel and work, encountered narratives and anecdotal evidence for how voting can produce a change of direction. Except that I disagree with that analysis. The world revolves around the money, it's backed up by organisations like the UN and defence partnerships like NATO. But nothing tangible can change or happen unless the irresponsible and greedy human race are killed off. It's like the moonraker film of the James Bond era. Except for the sake of the planet, it has to become a reality.

Striking workers back in the 1980's. Merit based social mobility:

Unfortunately, they shattered this illusion for me the day a traffic cop took a bribe. I was being ferried home from a cricket match by Ford Capri owner Alex, when he got a light flashing squad car up his backside. He loved his beer did Alex, you could tell by the smell of his breath. But one strategically placed £20 in his driver's licence was all the persuasion it required to proceed.

I have known people lose relatives and loved ones to drink driving, so I'm sorry but I don't accept that the police have a right to plead the fifth on this. It would be wrong for me to dedicate an entire chapter on the Bobby, which, bearing in mind how much of my life has been lived outside of the UK, but what I find irreconcilable is the modern copper!

There are of course a multitude of angles to best represent our figureheads, which if I allowed my frustrations would lead us on a tour of society! I'm tempted to make another list to get a wide representation of the duplicity found on the high street. Unfortunately, they are so multifaceted and commonplace it would probably use up half the book. Point is we are constantly directed to listen to our peers.

But what exactly does that line infer?

So even the upstanding members of the High Street, like bank managers who have always behaved with high standards and have proven themselves beyond reproach! BTW. I defy you to find an upstanding banker. Or more to the point an honest one. They are the modern-day Dick Turpin or "highway robbers," who have stolen our money by the integration of systems which they and they alone control. Look no further than stock exchanges! Investment banks, or even the institutions of the high street. Capitalism is a broken system and must be closed down at the earliest opportunity. Think the south sea bubble, 2008 financial crisis! The other badge wearers are the political figures with the gravy train following them on their every lie. Because let's be honest, who believes anything that is claimed. You can also add the doctors and pharmaceutical groups to the list (this includes veterinary). The major contention I have, is they are self-identifying drug pushers. No one really understands what harm these substances do to the body and possibly more relevantly no one knows what happens to these substances after excretion! Ever wondered why cancer is so prevalent?

Whatever your personal opinion is of the necessity to have a hierarchy just consider some of my prized examples of the old unethical, immoral behaviours. For starters what about the severe rule-breakers? Convention says they must be made an example of. Isn't it funny how things are different across the social spectrum. I knew a judge from my village who regularly drank before driving home! The same is true of 90% of Army officers.

So why do we tolerate this attitude? Well, let me give a synopsis of my take on being British, with all the ridiculous double standards fully exposed. It starts with sex education and the mind-blowing conflicting attitudes that accompany it. I, hand on heart, can swear I never received any sex talk. Not from my parents and not from my school. Which left me free to learn as I went along. The only reason I didn't wind up with an unexpected pregnancy was more down to luck than design. My learning came from newsagent top shelf magazines and any girlfriend that allowed me to cup a feel. This wasn't by choice of course. But the adults in my immediate social circle were AWOL when anything remotely sexual or of a delicate nature needed to be addressed.

I firmly believe that all these missed educational tit bits (no pun intended) probably helped me to become a better person. I don't shy away from the contents of your underwear drawer talk, obviously something which is taboo or frowned upon in some circles. My country has become infatuated with the whole conversation, with some advocating a more liberal education-based system. With the older fuddy daddies still stuck with Victorian attitudes.

The next piece of duplicity must apply to the financial restrictions. You see I grew up in Thatcher's Britain. A period not long out of the grubby seventies, where massive chunks of the working population were demanding a better, fairer remuneration package. Successive government's since, over the following 50 years, have overseen a decline in everything of any value, I deliberately include standards in this observation. But the point is, it's wrong to level any criticism at everyday members of the public. This entire failure is a direct result of the moment Britain handed the keys to the national identity to the financial institutions (b/wankers). The Foreign powers who helped us survive the Second World War, and the friendly nations (aligned to our monarchy) like the influencers at OPEC who helped overcome the energy crisis in 74.

What our entire existence is based on is the perpetuated lie that we are a self-sustaining wealthy country. The very idea that our systems are better than more progressive countries like Germany or Japan proves how crap we are. Don't forget they are the lands that lost the war!

Before anyone starts to question my logic, let me qualify this by admitting having lived in Germany for 25 years and also having a Japanese friend of 20 years, (hey Daisuke) everything looks better overseas, standard of housing, cost of living! But let me be clear where I stand. If two people or more if they are that way inclined, decide to get sexual with each other, then good luck to them. My only demand is that nation's must now enforce a population pledge. The concept I envisage would not only save millions of people the heartache of death by starvation or something equally avoidable, but it would also give the planet a chance to recover from 3.6 million years of humanity!

The first step would involve a world citizens charter. The entire population, YES, all 8 billion would commit to a massive collaboration project. Making the entire globe economy a division of skills. There would be a breadbasket. (Those totally devoted to food production) but done in a different way to communism. There would then be the technology sector, producing eco-friendly transportation means. Next could come educational centres.

My only interactions wouldn't go there with a barge pole. I can recall finding someone's porn stash whilst out walking the dog one day. It became my release point.

who said his goodbyes to my mother. Unlike previous times when we traipsed down their staircase to our car, it was strangely full of conversation, with my mum trying to fit little jewels of advice into the walk. The entire conversation was conducted at an ever-increasing distance, with my mothers' speech growing in volume the wider the distance. I particularly recall granddad standing at the top, as we finally reached the exit, still and thoughtful waiting for us to leave. I am sure my dad trivialised the impending surgery in a similar fashion to the way visits to the dentist used to be handled. One thing is certain, that drive home was final in more ways than I could comprehend!

But it was the eyes that gave the game away. The look of absence. It's something that you can't hide. It's a constant, like a poker player's, "tell" I have observed it in dozens of situations, something which is uncomfortable at the best of times.

So why do we have to change?

It's not even a conversation with you or your parliamentarians. This is, in my humble opinion. One for the brave! You see choices which need to be made have been given the widest berth. Humanity a weapon of mass extinction, treating the planet like a toilet. (Words of UN Secretary General). Woefully inadequate. Do the dance with no pants. Embarrassed?
I'm embarrassed for you. Is a derogatory expression, which is usually used to express contempt or dissatisfaction towards a service or performance which has been so poor, as to leave a foul taste in the mouth.
So, let's all take a deep breath and analyse the medical profession's recent performance during the Covid19 pandemic. I think an accurate analysis would classify all the doctors, not just locally, but globally, as being out of their depth. It reminds me in a way, of the Monty Python sketch, in the hospital with the machine that goes ping!
Now here's the thing, everyone knows how dedicated and hard working the nurses are worldwide. Or when, during things like warfare or natural disasters how the doctors perform an admiral service, in a bones and blood situation, but how many questions are there, elsewhere as to their competence?
I want to make it clear how much I dislike the white coats, yes, they do spend an extraordinary length of time studying. To then progress once qualified to specialise in an area which offers them a future.

What does that actually mean?

In their own minds this means a good financial opportunity. It is disguised by the official line, which is, "to make a difference or to pursue excellence!" Let me cynically destroy this myth of excellence! Because on the one hand we buy into this making a difference argument, but this pretence, that somehow all those years of study have made them into 'the oracle' striving for perfection! No, I'm sorry but, No Way!
Granted in some areas of medical science. There have been unparalleled success stories. I am mainly talking about surgery or conditions which show dramatically improved outcomes post-surgery, but what about the rest?

If you present with a life-threatening injury there is, in a limited number of cases in niche situations a little hope. Now this will either take the form of medication, or surgery, or a combination of both. But and I'm talking about a big But, with a capital B. For stuff outside the norm, like Ebola, or SARS or COVID19, we can't really make a difference, or rather the doctors can't. We, as the human race have supposedly cooperated as a species towards the pandemic.

But to what affect?

It is Now September 2021 and aside from using methods like total oxygenation, or a drug called REMDESIVIR, we are still blind tapping around in the dark, with very few effective therapies, we are hoping a vaccination programme might be the solution. But as of today, just in Britain, we have 10,000 in our hospitals and a daily death toll of 150. Which quite conveniently brings me back to the doctors. Because there is an almost incredible belief, they are infallible, (which, incidentally to a large extent, is where we have placed them!) Completely unwarranted in my opinion.

I would group them together with lawyers, priests, politicians and policemen, because somehow, these leeches have been elevated to stations far and above where they deserve. It's a bit like the old adage, "Blinded by science!"

When under scrutiny or when challenged, the default position is to place an element of uncertainty into things like the diagnosis, or expected prognosis, a bit like the old Witch Doctors in ancient tribes, or Divination in ancient Rome. Don't get me wrong. I have no doubt many of these people actually provide a service, but the vast majority are charlatans. It's all part of a fabric, which either encourages the absence of answerability or which deliberately practices a failure to recognise responsibility.

Now let's move onto the law. Another supposed pillar of society. I have, during my lifetime observed a plethora of examples of complete failure in the Rule of Law, of blatant double standards. Not just in the U.K, but also across the world. My first major bode of contention, revolves around the idea, you can be tried by a panel of your peers.

If a panel of 12 randomly selected university students is our society's way of achieving fairness. Then I say Fuck you! ... I have worked with some of these graduates. At best harmless, but spineless conforming robots. I admit some of them can demonstrate some ability in processing information, but a large percentage have zero common sense. The other side of the coin is the group, who are totally committed to playing the game. I.e. paying into the club/funds to become an accepted member of a particular socio-economic group. These are mostly right-wing latent homophobes, who given any judgement call, will usually side with the money or class! To which I expect many of you will question how I can comment on this.

Well quite simply, I can because this was the life I was born into and lived for my formative years. The majority of my parent's friends, were well-to-do Tory supporters, forever hanging on the coat tails of affluent and in some cases influential local dignitaries.

Watch the film, Twelve Angry Men, with Henry Fonda. It's set in New York, but the story is relevant the world over. It asks the question, "What If?" It's a very graphic illustration as to how the jury system is completely fallible. It highlights the imperfections from police investigation, to witness reliability,

The way either defence lawyers or prosecutors can become major factors in Trial outcomes. In real life cases like the OJ Simpson murder or the Birmingham 6 unsafe convictions there is always one constant. Namely ... TIME... Because of our system.

So anyhow, explain to me this. If countries like Myanmar are constantly oppressing their civilian populations, or if nations are guilty of crimes against humanity. Surely the United Nations if used correctly, could prevent any blatant abuses of power?

Don't you find it shameful that it took until 1807 to outlaw the slave trade and until 1834 to make it illegal anywhere in the British Empire to own or trade in slaves. But only until as recently as 2010 to ban it in England. At the time of writing there is also this. It is estimated that there are 27-million slaves held throughout the world.

There are lots of discrepancies within the world of justice too. For example, the US has 1% of its population imprisoned. Whereas even though other countries prison levels are lower, like GB. The actual true morality levels within nations are something which is open to interpretation. For example, there is no global agreement on what constitutes rape! Scandalous!

My theory on this which can also be transferred to any major crime, is that I truly believe the failure to be consistent globally, is a throwback to ancient times. So, there we have it. The cat is out of the bag. This baseless assumption we will somehow be better served by having individuals, of superior qualification, giving direction or providing moral compass, proves just how short-sighted and gullible we all are. I will give a few examples for each major influencer, and you be the judge.

I will start with the Police. Because from my early years I was educated to respect the law, so I tried to be, for the most part, an honest, law-abiding person. But my doubts about this arrangement soon became clear. I remember the exact moment in fact. I was being driven home from a Sunday cricket match. Which we had won and in which I had bowled well, consequently my chauffeur had drunk a few celebratory beers.

Anyway, after ten minutes or so of the homeward journey I heard a siren. Now I dare say this type of behaviour was repeated nationwide daily, during the late seventies. Either from a night out or sporting event, but as a passenger I quickly realised my elder teammate could potentially lose his license. So, still in his whites, he pulled over and wound down his side window. I saw in my rear mirror, a copper climbing out, and then to my amazement, what happened next left me flabbergasted. The guy who was driving, got out a twenty-pound note and placed it in his driver's license. This was then passed to PC Plod. It then miraculously disappeared. The officer just said, "drive carefully sir!' Knowing full well we should have been breathalysed.

The first major questions, surfaced around the Thatcher years. I mean sure, during the energy crisis, of the seventies we had seen unrest. There were also flash points during the industrial actions of union led disputes. But just look at the obstacles that polarised society in Britain.

The aggression against the miners, the unrest following the Brixton riots or the ineptitude of policing generally with a nod to Hillsborough or the Poll tax heavy handedness.

In fact, within a very short time span a number of key events occurred, but you must go back to 1977, when Home Secretary Merlyn Rees approved a pay package for the constabulary of a fifty per cent pay rise prompted by lobbyists who warned of growing civil disquiet about pay and conditions. This was essentially the birth of the countries division.

Anyway, after 1981 Toxteth, 1984/5 miners, or 1989 Hillsborough, this creepy bureaucracy serving system slumbered into motion. Oh sure, there have been improvements. We now had the Police and Criminal Evidence Act, which provided provision for the Police Complaints Authority (since replaced by the IPCC) Again based on a very laborious and time-consuming Lord Scarman report.

Shortly thereafter, The Prosecution of Offences act created the CPS, which you should look back on and think, you are pulling my chains! Because even after fifty-years in some cases, policing is an absolute joke! They have effectively been bought out by the politicians. With a bunch of Yes-Men/Women towing the party-political line. The recent findings of evidence tampering during the Hillsborough enquiry proves that. (An enquiry which has taken 30-years by the way!)

You then have ongoing situations like the Stephen Lawrence botched investigations. The failure to prosecute people involved in the Grenfell Tower fiasco, the Metropolitan Police being embroiled in unethical surveillance tactics, even one bastard cop who raped, killed then dismembered a young woman.

But again, on a personal level I have seen police on horses charging fans at QPR's Loftus Road, totally unprovoked! But perhaps most disturbing was a use of a personal friendship, between civilian and police, to catch an employee suspected of D&D purely on the bidding of an employer. An event I witnessed first-hand.

I would love to be convinced by successive media manipulation stories. Desperately trying to downplay the seriousness and extent of Police corruption, but I am annoyed and quite frankly feel vindicated after a lifetime of disappointment.

So that's one side of this web of deceit.

My second one concerns the schooling. I have recently watched an episode of QI. One of those programmes where you take enjoyment in Stephen Fry's command of directing a group of guests on a journey through various interesting topics. New world order. Breaking the Rules.

This is not intended to be anti-establishment propaganda, or even the hateful ramblings of some disaffected minority. But I want all the sane people on the planet to stop and think. I mean in a world emergency it's probably the only time we can ever do this. So, to that end I say, Thank you Covid19. Because hopefully some of you may have woken up, "no pun intended, "or even smelt the roses, "again no pun intended!"

I have a series of predictions, which do not attempt to drive any political narrative, or even to compare different nations, histories, even beliefs. I am a diseased middle-aged man. Not with coronavirus, like many would expect in 2020. But with a mystery illness which is slowly causing a degeneration of my body. We will deal with this later in the book. Suffice is to say I became ill in March 2012, and I have become very cynical with anything relating to modern medicine.

You have all probably had a bunch of free time on your hands lately, I am talking about the exceptional circumstances, resulting in nations going into lockdown. So let us begin there. I am no exception. This thing, (Covid 19), has caused radical changes everywhere. Putting some into total isolation, enormous restrictions were placed on populations.

Phrases such as social distancing became the new normal. We also were told to 'shield?' Now I do not want to repeat the claims and counter claims in the mainstream media. But we all have a duty and an opportunity to reconfigure. Now I am not going to be provocative, I'm just going to provide facts and let you be the judge. I demand every single world citizen understand the phrase, "Extinction Level Event!" I use this saying so that you can all understand how serious this is.

Right, here are the most widely accepted progressions of Covid-19. According to the WHO the first identifiable case was logged on 8th Dec 2019. It is a very hard claim to accurately be corroborated. This has been due to China showing reluctance to share information. The sticking point appears to be tracing the ground zero. One theory is this is a virus which mutated from severe acute respiratory syndrome, (SARS or COV-SARS). A mutation probably caused by a zoonotic (animal-human) transmission.

There are lots of coronaviruses, some of which have origins in obscure creatures. For example, during the SARS outbreak in 2003, it was speculated or hypothesized Civet cats or bats may be the carriers. But humans also have the ability to host nurture or infect corona. You may also have heard about domesticated animals becoming infected, like dogs and cats. There were also reports of mutations arising at slaughterhouses, even at a fur farm in Denmark.

Anyway the 2003 SARS outbreak only infected a few hundred thousand, killing an estimated 4,000, something you all need to understand and ponder, is that Wuhan is also the site of laboratories where researchers have been experimenting on SARS!

Wang Yanyl director of Wuhan institute of virology (WIV) admitted this to the Chinese state media, and it was confirmed by the Daily Express in June 20, they were working on 3 live Corona strains.

So first red flag:

Irrespective of who is implicated in the WIV admission. How come no-one has been arrested? Why are nations more worried about their economies?

What treatments have been made available to everyone infected? But for me the most important aspect of everything which has gone on over the last year, has been the bullshitting! Supposed peer groups and institutions have all gone AWOL, I hear approval of certain countries, and the way they have dealt with the pandemic.

New Zealand and Taiwan are two, who appear to have done well, but let's quantify that perception. Do we regard success as a direct link to the death toll?

Isn't a more accurate measure of who has achieved the better containment, the nations who have had the least infections? Now I'm no medical expert but surely the total isolation and subsequent reduction in cases has to reach zero before everyone can be sure the virus has run its race.

I am still not convinced the medical community has been telling us the whole story, or even if it can. I have been informed the accuracy of virus testing is only as good as the tester and the sample evaluation. So very quickly you see possible gaps opening up which I will expand upon very shortly, but a major doubt for me, has been the ineffective treatments given by doctors!

Now I will rarely question healthcare professionals. UNTIL NOW, but this crisis has proven to me the failings of modern medicine. It has also shown how poor humans are with personal hygiene. Even the basics like hand washing are too much effort for some individuals. So, let's delve into the world of the doctor.

Basic qualities include the ability to show an aptitude to pass exams? To which I say, WHY! What exactly qualifies anybody to be lauded and celebrated for being able to do nothing more than monkey see, monkey do! Or have a propensity to retain information, and by this, I mean in the most unfriendly way possible. The vast majority of these people are averagely knowledgeable gold diggers. A large percentage will take the default position, which is, they want to make a difference to the community.

Utter bullshit:

They are all playing the long game. Oh sure, they do sometimes work long hours. But who gives a crap, so do cab drivers or cleaners! They want the financial rewards, for doing the least amount of work. If you think back to your childhood, it's like painting by numbers. Or building a piece of IKEA furniture. Everyone can do it, as long as they have the diagram, colours and tools. Patient has xyz problem! The handbook says try cure no 1. If success, you are a hero. If not try cure 2. Repeat the process until a cure works or the patient dies!

What a crock of shit:

A doctor trains for between 4 and 7 years at medical school. There is then a chance to specialise into the various specialist categories of medicine, there are more than 60 of these to choose from. All in all, the studying and training can take over 10 years, with refresher courses and seminar to remain current. Now I recognise there are hundreds of different areas of health, where people can use experience and tried and tested methods to achieve a successful outcome. But let's try doing joined up writing! In the age of the Internet, how reliant should we be on old school medicine?

Has anyone ever questioned the doctor mafia about the long-term effects of their science? Now I realise many people throughout the globe are unsure, even worried. But let's put the recent pandemic into context. The virus is a Biohazard.

The area of medicine which should cover this emergency is, internal medicine or intensive medicine. What is strikingly clear are the similarities between the Novichok nerve agent poisoning in Salisbury, S. England and this virus. The immediate aftermath of Salisbury, was to isolate, trace the source, find potential infected. Treat them and perform biohazard remediation. This refers to (OPIM). Other potential infectious materials. It's a term commonly associated with crime scene investigation. So here is a quote. (Your alarm bells should be ringing by now.), this is direct from forensic science. A Biohazard refers to a type of biological material that threatens living organisms. Every country should have immediately closed borders.

But this was something, which not only required the action of governments it should have been demanded by WHO and every national health service. I have seen ideas from virologists and a university college London mathematical analyst, about the statistical likelihood of a devastating second wave, especially if Covid mutates as feared.

Let me make a distinction with my next comment. I do not trust certain parts of medical science! We find ourselves in the midst of a global pandemic, which on its own destructive way at the time of my writing has killed xxxxxx people. But then along comes a vaccine. The golden ticket! However, unlike the chocolate factory, the drugs developed to protect us are as understood as a novice skydiver. The chute may open! But what exactly are the consequences?

You only had to look around ICU wards to understand how utterly clueless these supposed bright sparks really have been. It's like trying to fight a forest fire with water pistols. Even the miraculous appearance of a vaccine, reminded me of Joseph Mengele. The Nazi scientist who carried out unethical experiments on concentration camp inmates a mixture of medications, just to see what the results would be! Ring any bells?

But you see the clue is in the name Covid 19 or SARS or COV-SARS (severe acute respiratory syndrome). In other words, a breathing affecting illness. So how come at the first initial peak, our so-called leaders and chief medical officer were surprised to learn the majority of critically ill patients required ventilators? Especially after the 2003 SARS outbreak.

Anyway, the most obvious shortcoming was every healthcare umbrella organisation. Even the WHO does not come out of this unscathed. The most beneficial statistic I think is the number of deaths above average. Which means in Britain with an official death toll of 64,000 people, this is wrong by about 25,000.

If you analyse the data coming from other countries, you can begin to get an idea where this is going. For example, the US has reported approx 15 million post-tests with 300,000 deaths. Which basically means every fiftieth person who catches the virus can die. World population 7 billion = potential death toll of 50 mil.

Ultimately, I hope to be proven wrong. But I think as a species we are too far into the abyss to recover. So, this is my gift if you like. It is my farewell to the planet I love. A final goodbye, to all the 7 billion misfits, wasters, and scumbags, and I hope you are all proud. On behalf of the remaining creatures on earth, I say good riddance!

Let's take the 50-cent tour of why!

We always like to place ourselves as the guardians of the planet. But hang on...A popular conclusion can be drawn on studies conducted with our genetically similar species, the chimpanzee. We now have documented evidence of these animals' ability to perform something, which until recently, we believed only human beings could. I'm talking about making tools. You see somewhere an ape discovered how to use a rock to open a nut!

We now know other animals are demonstrating similar skills. The birds such as crow that can open containers to get milk for example, or the squirrels who can not only scavenge, but also show planning techniques in preparations to hibernation. The more you look in nature the more you find.

Why does this matter?

Because arrogant and self-promoting homo sapiens, cannot admit that other creatures will eventually catch us, hopefully even overtake us. Or even that they are already more advanced than we are willing to concede. There have always been different dominators of the food chain, the dinosaurs are the most obvious example. But what about insects or simple single celled parasites. It makes you think, doesn't it? I will use the David and Goliath analogy. It is often used to describe how someone or something apparently inferior, can overcome overwhelming odds to defeat a supposedly superior being. Covid19?

So, let's go back to the ape's ability to learn. If you think about it, it's what humans place the highest value on. We have only just left the womb and yet policy dictates we must collect experiences and knowledge! Our whole lives we are forced into education. In actual fact, we are no longer allowed the privilege of breakthrough discoveries, like the nut cracking chimp. Oh no, we are put through a selection process. A kind of suitability test!

Let me throw my first prediction out there. Every species will eventually over time, develop thoughts, eventually leading to problem solving, which will lead to a social structure and awareness. What we have done is confuse the purpose of development!

Whereby a person's intelligence and suitability, dictate what options await later in life. If you agree then nod. Remember big brother is watching...He is always watching! ...So, who actually believes they are now in control of their lives? Let us analyse the worlds human education process. Irrespective of nationality, we are given the basic survival essentials.

There are early foundations taught, from potty training to physical education, basic language skills to safety and danger recognition. Following a number of reinforcement years our extended families or state institutions take over. This is where our species have lost the plot!

We have created a myriad of NGO's, Institutions and Organisations, whose sole purpose it is to steal our souls. Just imagine where the instruction comes from, to pursue technical advancement. Or the insatiable thirst for knowledge. Our entire raison d'être is based on a need to succeed! For me I kind of view everything with utter cynicism. After all, how many real "Eureka" moments have there ever been in human history?

Ok granted some things have been inspired, like the wheel, or agriculture. But step back and evaluate every breakthrough. For the entire lifespan of the human race, 99% of every advancement has its origins in some form of chance encounter, and the subsequent refinement and development of the original idea.

Let's explore one avenue, to demonstrate human intelligence. Or education. Imagine our first ancestors, in Africa. Probably Ethiopia. We live near to running water. One day a fallen branch flows past on the water. An idea forms. We could utilise other pieces of wood, to make a raft to go fishing on. Before long other useful suggestions materialise. The outcome is the first boat. Now obviously this is just a hypothetical example, but you can see how transferable everything is, one random event can lead to history changing inspirations.

Now I used water as an example, but it works just as well for the land with the wheel. So, I will defy anyone to give a reason why other creatures, over time, do not possess the chance to evolve into similar modifiers, like we have. Just imagine how great it would be if we could be living a peaceful co-existence with the other creatures. I also know, how mankind is too self-obsessed and utterly selfish, therefore, there will never be a shared eco-system.

The answer is simple. I have spent years trawling through the failings of British 'Governance and there is one constant repeating theme. Our country has been led by moronic, self-serving chinless bureaucrats for all my lifetime. Never tackling the real problems because they are unpalatable for our electorate. Always choosing to take the easy route. People have been applauded for their leadership within government. Which on reflection is possibly the greatest scandal of the past 60 years. Instead of leadership within the various sectors of society, the responsibility has been farmed out to regulators and private companies. Which means that when things eventually do go disastrously wrong. Which by the way is happening right now! The politicians and bureaucrats wash their hands and place the resolutions in the hands of public enquiries and legal teams.

A totally unacceptable situation?

I will give you a little taste of what is happening right now, so you can think about how utterly ridiculous our system is. Let's start with the Grenfell Tower enquiry. A clear-cut failure by a large number of groups. The house builders failed to install a system of emergency extinguishers! Something that is standard in all of Germany's high-rise buildings. The deadly incorporation of highly inflammable cladding was allowed to happen because no agency did the necessary checks on the installation!

The fire brigade had no plans for emergency evacuation of residents, despite warnings that the fire could, probably would escalate if allowed to spread unchecked! The council had forgotten about its duty of care and disregarded the warning signs of other examples of cladding failure. The key for all the agencies involved in this sorry process, was a massive shortsighted approach to the following of "Due Diligence." Yet, get this: - the fire was in 2017. Today is 2024 and the enquiry is still ongoing.

Next up is the sub postmaster and mistress scandal. Thankfully highlighted by a Mr Alan Bates.

A badly treated and disenfranchised group of Post Office employees. Most of whom had been harangued and pursued by the group. For committing crimes against a failing software system called "Horizon."

Some, if not all were forced into a legal process that in many cases resulted in convictions. Most of the time the postmasters were forced to pay money back which they didn't lose. It was a lose/lose situation and highlighted failings on so many levels that it showed how utterly ridiculous redress, and the legal process is in the United Kingdom in 2024.

For me it shows beyond doubt, that our entire society is based on boundaries and regulations that are programmed to failure.

We are not talking about little misdemeanours or anything trivial either. Some of the people affected by these events have lost everything. From reputation and personal relationships to insane financial losses and even in some cases liberty. Imagine being shamed "wrongly" for decades and having to wait for an Inquiry to exonerate your behaviour. UTTERLY SHAMEFUL '

I personally would want to see the whole plethora of deceiving idiots be sent to prison for twenty years and all their assets and those of their families being seized and given to the affected families?

Up next, comes one of my personal situations with all its ramifications and consequences and why I feel it is so important to highlight during this part of my story, because like the film

"PULP FICTION" it kind of links up my story in so many ways. It's all about the regulatory bodies of our island shores. I'm going to begin by going off on a tangent. In the Army we used to have a saying that described people who were given positions they were either unqualified for or were put there intentionally to keep them out of the way! We would describe them as sideways promotions. Usually occupying desks where the worst they could do was signing erroneous contracts or something similar.

It sounds a good idea in principle, but unfortunately the consequences of this policy would be to elevate absolute idiots into higher and higher positions. Which is inconsequential for the lower ranks and lower officer positions.

Unfortunately, I watched this practice continue until just before my leaving the service after the fall of the Berlin Wall, the inevitable implosion of communism! Or so we thought! I remember during my service years glancing around the parade grounds or watching joint operations or something that highlighted the inadequacies of certain groups.

It was usually the chinless wonders, or offspring of the officer types that made you sit bolt upright. The ones who had gone to university and got very mediocre degrees in stupid worthless subjects like history or geography. Sometimes when we deployed you would end up explaining how to do the basics and then plotting a course whereby you would never be in the proximity of them.

Sound familiar? Just look at people around the old conservative government like Boris or Liz or. But the sad truth is that this insanity stretches right out across all professions and qualifications. For me it reared its ugly head when I was 7 or 8.

Shortly after that car crash with my mother. I was shaking and jittering and sleeping incredibly unusual hours. On one occasion at my Nan's house, I slept for over 24 hours. Mirroring my mother's unusual sleep patterns. But obviously as a child you have different circadian rhythms and my situation was flagged as being the result of a strenuous fishing expedition with gramps, or the consequence of being in the outdoors of Beachy head. Or possibly the sea air? Oh, the joys of grandparents who lived on the outskirts of Eastbourne. A town I visited in 2010 whilst working as a union rep for UNITE.

Point is, it's one thing to hold a certificate or qualification. But it's something else when your performance is decisive in the wellbeing or outcome of somebody else. Let's go back to that Post Office scandal or the tower fire! I'm convinced that it would have taken just a small handful of individuals to make a noticeable change of outcome!

In my life it was that fateful day when my mother sped around the corner heading to Holmbury St Mary. To the picturesque thatched roofed cottage that nestled on the side of the road, with the streams and newts, a postcard picture of British middle class.

Unfortunately, my mother had panicked when the accident happened. The motorcycle had flown over our roof and apart from a few minor issues with paintwork and chrome we seemed to have survived! QUICK TIP, "NEVER ASSUME!"

I'm convinced my mother was petrified of the consequences of admitting the accident to dad. So, guess what... It was never reported... So fast forward two years and first debilitating symptoms of the accident started to appear on my mother. I on the other hand had been having some kind of character difficulties. I recall during those two years being more irritable than normal. Twice being kicked out the car and just having to wait for them to come and collect me.

On one occasion I ran away from my parents in Littlehampton, during a meeting with mum's mum. I remember the policeman driving me back and threatening me with "dire consequences?" I ran away from home a few times during this period, but I was small and a very naughty boy, so, nobody linked things together.

I remember at primary school in Godalming how fit I was becoming, driven by an internal desire to excel at sports, until one day I was playing football in the snow and my body just shut down. I suspected chill banes, but in hindsight it was the first time my condition had ever overpowered my internal system. Obviously, I could site hundreds of occasions during my life where the condition was winning and forced me to take a break.

The secondary school trip to Narbonne, in the south of France. Where I slept in the luggage rack above the seats for the entire return journey. As all sufferers who have this problem know it's all about management. Optic Neuritis is very difficult when you are powering down an icy Black run. On the slopes of Lake Louise. Or when the sun affects you while attempting to surf in Waikiki. The ones I got away with "just" were the endurance events. Like Vierssen marathon. Or the speed march at the end of my Sergeant's training course.

Scariest one was during a drive to England from Germany in 1985. In an Austin 1300, with no heating. I was going back for my posting to US & Canada. I pulled over in Duisburg at about 2 am, getting rescued about 5am, and then spending a small fortune to get towed to Zeebrugge.

I could of course go on. The fact is the debilitating episodes have become less frequent over the years, and I actually thought I was winning in 2003. When, in a stable relationship with my partner and kids I had my last 365 running year, completing at least 5km every single day. This included a triathlon, marathon, 30km hill race and the crowning glory "Sylvester Lauf," but unfortunately it was shortly after that when I realised that things were not as good as I expected.

I started to feel queasy around cigarettes and cigarette smoke. My partner was diagnosed with breast cancer, and I was taking more and more punishment in terms of hours spent working and parenting and keeping the family together! I always look at this period as the straw that broke the camel's back. In 92, I had organised a charity event to raise money for the cancer research charity and the Royal Marsden Hospital. Quite poetic when I reflect on how things have panned out. I think it was only a few years later that I lost my father, and that was when I knew I couldn't continue.

My grandfather used to refer to us as the gypsy family. Forever moving and unable to find comfort in familiar surroundings. Quite an accurate description in hindsight. Supported by the evidence of my travels. I believe that a child is moulded up to about 16/7. Which for me would total around 7 complete moves. Giving me integration skills that most people wouldn't necessarily experience. I'm quite proud of that little statistic, but it also means I have no childhood friendships that have lasted.

Some of the most enjoyable ones are those that relate to sports clubs or playground activities.

I will name a few to demonstrate how things worked out. Timothy (son of tv's James Herriot) was an interesting acquaintance. Sorry about the Elvis record collection! Conrad, funniest person I think I have ever met. In music lessons, when trying to recognise the instrument. Wrote synthesizer for every sound. Mr Wong, great tennis player. Jane hottest athlete in our year, with a wicked sense of humour. We once tried to blow the classroom up with lots and lots of sodium and magnesium. Sorry Mr Davies. I went back to Rodborough once in the 90's but the burn marks had all gone.

Anyway, the only reason to make this short diversion in my story is to explain how things were progressing in my life. I was finding concentration in my subjects at lessons becoming more and more difficult. I substituted academic achievement for physical activity.

I was so disengaged towards the end of my studies that I was solely focused on sports and travel. Oh yes and girls. My first girlfriend was the daughter of a formula one racing driver. I had left secondary school with virtually no qualifications but what I did have was the ability to lie through my back teeth. In fact, it is something I have always done.

I mean towards the end I was a dab hand at passing tests and the like. But in the years 16/17, I was utterly useless at fact retention and demonstration. I'm truly grateful to the Army for motivating me to "be all you can be" because 12 years and a whole bunch of qualifications later I was finally able to classify myself as normal. I have come a long way from travelling on trains to Waterloo without paying on an evening. By picking up discarded pink day return tickets at the local railway station and travelling up with my bicycle in the luggage compartment. Or going to visit my girlfriend at Walton on-Thames. Oh, happy days. I even recall hearing about the W Club from some random commuters as we pulled into Guildford.

The idea of being in the W Club, was to drink a Gin & Tonic at every station that had a W in the name. So, let's see.... Waterloo, Queenstown Road, Wimbledon, New Malden, Walton on-Thames, Weybridge, Byfleet, and new haw, West Byfleet, Woking, Worplesdon. An incredible number of stupid drinking by very irresponsible and overpaid city workers.

My old friend Pete tried this once and gave up at Weybridge! I bet the idiot stock exchange workers who regularly played this game are either dead now or have undergone kidney surgery. But happily, I learned from a young age that people who carry a condition cannot afford to dabble too badly in alcohol consumption. Something I was always scolding my mother for. I'm not going to say I haven't ever done it but for people who carry a condition. It does come with some significant side effects. On one occasion I got drinking Tequila with a group of Mexican tourists in London. I remember getting to Waterloo, but then it is a bit hazy. I woke up on a parked train at Yeovil Junction at about 6 in the morning.

On another occasion I went to a nightclub in Detmold in Germany to watch a band called "The Damned". If memory serves me correctly it was 1985 and the club was Hunky-dory. On this occasion I woke up on a toilet in a pitch dark and locked up venue. I triggered some kind of silent alarm and sure enough a couple of Polizei picked me up. So, I learnt a very useful lesson that night and one I have only failed to follow on one occasion.

It was 1988 and my friend Fletch had organised a canal boat holiday to do the Cheshire Ring. It began in Stoke and went up to Wolverhampton and then down through Stafford. We were a very unusual group. One more squaddie, two Posties, Malc the Alc, two lads from London, the Fat controller from Waterloo, Fletcher's wife Bee and a Morris dancer called Psycho! Now not everyone was a drinker! (I include myself in this) but Airtech Ian got me into trying the local beer!

Before long Malcolm (who I think worked for SEALINK) started to make it his mission to beat the soldiers. Then before long, the whole boat got lost in a kind of liquid diet.

The two Posties, Graham and Gary, were in a state of permanent depression, whereas the Peckham guys had permanent smiles on their faces. What happened in Wolverhampton however should never be forgotten. I'm not sure how it started but the whole McDonalds restaurant has probably never experienced a war like it. I was sat with Glynn and Bee, and everyone had their massive meals in front of them. I think the first attack was started by our morris dancing friend Psycho. He quite purposefully dipped a chicken McNugget in a sticky sauce and complained about the boat sleeping arrangements. Citing how Fletch and his wife had taken all the room.

Next thing you know Bee is clutching her blouse with the stain of a full-frontal assault showing off her body. There was a slightly uncomfortable moment that followed this until all hell broke loose. People were hiding behind tables and fittings and throwing stuff at each other. Until eventually the entire restaurant had been dragged down into this mess. I'm not going lie, but this was simultaneously the funniest and most embarrassing ten minutes of my life. We eventually got the heck out of there. Just before the police arrived. But to all the participants in the battle of Wolverhampton I thank you for being such good sports. Funnily enough only Glynn was questioned by the cops. So, remember if you have MS don't drink!

Going back to the chinless wonder brigade I have a lot more to say about this, before I got distracted by the drinking. Maybe it's because I mentioned Boris that I was sidetracked. Anyway, it is not rocket science when you look at the examples, I have mentioned about regulatory bodies and the supporting mechanisms and support that supposedly exist to protect and prevent miscarriages of justice. You surely must recognise that our system has failed. I could go on a rant about hundreds of areas where even the blindest people have started to wake up to what is wrong in our land. But I don't want to distract from my concerns and story, so here is the next section.

One area that concerns me most about the whole process of my life post 2012, is the white coats. A group of overpaid underperforming individuals. Who for the most part is following strict guidelines and policy decisions that dictate how they should treat patients. Now we have all read about the marvellous contributions that the doctors and nurses made during the pandemic. But understand this. If the so-called leaders of the NHS had actually listened and done their job before the cracks in the system became vast chasms we wouldn't even be talking about a crisis?

You see even after my suspected stroke of 2012 and the dereliction of duty with regards to the timely treatment that I received. I am utterly devastated that twelve years later I am still waiting for a proper explanation as to why my family has been so badly affected.

I wasn't included on any investigation after my mother first started showing symptoms of MS, but probably more to the point I was always left out of any discussion, despite sharing the similar symptoms as my mother.

In hindsight this was a blessing in disguise because I dare say if I had been forced into sharing her journey of intrusive procedures like the spinal tap or lumbar puncture. Or the experimental drug cocktails she was given, and which ultimately resulted in her demise. I dare say I would have succumbed to dark thoughts and anxiety could have tipped me over the edge.

Whenever I talk to fellow sufferers about their experiences it is always the same. Being driven into a lifetime of the same money-go-round drug adventures that mum had to endure. With white coats doing the bidding for the pharmaceutical companies.

It will come as no surprise to you that I have no sympathy for this band of charlatans. The ones that love to call themselves neurologists. I don't know what their remuneration packages are, but I'm sure they're earning 100 times too much. Because remember when I spoke about managing my symptoms myself? Well, I did. I got incredibly fit, and I didn't need a white coat consultation or anything of the kind. Until the contracting of glandular fever in 2008. This was the beginning of my deterioration.

You see it always strikes me as funny in a perverse kind of way, when the white coats carry on about the different pathologies of MS patients. How everyone is different... The answer is no they are not. The problem is the deterioration is set at different levels until they have been exposed to a secondary infection. Which for me was the virus responsible for glandular fever!

I recently had a neurological consultation with a white coat, who essentially admitted that there was increasingly more evidence to support this hypothesis. But given that co-morbidity is an important factor in diagnosis and treatment. Surely this is where R&D and funding should be focused on. I mean it's not rocket science!

The State of Affairs Email:

From: "REESMOGG, Jacob: **Date:** 11 September 2014:
To: Ross **Subject: RE: The state of affairs**

Thank you for your email addressed to Jacob Rees-Mogg. If you have not previously done so, please send your full postal address. If you are a constituent Jacob will write to you once answers to your enquiries have been found.

From: Ross:
Sent: 11 September 2014:
To: REESMOGG, Jacob and others:
Subject: The state of affairs

This is a considered appraisal of my experience of the NHS and other agencies in and around the Bath/Bristol area. It is a detailed, methodical account of **my** treatment at two hospitals, a community care team, physiotherapy, at two establishments and the general support from neurology and MS advisors (nurses), over the course of two and a half years and the failure of any one group, institution or agency to take full control of the advice, support and disease management of my care.

I am Ross Bowran (NHS ID and details supplied): This is to raise issues surrounding my treatment, but more importantly to allow the relevant powers to instigate changes in procedure to allow people who find themselves in similar circumstances as mine to be treated with the dignity and care they deserve.

WHY? Because the Services for MS sufferers as they currently stand are "NOT FIT FOR PURPOSE!" overloaded and unable to cope with the management of individuals like me. This is not conjecture or opinion, this is "**FACT.**"

It is borne out by conversations I have had with healthcare professionals from across the medical spectrum, from my own experiences with fellow sufferers at the MS Therapy centre in Bradley Stoke, fellow sufferers who I tried to bring together in South Bristol forming a group with the MS society and from nurses, physiotherapists, OT's, doctors, specialists and even management. (The latter being off the record) also from different agencies who undertake various roles as private companies (Sirona care and health) being one supposedly easing the NHS burden? In my opinion it does nothing but confuse the situation. Splitting the responsibilities and making it very unclear as to who is actually in charge.

This is not meant to be a damning indictment of the policies in place to manage services and treatments, **BUT** it is clear to me now this division is deliberate so as to deflect any criticism from any one agency. As a result, causing patients (me included) to lose faith in one of the most important pillars of our society.

RAISING A GRIEVANCE OR CONCERN:

Because of this dividing up of responsibilities, when things do go wrong the hardest part is picking one individual or department to actually shoulder the blame. It is more often than not a collective failure.

Patients who put themselves in this "**challenging the system,**" category automatically feel vulnerable with respect to any future treatment they may receive, or perhaps it is the effort required to raise a concern in the first place, or, like me, their complaints were blamed on Admin short comings or communication errors or part accepted as a collective.

What disturbs me, however, is there is no attempt to rectify the situation, or apologize. Instead, the response is **hollow** unwilling to do anything more than lose itself in the machinery. This is in most cases in my opinion, is not just a "**deflection of responsibility**" .... more like a... "**Dereliction of duty!**" Good Health does not grow on trees, if you lose it through negligence, you can't simply go and pick another one.

It is **unacceptable** to hide behind them, "you should have raised this in a timely manner!" Many MS sufferers are incapable of expressing their misgivings in a timely manner! This also applies to the frail and infirm. They sometimes forget points which they would have liked to talk about and only remember them when the opportunity has passed.

It sometimes appears the advocacy, PALS, SEAP and all health complaint services half-heartedly investigate a grievance knowing the complainant is unlikely to pursue the matter further due to the nature of their illness or their mental capacity, or in the hope the passage of time will pacify. They will never accept fault. Because to do so would tarnish the reputation of not just their establishment but also the whole system.

Another favourite is, "We were unaware of these concerns!" My answer is: I have repeatedly voiced my concern, and I have also tried to use the complaints procedure, both in and out of hospital. Other MS sufferers have encountered the same.

It has proved fruitless on all levels. So, what chance have the less able, or more vulnerable? Every part of the complaint's procedure is designed to be draining, both mentally and physically. "**This is unacceptable**!" See Admission 4!

So why me and why now?

I have tried to be reasonable on all matters but am now beyond frustrated by the events of the last half year. No one has taken a lead in my treatment or my general deterioration through the past two and a half years. My last experience has left me both emotionally and physically scarred, I have lost 20% vision in my left eye down to my last hospitalization **see Admission** 4!

It is unacceptable to expect patients to have to wait **months** or years to speak at length to specialists. Or have to travel long distances or deal with endless streams of letters or referrals. Especially when they are clearly suffering because of it.

RECOMMENDATION 1.

*There should be **ONE Specialist** be that a GP, or a specialist (Neurologist) or MS nurse who coordinates everything for MS patients. Don't say we can't do that! Or We do that already!*

What do I want?

I would like a formal apology over my treatment and a written acceptance of the validity of the issues I raise. I also would like my healthcare/neurology team to formally accept in writing the failings which I have raised and for them to become more proactive in managing my care/treatment. If possible, putting me in the hands of specialist neurophysiotherapy.

In respect of DMT I want assurances any future treatment will be properly monitored. Then after 2 and a half years of avoidable stupidity finally to take

my disease management seriously and find a course of action found which provides me with some quality of life. This doesn't mean sending an MS nurse to try and empathize with me or to discourage me from complaining! It means better advice and monitoring.
I also would like my recommendations assessed and reasons given as to why they can or cannot be implemented.

I shouldn't have to complain, but I feel I need to, not just for myself but also for those less able.
I imagine your reply will be in corporate speak about your inability to find any **FAILURE** but what you have to realise is people like me **DO NOT** I repeat **DO NOT** have the slightest interest in you finding out who, where, what, why, or how it went wrong! ******* **IT HAS GONE WRONG** *******
This is. "**Real people**" with "**Real problems**" Confronted by situations designed to obscure the short-comings and failings of "YOUR SYSTEM!".
It's not about identifying the cause, it's learning from the mistakes and ensuring they do not repeat. Which up until now **YOU HAVE NOT**!

ADMISSION 1 RUH BATH 3.2.12:

I was admitted to the RUH in Bath 3.2.12, having had what I suspected as being either an epileptic episode or a stroke. I had recently had 2 injuries which my body seemed to have overcome. One was being assaulted in a pub, the other was being injured in a gardening accident lifting a disabled neighbour's garden waste (including concrete posts) late 2011, I suffered my first continence problems, 12th January, I suffered my first back spasm. My GP assessed me and realising I needed immediate tests referred me straight away to the A&E, RUH in Bath. However, this being a Friday I was left to wait 7 hours only to be given a head-to-toe examination and a function/perception test.

I was not actually seen and examined until Monday the 6.2.12 when I was given CAT scan and MRI scan. During this time, I was placed on the MAU ward which I can only describe as a hectic noisy chaotic environment. The nurses and doctors on this ward have my utmost respect but putting patients into this ward who would benefit more from a relatively more sedate atmosphere must be revisited. At one point the patient to my right took the mattress off his bed and was sleeping on the floor.

Whilst on this ward there was a constant ringing of alarms whether they be bedside or machine or call bell with patients crying out or moaning from their pain/discomfort. I was placed between the doctors/nurses' station and the entrance to ambulatory care ward, which resulted in a constant flow of doctors/nurses and patients or relatives/visitors.

Eventually I was moved to a more sedate ward but after a day of relative quiet I was transferred to Helena ward, another noisy chaotic kind of place. With patients wandering around unsupervised in various states, with crying out and confused mutterings the order of the day. One older lady was constantly moving unsupervised in between male and female wards in an agitated and confused state.

For the purpose of communicating my diagnosis and in line with NICE guidelines I was moved temporarily into a private room. A Dr Giffin then gave me the news that it was suspected I had MS. She informed me that my notes would be passed onto a Dr Lyons, and the results of my scans would be sent along with a referral for a specialist consultant as soon as possible. I underwent 3 sessions of specialist Neuro physiotherapy which I found very beneficial, each consisting of 20mins on a highly sensitive type of balance board (rather like the Nintendo Wii) over a three-day period. This was done with me simultaneously being given a 5-day course of high dose steroids.

I was discharged on 10.2.12 and after intense self-help using the Nintendo Wii fit programme at home on the advice of Pete Bishop-Ponte the RUH Neuro-Physio my balance improved so far as to allow me to return to work.

OBSERVATIONS:

This visit raised some serious issues. Now I realise my injuries appeared to be non-life threatening but to have my GP refer me on Friday morning for same day testing makes very poor reading in terms of the Mon-Fri 9-5 service/policy in place and the fact I was only really dealt with on Monday.

Because of the lack of beds, I was placed on a ward wholly unsuitable for someone in an anxious and agitated state. Far better would have to explain the situation and sent me home to bring me in on Monday instead of making me endure the environments I was put in.

Not actually being seen for 6 hours was very poor and could have been avoided if GP/hospital liaison worked better.

Also, the fact patients were allowed to wander unsupervised raised many concerns. One of which was constantly being disturbed in my bed.

The results service was very slow in coming and the referral to speak to a consultant even slower. I also had the misfortune of going to the Dr/nursing station to request a sandwich only to see my details on a symptom checker website. Not confidence inspiring. I also had a fall whilst in the shower due to imbalance again due to lack of advice and proper supervision.

FOLLOW-UP:

The follow-up was very slow, and I had to wait until mid-May 2012 to receive the results letter of my scans and about referring me to speak to Dr Lyons However, the referral to speak to a qualified consultant (Dr Lyons) was not until Feb 2013. A whole year since my initial episode.

My first meeting with the **MS Nurse** Bev Bowers was on 21.07.12 where I was advised to take B12 supplements, vitamin D and try eating oily fish. Which I do. She also mentioned discussing with Dr Lyons going onto disease modifying therapies. I came out wondering why I hadn't had a discussion with the consultant over such a life changing course of action.

So, what is Bev? and all **MS nurses** I have encountered.

Answer: They are the gatekeepers, designed to shield the Neurologists from valid concerns and protect their time for more pressing issues. What these are I do not know, but my suspicion is they have too many patients to be able to manage. They probably also have a private clinic for private patients.

My next meeting with Bev Bowers came on 13.09.12, this basically centred around my deterioration and the accompanying symptoms as were being presented. Again, I was deferred to my up-and-coming neurology appointment and DMT which wasn't until Feb 2013, where again I thought why am I having this conversation with an MS nurse as opposed to a qualified neurologist?

Finally, on 19.12.12, I presented myself to the Neuro outpatients' clinic at RUH Bath desperate for something to halt my deteriorating condition. Quite by chance I saw Dr Lyons who prescribed steroids. We also briefly discussed DMT (disease modifying Therapies). I accepted this opportunity. I next spoke to my MS nurse in clinic on 3.1.13. I attended a Baseline neuroimaging on 18.1.13 which allowed me to commence DMT treatment.

I also saw Dr Lyons for a follow up consultation on 7.2.13 where we discussed my impending treatment. Eventually I got the go-ahead to begin my Tysabri (DMT) infusions on 11.3.13, another avoidable example of stupidity resulted in my attending the clinic in Ambulatory care at RUH only to find after having a cannula inserted, the drugs had not been ordered. This wasted not only my time but also a colleague from work who had accompanied me.

Before my infusion was due to commence, I caught Bev Bowers quite by chance, which was described completely differently in the reply I got from SEAP. More later... Having eventually received my first infusion on 13.3.13 I suffered what can only be described as a **reaction.** My whole body went weak, and I was unable to move. I phoned 999 at approx 18:00 on 23.3.13 to get an Ambulance to take me to A&E however NONE were available.

Luckily after 4 hours the central heating kicked in and I managed to recover well enough to drive myself to A&E at Frenchay. I arrived at 22:30 where I had to explain my story 3 times before being seen at approx 01:30 on 24.3.13. After wiring me up to an electrical functions device to check I think for epilepsy The doctors decided (NFA) no further action. I informed them of my recent DMT infusion, the staff at Frenchay informed me I should divulge the incident too.

I attended 3 sessions of (DMT) in total and each time informed the staff my condition had worsened but nothing was said or done. Feeling at best NEGLECTED I decided not to pursue this course any further. Which ties in with my concerns surrounding redress.

ACTION TAKEN:

After the failure to monitor my DMT and because of the wasted journey on my first attempt to receive DMT and also the issues I had on my initial Admission I raised a grievance with SEAP the patient's advocacy service. Unfortunately, my concerns were not adequately addressed. Including why, for such a serious issue I was not seeing a more experienced medical advisor (neurologist). Also, the amount of contact I was having with specialist professionals was negligible.

The reply I got was a total whitewash of the truth. Especially the claimed amount of contact I had had with Bev Bowers. Who apart from a couple of phone conversations and our clinic visits did nothing of practical use. (Once again, the gatekeeper-aimed at empathizing and deflecting any short comings!.) this highlights the serious lack of neurologist's time to take control of the situation!

FAILINGS:

The passage of information between A&E Frenchay and the RUH was made by me at my second infusion However no action was taken! There is no information sharing between these two establishments. I also raised my concerns in the infusion suite on all my visits, however no action was ever made to address my concerns!

Why did it take from 3.2.12 to 9.12.12, when I presented myself to Neuro at RUH to speak to a neurologist, even though the MS nurse was aware of my concerns?

The service is obviously overstretched. For it to be acceptable to leave someone on a cold floor in a cold house and to put the onus on the patient to call back if the situation worsens is unacceptable. My neighbour was on holiday and all the people I tried to contact were either working or unobtainable. What would have happened if I was elderly and frail/infirm etc..?.

The SEAP complaints procedure was flawed from the outset. With genuine concerns dismissed without proper consideration. However, as I was preoccupied with the death of my mother and other serious issues such as my inability to continue my job in my current state, moving house and trying to negotiate the benefits system for the first time, I could not raise a protest about the way the complaint was handled. They even got my admission date wrong in the written response.

The results of my blood test to determine whether or not I had the JC virus did not get to me until AFTER I began my infusions. The letter informing me was dated 19.3.13.

It also states in the letter that nurses "monitor for early signs of the active virus" which considering the concerns I raised at every infusion seems completely false. Believe me when I acknowledge: - It is **wrong!!!!** To tie up healthcare professionals in investigations about people's healthcare treatment but blaming the system is a poor excuse.

RECOMMENDATION 2.

All healthcare agencies GP surgeries and hospitals should be linked into a computer note sharing system. Surely in this age of technology the passage of information should be taken as read.

POST TYSABRI (DMT):

After the events surrounding my trial of (DMT) I had a follow up on 13.5.13 where we discussed the events surrounding my (DMT) treatment and the fact I had ceased them.

However, at no point were my concerns addressed about the overall departmental liaison between Frenchay A&E and Neurology, or the DMT suite and Neurology.

This was made even easier due to a continual deterioration of my condition.

Q. How could I continue when my concerns were not addressed? We also discussed the fact I was seeking a second opinion in Bristol.

ADMISSION 2 RUH BATH 6.9.13:

I was readmitted to the RUH on 6.9.13 via A&E, where once again after an initial assessment I ended up on MAU ward. One of my local surgery GP's (Dr Karensa Branfoot) did a house visit and realised I was in a bad way after a fall, with weakness and numbness of legs and arms, she did the right thing and called the paramedics. After some basic SATS and Bp, it was agreed to get an ambulance. After a long wait........one turned up to take me to hospital. The Ambulance crew explained the (and I quote) " chronic shortage " of fully equipped ambulances!

This was not another "episode" but more to do with my increasing deterioration which had caused a fall at home. Once again, I was processed through A&E 1&1/2 years after my first encounter but still the same issues! Long waiting and a plethora of faces constantly asking the same questions.

I was moved from A&E to MAU and given an intravenous saline drip because my levels were so low. I couldn't help feeling a sense of déjà vu on MAU ward. Hectic loud and a constant stream of comings and goings.

Fortunately, I only spent a short time on MAU before I was moved to a quieter ward. After a couple of days and some more function tests and a revisit of my medication, one of the doctors approached me because they desperately needed my bed!!! I was asked if I was feeling able to would I mind giving my bed up as there was a shortage! I was discharged on 8.9.13.

OBSERVATIONS:

Once again, this stay raised some serious issues. One and a half years later and lots of similarities with my first experience. Totally underwhelmed with the ambulance availability.

Extremely appreciative and grateful to Dr Branfoot for her patience and the care shown to stay with me until the ambulance arrived.

Overwhelmed by the questioning in A&E despite a comprehensive handover by the Ambulance crew. I know what the answer is going to be "these are our SOP's!"

Well revisit them!!!! Because "If, I" find them laborious and tiresome then frail or elderly patients certainly will. Don't just verbally interrogate!!! WRITE IT DOWN so that other nurses and doctors can read it. Virtually impossible to get any rest, never mind sleep on MAU ward.

No inter-Departmental liaison again, or if there were no eyebrows were raised.

Follow-up:

For this brief stay, no new consultations were planned. With not so much as a phone call from Neurology to ascertain if there had been any new changes in my condition.

ACTION TAKEN

My concerns were briefly discussed with MS nurse who visited me post Admission 4.

FAILINGS

Once again confronted by too many people asking the same questions. I know what the answer is going to be "these are our SOP's!"

Well revisit them!!!! Because "If I" find them laborious and tiresome then frail or elderly patients certainly will. Don't just verbally interrogate!!! WRITE IT DOWN!!!! Or look up notes or better still get Neurology involved.

This idea of managing casualty assessment is obviously aimed at speeding things up "Ticking boxes again (time spent on patient assessment)" when all this does is slow things down.

Once again there was no inter-department liaison and no visit by my MS nurse or a neurologist.

Being asked to vacate a bed point to an acutely overstretched service.

RECOMMENDATION 3.

Procedures for ascertaining information from MS patients should consider their agitation and wherever possible place them in a sedate environment. At the earliest opportunity the responsible MS nurse or care team should be involved.

Flying in a Lynx helicopter over the Rhine.

Harry's Bar in Venice with my carer Ashelle.

Holding a croc.

Me in EasyJet mode.

Me in Moron, Cuba, with my first carer Ashelle.

My Army Regiment cricket team with me on the back row.

My friend and ex-fiancee Stacy, a former England netball player, in the Maldives.

My little friend in Cuba.

On a boat in Bonnaire.

On a beach in Cuba.

Parked in a Norwegian Fjord.

Swimming in St Lucia by the Pietons.

Swimming with the turtles in Barbados.

The set for Pirates of the Caribbean at St Vincent.

A selection of my paintings

Florence hillside view

My pet magpie in honour of Newcastle fans

Verona amphitheatre

Verona - River Adige outside the centre

Venice bridge of sighs

My current carer Lucy, I am really grateful for all her support

A&E visit RUH approx 12.10.13:

During the afternoon of approx 12.10.13 I was again in some discomfort. This time I suspected a UTI. I also had back pain and numbness. So not wanting to cheat the system I dialled 111.

After passing my details to the phone operator, she advised me to stay by the phone and await further instructions. Three times I was phoned back, ensuring targets were met ....

Eventually I was instructed to proceed to A&E using my own initiative (fortunately a friend was with me) and I was told I had an appointment at 22:15 to see a doctor

Well on arrival I looked at the other walking wounded and thought "good job I have an appointment"

I had to describe my situation to the duty registrar. 22:15 came and went......as did all the other patients.......!!!! Eventually a nurse called me over at 23:45. Once again I had to describe the problem only for the nurse to decide because of the complexity and the fact I have MS to refer me to a doctor.

I eventually saw a doctor at 01:100 who wanted the full story again, I was asked to give a urine sample. Having passed water only a half hour previous it then took copious amounts of drinking to facilitate the required sample.

The dipped sample showed no infection, so I was discharged with a prescription for back pain relief 01:35. Advised to speak to my GP if it worsened.

OBSERVATIONS:

The whole 111 process was flawed from the outset. The reporting of my complaint was not passed down the chain. Hence my constantly having to repeat my story.

As the doctor who eventually saw me said "it was blatantly obvious " I needed to give a sample, but this was overlooked by all parties until the doctor requested one, it could have been made clear on arrival this was required. Or even 111 advisors.

People with MS get anxious and agitated very easily, so wherever possible the constant bombardment of demands for history should be annotated and made available on some kind of centralized patient notes system.

To make patients constantly have to repeat their story needs revisiting.

Why do patients by-pass 111?

Well, if my experience is anything to go by it is because it doesn't do anything other than allow for massaging of A&E figures. Unacceptable!

RECOMMENDATION 4.
Any admissions of this nature should be passed to GP's and Neuro/MS care team as a matter of routine. The Onus being pushed on the patient must STOP.

ADMISSION 3:

Again, taken poorly, this time lumbar pain/discomfort.my GP visited and prescribed pain relief.
Unable to function properly. Again, I waited for hours for an Ambulance. When they came out, they tested me and decided on hospital. I was admitted on 21.5.14

As I was due to see Professor Scolding at Southmead for advice, the possibility of Stem Cell Trials and a second opinion that week, so it was decided to proceed there.

It was unfortunately it was only day 2 or 3 of Southmead being in existence as a front-line A&E all-purpose hospital due to the transfer of services from Frenchay.
waited for hours on a stretcher logjam. With multiple ambulance crews lined up to handover patients, I then had the same experience as previously in the RUH.
where despite a very accurate handover by the ambulance crew I was permanently having to repeat my symptoms to various nurses/doctors until I spoke to a duty physician. He once again made me recount my story.

At this point having been formally processed I was placed in a "waiting" area of A&E until a ward bed could be allocated. I was moved to Bay 6 room 41. After many nurse/specialists visits I eventually had an MRI scan of my spine from Th10 to the sacrum.

During my stay on this ward, I was attended by many different professionals from Neurologists to Neurosurgeons. Physiotherapists to OT's. I was also able to have a brief chat with Professor Scolding a leading specialist on MS. There was also a registrar present called Diane whose surname escapes me, who dutifully notated all of my discussions with doctors.
I was discharged 29.5.14

OBSERVATIONS:

Despite having to go through a tiring admission process **All** things considered and the fact this was a massive transition period for this hospital I felt in safe hands.

On 7.5.14 I had spoken with a Dr Kirsty Inglis at Frenchay BRAMS centre who noted I complained of "ongoing chronic back pain with right lower limb symptoms constant for the last 2 years"

She goes on to say my GP should arrange a local musculoskeletal specialist referral.

I have also spoken to and been advised by Tania Burge MS Specialist Physiotherapist.

The pathological outcome of my Southmead stay was one of mixed signals.

Professor Scolding noted on my discharge notes: - "His symptoms and difficulties are disproportionate to his neurological findings."

It also stated on my discharge notes "there was no history of injury" despite me repeating during admission how I had injured my back during a gardening incident in 2011.

FAILINGS:

Now for whatever reason I cannot fathom out and despite me recounting my history to tens of healthcare professionals it appears my history of illness has been trumped by MS!

It is inconceivable ALL my deficiencies can be attributed to this one thing.

It is quite clear from what Professor Scolding writes in my discharge notes there must be something which needs more investigation.

I was advised by a staff nurse to drink much more fluid, which caused my continence issues to become accelerated. "Is this normal?".

With regards the nurses on this ward the only negative I encountered was their ability to maintain an overview of their charges. This is in part due to everyone being in single rooms and part due to the distances needed to be covered by the staff for each call bell.

This admission occurred on a Bank Holiday so once again nothing could be done in terms of detailed examination until Tuesday.

FOLLOW UP:

I have a pre-planned follow up meeting planned with Neurology in Southmead for 25.9.14

I have also recently discovered why some referrals haven't been actioned by my GP. She is on maternity leave.

RECOMMENDATION 5.

The liaison between specialists and MS care teams must work better.

If a leading specialist writes his concerns on discharge notes surely this must warrant further investigation.

ADMISSION 4:

On 9.6.14 Shortly after my stay in Southmead, I was taken ill again. This time more stroke like than Feb 12. Right sided weakness (including hand tremor) facial changes (including speech difficulties, severe headaches) classic FAST symptoms. Luckily my neighbour was visiting at the time.

After going through the 999 process once more and negotiating the operator assessment process I was told to await a callback! Now I was lucky my neighbour was around. I certainly would not have liked to be an infirm or frail or vulnerable elderly patient.

Eventually after lots of callbacks and apologies a paramedic arrived who, after a very efficient assessment called for an ambulance. This took not minutes but hours too.

Eventually an ambulance arrived, and the paramedic handed over my information. However, the ambulance crew did not have the necessary monitoring equipment on board their vehicle so a second was ordered.

On 10.6.14 at 04:30 I was able to text a friend I had finally made it to A&E RUH and was being attended to! Once again, I endured the lengthy and physically draining process that is Admission! In the two and a half years since I was first admitted NOTHING has changed.

With a long wait to be processed, followed by a constant barrage of questions by lots of different nurses/doctors. All of which is avoidable if the processing nurse had listened to the ambulance crew in the first place. At one point a doctor came in and begin questioning only to be dragged off to treat someone more urgent. It was a middle-aged woman who had burned her arm on a saucepan whilst cooking!!!!! Her partner was being very loud and agitated.

Really!... I thought casualty assessment went breathing, bleeding, brakes and burns?

I will only add that the process had not improved over time because everyone is so focused on time targets and placement strategies. The work is carried out more like stock market traders chasing sales bonuses, than healthcare professionals!

Fortunately, and after the first breaking of Dawn I was moved to ward C1. Once here I had a spine head and neck MRI on 11.6.14

I tried to use the complaint procedure here in the hospital on this ward not just about the admission and the time factor but also about the questioning process. I tried to get some sort of control stating "I am a known patient, get me someone from my neurology team. I have just come out from Southmead. Please consider that visit!"

These protests were dismissed off-hand!!!

I was also placed on a special mattress because of my back issues.

On 12.6.14 a.m. a doctor visited to inform me a stroke had been ruled out. Later that day I was moved to Helena ward B52. *See WARD ISSUES.

Failings: The **usual** ones are here again, Ambulance difficulties. Having to repeat my history on numerous occasions. The time taken to process me. Liaison with other agencies. Failure of Neurology to be consistent. No input from my MS nurse during my stay. Failure of the in-house complaint's procedure.

WARD ISSUES:

Now for the purpose of this account I have left out many details, but I did inform the ward Senior nurse a Mrs Rosie Lloyd of my concerns. Who assured me they would be addressed...???

But for this account I will divulge some of my major issues.

1) lost a tooth (bridge) on hospital food. It took the staff a week to find me a doctor to ensure this had no infection risk. I was woken during one night in the dark to have a junior doctor shine a torch into my mouth to then proclaim the mouth is fine!!! Are you a dentist? "No," but if you are still concerned, I shall arrange to get some mouthwash sent up.

I ended up with a 3/4 full bottle from ?!!! Reassured?... "No!"

2) I had sleep deprivation of 4 days due firstly to another patient being moved out of my room, which due to a mix up with the correct type of ambulance and stretcher being organised lasted two days, there followed further

disruption due to new patients being moved into the spare bed space. On two consecutive days. Plus, other hair-raising incidents which I left to the ward Sisters discretion.
3) Owing to a lack of meaningful communication between the neurologist and myself, I tried desperately to work out what this episode together with ADMISSION 3 in Southmead had to do with each other. I tried various ways to get the neurologist back to explain but she didn't come.
I did however meet the registrar who I encountered at Southmead and hoped for some kind of information sharing. But now I see her as nothing more than complaint reduction!!!!!!!!!!
4) 23.06.14 I used the hospitals own IFE system to do a "PRIVATE and CONFIDENTIAL " survey on the hospitals performance marking the worst possible option for all categories. It was intended to gain a reaction and "IT DID." **Boy did it**. Most noticeable were the disturbances.
24.6.14 I had 40 (yes forty disturbances from 06:30 to15:30) until eventually the registrar turned up to inform me the neurologist would come to talk to me later.

During that meeting the registrar Diane took notes and Mr Bishop-Ponte the neuro physiotherapist, and Rosie the ward senior nurse, were also present. Diane seemed pre-occupied with trying to establish if I was completely satisfied with my treatment? **Hmmm I wonder why?** Whilst the neurologist focused on DMT blissfully unaware of professor Scoldings input. Then she did something which caused me to do a double take. She wanted me to speak with Dr Lyons who was more specialised with MS patients, irrespective of any secondary underlining injuries I might have and then when she realised, I had been speaking to BRAMS, suggested I move ALL my treatment over there. After my positive constructive feedback about the neurophysiotherapy She then proceeded to rubbish them as well. So much for a PRIVATE AND CONFIDENTIAL survey!
5) it was during the periods of my intravenous drip which I assumed was a saline drip but subsequently turned out to be steroid administration and the issues raised in bullet points 1-4
That my left eye started to cloud over. I informed several people including Dr Nichola Giffin however her answer was to wait and see how it progresses.
However, and thanks mainly to the neurophysio work (they got me walking again unaided in 20mins) I was dismayed at only managing 3 sessions with Mr Bishop-Ponte and his assistant Ruby. I got discharged on 27.6.14 with the understanding that all agencies were informed of my discharge and that my rehabilitation would continue seamlessly.

Well, it hasn't!

RECOMMENDATION 6.

The process of transition between a hospital and a community care team should be seamless.
It shouldn't be that a patient has to organise his ongoing rehabilitation
A hospital in-house survey which purports to be ***CONFIDENTIAL*** should be just that.

I would welcome any comments on what a very difficult time for me has been but to put things into perspective. I was informed of The MS Therapy Centre in Bradley Stoke a while back.

Not by my Neurologist or my MS nurse but purely by chance at a military charity function in Ascot. This centre is completely funded by donations and is increasingly becoming the centre of excellence for not just this region, but with other similar centres opening up across the U.K.
It is well run and occasionally trains students on placement from UWE.

Without their support and the opportunity to talk to fellow sufferers the stresses and strains from the last few years would have been much harder.

So why is it MS nurses do not promote it or support it through grants etc. Or is it just a case of more patients for them less work and expenditure for us? I have copied the MS Therapy centres manager into this mail along with many others to see what response I get and also to receive feedback.

Everyone I have copied into this letter is more than welcome to not only pass comment, but also pass on advice, indeed I welcome it. I have whilst writing this mail attempted to leave emotion out. The facts are as accurate as my records allow and as for the timely nature in sending this out, please bear in mind my disabilities and the fact I am writing with a major visual disturbance.

ACKNOWLEDGEMENTS:

One final thing I wish to do is write my thanks to certain individuals and organisations who have tried their hardest under very challenging circumstances to provide a high level of care and support and who I would like to offer my sincere thanks.

1) to **ALL** the staff and GPs in Temple house practice, Keynsham
2) to **ALL** the ambulance crews and paramedics that have ever dealt with me

3) to **ALL** the staff in BRAMS and Southmead, and the RUH who have ever had to deal with me.

I fully understand the parameters which you have to work under. You are not the problem. It's the procedures and policies which limit your time to actually do proper caring and nursing.

I have witnessed first-hand the constant paper trail you must adhere by.

4) to the physiotherapy departments which have tried to help. But again, the system dictates how much and how often. It is also incredible that if (like me) you have to move out of area there is no way your ongoing treatment can be transferred.

Special mention to Cheryl at Frome community hospital. Special mention to Mr Pete Bishop-Ponte at RUH and Ruby his assistant. Who runs a fantastic ship, underfunded and overworked and probably for the most part unappreciated. I really appreciate your advice and work. It gave me belief that this is reversible.

5) to the nurses and doctors at RUH who do a great job in very difficult circumstances especially the group who dealt with me on Helena Ward and DID NOT get involved in my feedback (patient survey) issue. Namely Rosario Fajardo, Harriet Owen, Edyta Sobilo, Sharon Ferguson, Jenny Wilson, Sara Ferreira, Norm Tion, Lorraine Dury, Laura Blore, Buddy Soriano, Laila Reyes.

There are others but I did not manage to collect all the names, but my biggest thanks go to Dr Katherine Stewart who "listened" and confirmed there may well be an underlying secondary injury. Which is basically what Professor Scolding eluded to in Admission 3 in Southmead.

5) to all the staff at the MS therapy centre in Bradley Stoke. For all their patience and help. Especially Amrik, Mary Jane Nathalie and Doro.

And to all those involved in my Neuro care I say this: -

1) do not hide behind financial or personnel constraints, or different agencies **change it**.
2) be honest and realistic.
3) give patients more access to specialists instead of rationing them and hiding the true shortcomings behind overstretched nurses (this includes MS nurses) and specialists (including specialist services).
4) If: - (and I know they exist) staff are forever chasing targets because of performance statistics.
   Change the focus away from them and move back to patient care.
5) the ratio between patients and specialists is unacceptable.......**change it**.

6) if the system is overstretched (and I know it is) **admit** it!
7) stop trying to kid yourselves and me/us you are coping **ADMIT THAT YOU ARE NOT!**
8) stop trying to over-complicate a system with different agencies and the admin machine and give it back to the professionals. By constantly working towards targets you are neglecting the patients!
9) place patients using a bit more intelligence (this refers to wards and also hospitals which you will read more on later. Also liaise more with each other, this includes between hospital and GP's.
10) Probably the most important one...LISTEN!

I don't mean paying lip service to someone, or deciding if it may affect your agency, or may affect ratings! I mean taking people seriously.

This is not just my opinion; it is one shared by most of the fellow sufferers at **The MS Therapy centre** in Bradley Stoke and also by the fellow sufferers I met through a self-help group I set up with the **MS society** in South Bristol

This is a story of failings in all sorts of different ways. I know nothing is perfect but look at yourselves, since being discharged by RUH on 27.6.14.

No Physio was in place, Emily Wilford a fantastic lady from the community care team in Keynsham gave me a frank account of what they could or couldn't do. Apparently if I was older then more could be arranged. I QUOTE "due to training and financial constraints, we can offer no more". So, this body need more funding!

I am now totally reliant on the MS therapy centre and my neighbour who takes me swimming.

I went to St Martin's Clinic in Bath to receive physiotherapy only to be party to another administrative faux pas. Wrong appointment time. Despite me putting it in my diary as witnessed by a friend. The phone number I was given was not manned as it was Friday afternoon, and after I was escorted to a waiting area nothing happened for 40 mins. I eventually did see someone called Steffi for an assessment but as the majority of my appointment had been missed, we ended up doing a half-hearted one.

I then had my walker was taken away, and with it I found afterwards my spectacles too. It turned out this walker wasn't St Martin's property either, it belonged to the community team in Keynsham.

So, you see despite being visited by MS nurse Bowers three times since my discharge who has empathized and tried to get an overview of what is going on, verbally accepting some of the short comings and despite Prof

Scolding and Dr Katherine Stewart agreeing there might be an as yet undiagnosed underlining injury.
2 and 1/2 years later...Lots of unanswered questions.

Bev Bowers has my utmost respect and sympathy, being at the sharp end of people's frustrations (mine included) She also understands the phrase: - "Papering up the cracks!"
Her department are completely overwhelmed with patient to nurse ratios. "Stretched" is an understate YOUR THOUGHTS PLEASE?

Abinger Hammer Swimming:

I've had long distance friendships, pen pal, and holiday connections. It's just one of those things where I've become a very silent partner, ever since my diagnosis. The thing that got me started on this type of collecting was the house my parents moved to from Cheam. It sat around twenty minutes away from Guildford and I think was chosen because of the proximity to dads work and the fact that we would be effectively living "off grid!" It was in a little village called Holmbury St Mary's.

My memory of that place is limited to be honest, what I do know is the areas where I could go exploring were massive. The house itself was an oak beam, listed building with a thatched roof. I would imagine it would be highly desirable for any family with young children. It had a driveway down from the road. An imposing wooden garage with a medium sized garden, it also had wild strawberries growing on the bank side of the grass.

Our neighbours were a lovely Spanish lady and her daughter. Which was handy as were able to use her garden to access the woods. I went back there in 10 to see if I could remember anything. It was still a gorgeous location. I can remember catching newts and grass snakes on some of the fields. I've also got a memory of a village fete there in one summer. They had a lucky prize wheel. With numbers from 1 to 12. My favourite number 3 was already gone so I picked 10 instead and it won me a basket of fruit. I knew there and then, I was a lucky sod.

The reason for me choosing this story is because it links lots of elements in my life. The senorita from next door was the first time I had close contact to a foreign national. I think my sister still has a Christmas card relationship with the daughter all these years later.

I'm certain that she was the motivation for me to endeavour to become the opposite of the xenophobic attitude of most of my family and friends.

You only have to stream the old comedy series of the 1970's and 80's to understand what I'm talking about.

I remember on one trip home from the school in Guildford when we saw a soldier in (DPM) riding his thumb. I got really agitated and aggressive when mum showed signs that she wasn't going to stop. Turned out to be a Gurkha from Nepal, trying to get to a colleague's place. It was an officer's house in Abinger Hangar. He was so grateful for our act of kindness that we were given the privilege of using his swimming pool.

Which in the late 1970's was a rarity in Britain I can tell you. He had lovely gardens, and the television actress Prunella Scales lived close by. My dad loved her because she was Basil Fawlty's wife in the classic comedy series of Fawlty Towers. Who both me and dad absolutely loved. The point is, that little act of kindness showed me how much harder average people of England are prepared to fight for their white only mentality.

The Gurkha we picked up, had heavily tanned skin, as did our neighbour by the way. Much to the dismay of some of the residents of Holmbury. Which I think is why we needed to move! Isn't that shocking. The mentality is still here by the way, it's just gone underground. You can hear it most in football grounds, despite taking the knee etc.

What is the point of this short paragraph? Is it a glimpse into a child's perspective. Or is that quiet xenophobia a very real phenomenon. One thing is crystal clear it is time to get real about British population change.

I just read the headline of the 2021 census which was 2% fewer white British citizens than 2011. Which is a drop of 1,200,000 less (fewer) than a decade ago. I'm more aware of this than most of you. Because you can see it reflected around the world.

In places I've lived, British migration is a big deal. For example, just look at how many Brits have moved to Spain, Australia or a host of European countries. Then of course there is the pull of the green card. Moving to the U.S. Something which more people seem to be considering. Which begs the question, is this a recent trend? Of course not. It's something which can be traced back to post-world war years.

Zero prospects, zero money, zero food. It's no coincidence that the end of empire talks divided opinions. The wealthy and power-hungry saw massive opportunities.

There was a massive structural deficit throughout the world. Every country had experienced loses and normal economic conditions were non-existent. I'm only going on information that I've gleaned from conversations with grandparents, the internet and veterans, but the general consensus was the old career paths were difficult to impossible, the key to middle classed success seems to have been nepotism, old school ties and military connections. What happened in reality is another missed opportunity to make unifying changes. A worldwide set of conditions set by the "chocolate teapot brigade!" (a reference to a joke about useless utensils!), which, I believe, also had something to do with Rifkind's throwaway remarks during the Thatcher years!

What we failed to understand in those early years of war free Europe was how the maps had changed. We were not an empirical phenomenon any longer. The old alliances were either gone or quickly disappearing. But instead of being aware of our new position in the world, we were forced into uncomfortable reality checks.

It is something I love to compare to rock climbing. The three point of contact rule, A very simple guide for novice rock climbers. Always try to keep three limbs or grips on the wall as much as possible. Because with every movement you take with two or fewer holds on the rock, the likelihood of a fall increases. You can smell our influence and position being not too dissimilar to a climber clinging on by the fingernails. I can also compare our new position as a bit like the dinner party guest, who overstays his welcome and tries to get one more drink!

That simplistic explanation translated into a period of consolidation and head scratching, when we still had some European alliances and some Asia friendly countries. Our main focus centred on cementing relations with our financial backers during the war. Namely the Americans and being civil to our French and Russian counterparts. We then tried to find new positions with nationals who were part of the coalition, and....and....and we kept friendly with Japan and Germany?

It's strange isn't it, we have to fight two World Wars and affect millions of people worldwide in our pursuit of control! And for what?

I recently read that it took until the 31st of December 2006, for Britain to finally finished repaying the World War debt owed to the United States. Which is staggering when you consider how many years ago it goes back to but think about it logically the date when the loan was taken out is 'Britian's "ground zero!

It was when the government, foreign office and our ancestors put the first nail in the coffin. Just think about the sequence of events that were unleashed on us as a nation, then us as a world. When we were bailed out by the US there was a huge shift in world power.

We've witnessed many magnificent civilization's, in Asia it's Chinese, Japanese and Vietnamese. To name some, In Africa we've had the Egyptian, Ethiopian and Sudanese to name just a few and Europe can claim even more influential empires. The Romans, the Spanish conquistadors, Alexander and his armies. Even South American civilizations like the Mayan or Aztec. But nobody of note had ever been championed from North America, until now.

It was something unprecedented in British and world history too. A nation that had almost always been able to project a dominant position and image. But come the day, where swastika flags flying over Buckingham Palace looked a real possibility, we took an unprecedented position of alliance with the newest superpower.

As with any untested military pact, there were teething problems, but happily on the 8th of May 1945 it was announced the end of the war in Europe. Which we all know was not a matter for smooth transition back to normality. It's still a work in progress.

Which is my point really. Humanity is a very sad species, I don't want to go into history sound bites, but right across the continents our cruelty, savagery, imperfections and insanity is etched into the landscapes throughout the globe.

It's so apparent and obvious, that even primary school children have figured it out. When a so-called civilized country like Russia invaded Ukraine, it was just another episode of human stupidity. Which brings me nicely onto the path to enlightenment... The crisis we are experiencing is not a blip. It's part of the genetic makeup of human beings. I for the life of me can't remember a single moment outside of the celebration for the world wars ending, when our species wanted a peace!

But here is the crux of the problem. I will use the US as the measuring point. If you type into any search engine, "Duties of a government towards its citizens" the actual suggestions are mind blowing. I'll list a few for your contemplation: -

1) defending the country against attacks by foreign nations

2) defending the country against natural calamity, such as floods, drought or infectious diseases to name a few. 3) protecting human rights 4) safeguarding freedoms such as life, liberty, property.

5) facilitating the means to solve disputes among individuals and the government by using the justice system.

I'm not going to do the groundwork on this. You are going to have to research yourself and draw your own conclusions. What I will say is this, just think the Twin Towers, Hurricane Katrina, tornadoes in Tennessee, forest fires in Oregon, (D'ya see)? George Floyd asphyxiation, national lockdown, storming of D.C.!

I have just used Americans for the example, but it applies equally as well in every country around the world. Doesn't this make it clear to all of you, you muppets!

The French public have recently got the right idea, protesting against the raising of the retirement age to 64, but you can see how quickly their government and all countries governments, employ specialist security personnel. With the clear intention of clamping down on any civil disobedience! Or to use the correct terminology, strike busters.

It therefore boggles me why anyone would want to do the bigger challenges. If you look up the responsibilities and duties of a government towards the public, you will see very quickly how totally unenforceable and dishonest they are.

A lot of contemporary paradoxical stand offs are fuelled by the fact that our so-called leaders are playing a duplicitous game of contradiction. Whereby they will only allow the truth out into the public domain when it suits them.

Just look recently at some of these politicians bare faced lies. There were the expenses scandal the misinformation around Brexit, the corruption of awarding PPE contracts, the delaying tactics in producing enquiry findings. (Police misogyny and racism, Grenfell Tower, Party Gate), and now when the climate emergency should be centre stage, we have a national scandal on power, water in fact every utility. I'm sorry to you shareholder crooks, but enough is enough, paying dividends to modern day highwaymen is disgusting.

Another way of looking at this is to understand that the umbrella organisations that should be keeping us safe are in cahoots with their political masters. So, groups like Ofsted, Ofcom, Ofgem and Ofwat are toothless nonentities, but guess what! Until the cost-of-living crisis really starts to hurt you won't complain, because you are stupid MUPPETS!

This reverts to the piece I wrote earlier about the escalating number of weapons in society and more tellingly in the hands of the psychopaths. I'm not aiming this at anyone either, because I know from just watching news reports how many "wrong uns," are in all levels of society.

I read a recent study of school shootings in America the other day and it is staggering how frequently they are dealing with mass killings in the confines of classrooms and playgrounds. But does this surprise anyone? Of course not. It's the same in British public places too, but the media don't want to highlight it here, in case it causes mass dissatisfaction and demands for a more intrusive response.

All I will add to this is to remind you all how many incidents of police improprieties have been committed in the last decade! I touched on this issue in a previous chapter, but what has changed? Of course, nothing!

So, my question is knowing what you know now about the state of this joke for a country, why doesn't anyone go to the gun armoury and head for Parliament?

The problem with modern day anywhere is that there is no identity anymore. The hoards from population explosion in countries like Nigeria shows that the current trajectory of global population is heading for collapse. It should come as no surprise to anyone on this planet either. I'm convinced this is what will drive the next wave of death and destruction. With global food shortages and rising effects of climate change reducing our ability to cope.

I am reminded of two kids I was friends with at school. Gavin Wong and Kazu Ito. For all intents and purposes, they were the outsiders, something that I identified with, it was difficult for me to be anything else. Because of the way my parents had moved me from here to there, I was the stranger and just as much an outsider as they were. However, I found my best integration opportunities were centred around sports. Another reason for acceptance was my understanding of British comedy.

Which leads nicely onto the migration dilemma. It goes without saying that everyone is acutely aware that there is a national crisis now in terms of immigration. I think the figures at present for Britain are unprecedented. Which is not surprising, but what is, is that this has taken so long to be recognised as a serious issue. What does this actually mean? If you just glance around the world, you'll notice that there is growing amounts of population movement.

It's funny isn't it. When you break down the whole discussion of what does it mean to be a migrant or an asylum seeker. I'm actually quite well placed to enter into this debate. Because in 1992 during the days when Windsor castle was burning, I had literally just walked out of my last Army barracks, and out of my country!

The M4 motorway experienced a very severe crash the day I left, it was in that morning's rush hour just outside Chippenham and mainly due to fog. There was also a kind of apathy displayed by the soldiers I had just been saying goodbye to, probably because they were being sent to the Bosnian war or the Yugoslav conflict. It was the major issue of the day, and all the soldiers were unhappy about once again becoming mixed up in somebody else's war!

It was a strange drive home that day. I've got a vivid mind's eye picture of the smoke billowing out from the ramparts of Windsor Castle shortly before I turned onto the M25. I also remember almost becoming a target for road rage, by some numpty in a white van. Who seemed to think that he was exempt from following the Highway Code. (White van man)

I made my hellos and goodbyes to the folks (parents) shortly before setting out on my evacuation from Britain. I gave instructions to dad to sell my car, and I remember conversations with them about, how since the fall of communism and the Berlin Wall, there were suddenly thousands of Eastern Europeans looking for a new life.

They had also noticed other people from the knock-on effect of the Kuwaiti crisis and those disaffected Kurds from the north of Iraq, who Saddam Hussein and his followers had declared war on, probably as a distraction from the illegal Kuwaiti occupation. All this coupled together with the overspill from Africa and now the Balkan's. It was if you like the perfect storm.

I was just happy to be getting away!

I remember getting onto the boat at Ramsgate heading to my new life in Germany, thinking how unusual it had been seeing the first signs of gatherings in Calais, on my return to the UK. They weren't visible at Oostende, my arrival port in Belgium. Which was the cheapest place to cross over the channel. Which even today produces one of those vacant expressions you make when confronted with a deeply challenging conundrum. I thought, what are all these strange people doing, gathering around ports?

I remember on occasional visits back to England during the late 90's how more and more frequently we would see travellers without vehicles, not just in the ports but also around service stations on the autobahns. This prevalence of travellers was hammered home one time, when after nipping out for a pee, I caught one would be illegal, sniffing around our ford focus!

I was recently quietly hoping that the pandemic might go some way towards addressing the imbalance currently facing the world populations. It is no secret that we are now at eight billion and climbing. Which throws up lots of difficult questions, for example how we create a sustainable world. Where is the tipping point or should countries consider enforced sterilization? I personally don't think it will ever come to any kind of agreement or even debate but hopefully the next Covid will be as effective as bubonic plague was! Too grim?

This population wandering is not a new phenomenon, but it has certainly changed people's attitudes about growth. Because when you combine these movements together with climate change, national disasters, the warring groups like ISIS, or Russia and throw economic forces into the mix. I'm sure you can see that this will only go one way!

I have no doubt that your governments are determined to be upbeat and positive about the outlook. But understand this, the world is a hairs breadth away from implosion. If climate emergencies don't get us, you can always rely on our own stupidity. Which is why the whole make-up of the planet has to change.

All it will take is for every country to sign up to a new structure. Let's call it "Arc" as in the one supposedly built to rescue all the species in ancient times due to flooding.

I dare say that some countries will have already started on this kind of planning but the difficulty with such a project is going to be reverting back to my analogy about Army officers. "TRAIN SET "remember!

The recent international crisis which we have been served up, like Ukraine, Iran or North Korea shows how dysfunctional the umbrella organisations are around the world. But even me just writing about them makes zero difference. It's like sitting on a ticking time bomb. It would take just one second of frustration and we would be transported back to the meteor impact that finished off the dinosaurs.

Do we have the ability as a species to make the changes that need to be made? Personally, I don't think we do. But I'm dying anyway so I really don't care! But for anybody out there who wants a fighting chance here's the clue. AI has to be switched to a controlled level and given the correct amount of access to any data. Otherwise, the terminator will be born.

The scary truth is. Pandora's box is just a collection of binary code. But all of you gaming developers/ enthusiasts/ programmers knew that already didn't you! It'll be poetic justice for anyone off grid when the ICBM's plough into the cities. I hope I'm scaring you, because this scenario has been coming for a long while.

So, let's go back to the population wandering situation, people who are dissatisfied with their country, government or even system have basically got a few choices. You can knuckle down and conform to the way the powers that be, dictate is acceptable. Hoping to get a good slice of the pie. Or maybe you can attempt to make a life outside of the land of your father's. Probably requiring learning another language and maybe even retraining yourself in some other skill to be able to achieve acceptance and accessibility to work. Or thirdly maybe you can play the ghetto game. A nasty term which I have borrowed from the Nazis, when they used to corral foreign immigrants into cheap, undesirable communities. Deliberately segregated for effect and humiliation. This was in the 1930's a very widespread phenomenon, it's incidentally also the way the Arabs in Saudi Arabia treat their foreign workers!

Looks however, can be deceptive, and I think that every country should be held to account. I'm sure there are kindergarten kids out there who have seen this exodus from their parent's living rooms and are questioning how it's possible they can eventually be replaced by these invaders, who work for the lowest rates of pay, because as is the case with most employers in the Eu and US it's all about the bottom line. If the workforce is low paid, then the company's profitability and margins climb. Basic economics.

You see it's the overspill conundrum. Countries show their tolerance and help, by finding ways to safely house the vulnerable and oppressed wanderers, but they cannot take an unlimited quantity of people. House and feed them with very little financial assistance. Despite knowing that it's a very good business model if you don't have to pay a living wage!

I mean think about it, At the very least the population of the country providing shelter has to be reimbursed for any rescue, healthcare and housing. Which brings me nicely onto the "elephant in the room" for the whole scenario. Religious groups. I don't care what you follow for a religion, but this whole "help your neighbour" narrative is fine up to a point but is deeply flawed. For example, the idea that everyone has a moral obligation to stand up for the less fortunate is the biggest load of crap since sliced bread. It's portrayed as being the modus operandi for more developed and the more fortunate section of societies. But the obligation to be a caring and responsible person or county is riddled with problems.

Now I'm no expert but when during the whole of the planet's history has there been a unifying force for good?

For the ones that have escaped oppression and harm, I say welcome to peace and safety, but if you live in one country and don't claim assistance or asylum in a neighbouring country and travel on to a financially preferable destination. I say this! You have to go to a neighbouring country. FULL STOP! No economic migration unless due to invitation.

The UN should pick up the bill for implementing this, as well as any religious groups that spout brotherly love rhetoric. By the way if you've never been, go to St Peter's Square in Rome to the Tombs of the Popes. It's a tiled floor swimming in treasure. I was so shocked when I saw this, it made me want a new lesson for schools. "The Evil of The Church"

He even has his own airline! Which forced my own work airline to divert on a few occasions. Because they are so important. The fact is this; because travel has become synonymous with post 20th century norms, it has fuelled ghetto building, partly due to lack of integration skills and partly down to the old favourite "safety in numbers".

The obvious problem with this, is that at some point, if a nation is swamped by excessive amounts of foreigners from a particular geographic region. There will eventually be an uprising and a revolt against them. I've only been back in England since 2008, and it is currently bubbling around under the surface. Like I have already indicated I'm quite happy with allowing people from different cultures and countries to come here, but there are some things that truly trouble me.

For instance, I have observed that foreign nationals are buying to let properties, which is one of the craziest ideas I have ever heard of. It's taken years of incredibly hopeless leadership of the country for this even to become an issue. (Hey, you Tory and Labour muppets, I mean you!)

It's not just been the carrot dangling in front of the donkeys (euphemism for the general public), it's this idea that owning a property somehow makes you a successful person.

What a pile of dog poop! What it means is you have participated in the greatest swindle ever seen. You have bought into conformity and consumerism, which essentially is what will kill the planet if we allow it to continue!

Couple of observations, I came on a visit to London in 2007, our hotel was in Knightsbridge, and I was gob smacked by the amount of foreign money there. Rich Arabs, rich Asian people, possibly Chinese and Japanese, and then definitely Eastern European, which made me realise how much damage the introduction of the money tree had been to Britain.

I'm sure it is a very exclusive private club. Where all the old exclusive addresses have been bought by Saudi Princes or Russian oligarchs. Mind you, the same is true of old fishermen's villages in Cornwall, in fact just look around. This exchange of population is not an exclusively British thing, it's mirrored by our old pensioners who have chased the sun in Spain!

Bloody well wake up, it's global and it's coming to your doorstep. The first time I realised this was on my emigration to Europe. I'm not big on money or expenses so it was the first thing I noticed crossing borders. I just kept repeating "how much!" It was how expensive I had found the travelling, so that then throws up a whole bunch of different questions applicable to the modern-day travellers. If these people really were asylum seekers or were they economic migrants. how can they have the funds?

It's one of those "you can think it" scenarios, but God help anybody stupid enough to actually express their feelings out loud. Just look around the planet at this moment in time, with increasing desperation amongst the low paid and lower classes.

Just on the South American continent and swathes of countries in Central America we are witnessing a very troubling trend towards the development exodus North. It gets reported on by strangely biased media outlets. Firmly placing the blame on the governments and industries that have always used the cheap labour and badly managed companies who are quite ruthless when it becomes an unprofitable sector.

What is particularly obvious is that the global community is broken. We are all slaves to the dollar and money generally. I predict that we will have a third world war within the next 25 years, and it will start with infighting and overthrowing of a declining countries military.

Best guess is somewhere unexpected like India or Pakistan! But as we've witnessed in Ukraine it's not inconceivable that Iran or Israel might have a go. It's never who you think; is it!

If you try to make predictions you run the risk of denunciation, be that the media or the so-called experts. (Who by the way I don't think exist) it's a very grey area in most fields. The problem I have with this is very easily demonstrated by Michael Fish, the weather "expert" for the BBC, who on October the 15th 1987, made his prediction that there was not going to be a hurricane. I was literally just loading onto a Royal Navy boat bound for Cuxhaven in Germany.

Fortunately, the worst of the weather hit the mainland, which we then realised on our return home. But it proved that even with supercomputers and a dedicated team of specialists, deciphering the data can be a fool's errand! Which is why one of the reasons why I don't like to believe anything on face value. Another example is Stephen Fry, of QI fame. Who proudly boasted that the earth had more than one moon.

A statement he has been forced to correct on at least two occasions on his program as more accurate information became available. I'm not saying that everything you learn is wrong. But be careful because if you reflect on something after say fifty years, there's a good chance you'll learn something new! You all thought I was mad when I slagged off the school classroom? But the great thing about that little revelation is, it applies equally to many fields including health. Overlapping ideas of medicine, science, magic and religion as the most accepted progression of what we would today call healthcare. Although in reality as marvellously demonstrated in the recent pandemic episode, we might as well have resorted to village shamans or witch doctors, because as much as the white coat brigade like to blow their own trumpets they proved quite categorically how much a joke they really are.

I don't know what the actual death toll was or even care, but what it demonstrated incredibly clearly was, the wages that they earn is in no way justified! I have heard seven million people approximately is the number reported by the WHO, which although tragic is a fraction of the real numbers of infections. Which raises the biggest concern of mine.

What would have happened if this thing was really (nerve agent) serious? I am struggling with the whole way this played out. Detection, alarms raised, isolation and then the panic in finding an effective solution.

I'm sure the vaccines will have helped some people in society, but surely all the world must now know that a disease has to run its course! Acceptance of vaccines and the drugs of the licensed drug dealers (doctors and chemists) is not the answer!

Another situation that I observed during the whole pandemic crisis which took a different direction once we had all been offered the drug (injections). It was a kind of crossover moment where science fiction became science maybe?

If you recall the lockdown early days, governments were always trying, together with the health industries to find a magic pill, therapy or other alternative solutions. I can remember the chief medical officer for the country, quite clearly stating that the health sector was experimenting with already approved treatments, vaccines and drugs. To assess whether anything might actually have any impact against the virus!

Why bring this up? Well, I will tell you why. Because funnily enough it had brought back memories of when I went fund raising for the cancer research charity and the Royal Marsden Hospital in London. I finished my marathon event actually at the hospital and after paying my respects to the patients and staff I had a very revealing chat with one of the cancer specialists. Who told me about the costs for some of the treatments and how sometimes they repurposed medication from other treatments to see if it made any difference.

I read yesterday that they were doing the same for MS sufferers and were touting this as a potential monumental event. A breakthrough if you like. What this proves to me is that the pharmaceutical industry is in league with the white coats and governments.

Pills are NOT THE ANSWER! It's got to move into the 21st century, with carefully tailored therapies and much more focus on rehabilitation and physiotherapy. A dear old contact of mine from Lyme Regis, confided in me her distrust of modern medication! I also have had countless conversations with cancer survivors. Including my ex longtime partner, who underwent chemotherapy and radiotherapy for breast cancer; she was a nurse in intensive care and was also a doubting Thomas with some of the things she knew about!

Almost every talk I've had with people who had been hospitalized revealed dissatisfaction with the process. These supposedly intelligent people (Doctors and Specialists) are playing games with people's lives. Using the old mantra of breaking something first to be able to fix it! WHAT A LOAD OF BULLSHIT! The painful truth is 90% of the time they have no idea. But you can bet your bottom dollar that they have a tablet or medicine that "should help" Now call me judgmental or reactionary. Surely, we deserve better than this!

Which brings me to modern Pharma!

Now I don't want you (the reader) believing all drugs are about as useful as a chocolate teapot! The majority will perform some positive function, I'm sure. What concerns me is how reliant we as a society have become towards occupations like the chemists and massive organisation lobbyist groups like the petrochemical industry? I'll give one or two examples to highlight my frustrations, I have recently been diagnosed with MS. Now I don't agree with this, more likely it is a fractured spine caused by a heavy landing whilst working for an airline.

Now I could not challenge this because doctors like radiographers, neurologists even back specialists are lazy, inept, overpaid prima donnas. Not my words ... These are a comment left by an MS Trust regional manager, and incidentally an opinion allegedly supported by J K Rowling.

Anyway, I initially was treated with a course of steroids **alarm bell** right! I have since taken paracetamol, ibuprofen, amitriptyline, baclofen and I was steered towards a modern (DMT) disease modifying therapy called Natalizumab or Tysabri as its product name.

This, as you may recognise is a mind-boggling mix of pain relief, opiate, steroid, anti-spasticity, anti-depressant and a chemically laced infusion. All of which I have now stopped. Luckily, I had the good sense to be ultra-cautious about using this stuff. Now I am not supposed to be the healthcare professional, but after the last 9 years, I now know what is going on. I am a cash-cow for big Pharma. Despite my reservations about the effectiveness of all these things I was constantly told you need to experience them for longer to really appreciate their effectiveness. Or I was frequently told the drugs don't all work the same for everyone.

What the F... ! To which I say you are just being lazy, the reason why there are such differences is because MS patients have a large number of different conditions, it depends on where the spine is injured. BTW, I only want 10%. All of which I will donate to a children's charity, as Opposed to Fantasy

One of the first lessons which you learn when dealing with an illness. Is getting real about stuff. The definition for reality (or getting real) in the dictionary is the state of things as they actually exist, as opposed to an idealistic or notional state. It's about the A to Z of time management. If you have ever had to deal with anything serious, you'll probably know what I'm referring to. It also doesn't happen automatically or immediately either. It's what I like to refer to as the 3 R's.

Not the school acronym for reading, writing and arithmetic. No this is far more subtle and punchy. I'm talking about relevance, reticence and refusal to accept the inevitable. Because I promise you that any acceptance of "a truth" will only have one consequence. You will immediately begin down a road of decline and the consequences for you and your family's mental health will be irreversible.

But hang on, you're not medically qualified to make those assertions. The fact that this is true, is irrelevant, in my defence I think I'm more qualified than some of the stethoscope carriers. I've lived my story and done my research for fifty years. I'm not just talking about on me either because I'm in the unusual position of having witnessed this with my mother who I believe was invalided on the same day I was. In this respect I'm kind of unique. I learned how to make body management decisions from a very young age, all the while being motivated to prevent my life from being overwhelmed by the disease.

So, there you have it, staying fit and mobile guarantees a better quality of health. It also means that your body becomes ultra-sensitive to minuscule changes in environment and the potential of hazardous materials and foodstuffs.

If you think about it, it's good advice, keeping things simple and real or relevant. I'm immediately drawn to "the rule of law," whenever I think about this. You see on the one hand you are drawn towards laws and ethics of living. But on the other you are immediately confronted with the exact opposite. Which I don't think I need to remind you is "fantasy," or to coin an expression, "Trump world" or "Boris's world "

You see, I firmly believe that once you have been given a piece of unsettling information, or perhaps a terrible diagnosis. It is important to adapt your mindset, it's also imperative you start building defensive blocks into your routine.

I have used our legal profession "rule of law," as a comparison because in a weird and perverted sort of way it kind of highlights how you can change the rules to suit yourself!

Look at how rules and regulations apply differently to different sections of society, or perhaps how sentencing guidelines and punishment varies depending on what level of personal status or friendships and positional influence you possess. I'm convinced that these irreconcilable failures in the judicial system. Like when a judge passes different sentences for equivalent crimes is something that equates directly to how people are treated in the British healthcare community.

In my experience and lifetime, I have been fortunate to have never played the game according to the rules of the "grown-ups," if I had, I am certain I would never have been able to do all those bucket list moments. Sailing the Great Lakes in Canada, climbing in the mountains in Morocco, watching a Mozart concert in Salzburg or diving with sharks in The Maldives.

You see I've met people who have been given the same diagnosis as myself, but the difference is, much like my mother the diagnosis harboured a death sentence. Unable to work, unable to drive even in her later years it was one line of restrictions after the last. The doctors and healthcare system were utterly overwhelmed and useless. In fact, the biggest help she got was a worthless bunch of ineffective medications. What all these occurrences meant for me was to take positions on how I could avoid seeing any medical professionals. Who incidentally I do not trust or respect.

The only thing I ever followed and accepted with my dealings with MS sufferers was the golden rule. NEVER SURRENDER/DON'T GIVE UP! The day you stop trying to exercise is the second you start losing the battle.

Other big factors in the legal profession are intelligence, and communication skills. Which in a roundabout way can be translated directly towards the medical adventure. It's common knowledge that the doctors, neuroscientists, neurologists and other related specialists are well qualified. But so too are the barristers, judges and police!

I'm not going to be nice about this because I'm completely convinced that it needs to be said. In fact, I think most people would agree it's long overdue. What amazes me about British culture is how divided we all are. When I first got into difficulty, I had the wherewithal to self-diagnose. It was like glimpses into Pandora's box. You see I'm not a wannabe rock star, or a footballer who plays for a Premier League club. If I'm honest I realised this fact after the first hour of becoming sick. It's because I am rated as a third-class citizen, something I don't think I completely understood until I entered the NHS hospital. Even though I was not seen properly for three days.

I have watched how politicians and celebrities are fast tracked through the legal system. Even having been forced to pay compensation and costs they are still treated with respect and dignity. Something that you won't get from legal aid. But even when you have a valid case or argument you have no chance. It's mirrored perfectly in hospitals. If you are a private patient, you get priority care and treatment. In fact, I think the only NHS personnel who deal with private patients are radiologists and admin staff.

Whereas I have been moved from pillar to post during my experiences with the NHS, so it's fair to say I have zero empathy or respect towards them. "Nurses excepted!" A truly broken and dangerous system. Even long before you are confronted with a diagnosis, you are faced with navigating your way through a maze of appointments, meetings and tests.

This can be translated directly to the actions of our legal experts right down to a police force, or some other law enforcement agency, because for anyone who watches the news on a regular basis, you will have seen multiple examples of double standards. When despite literally identical crimes being committed by various people. It is always a perverse kind of game.

Sometimes the charges are dropped, sometimes the severity is reduced, sometimes the barrister finds an excuse or escape route, sometimes the criminal is pardoned by default, or insanity prevails like expired deadlines or misfiled paperwork is submitted. But tellingly they are all connected by one factor.

It all depends on who is the person being investigated! Just look at the Metropolitan Police force who have in my eyes always had questionable ethics and standards. I'm not just talking about the criminal elements like in the investigations involving bung taking or turning blind eyes to organised crime. There is also a degenerate element, like the misappropriation of undercover work. Misogynistic behaviour towards women and handling of female employees, racism on an industrial scale. I could go further but it would only get worse. The point is when any of these things come to light you can be sure that they won't get realistic punishments and consequences, when compared to the average citizen. The affected list of these double standards is extremely extensive too.

It includes the following, serving and retired police officers, legal practitioners of the courts, the political establishment, including home office staff, members of parliament, members of the House of Lords (serving and retired), the royal family, the extended family of various churches and perhaps most disturbing of all, members of the health service. It's like a role call for every level of what our so-called democratic society champions, as being above reproach. When in actual fact they're the ones who should be sitting behind bars!

Just for clarification when dealing with an illness. It's a fight for survival. It's bad enough that you are vulnerable and hoping for answers, but what disgusts me, and I find inexcusable is the fact that you have to play along with "the game!"

This relates to, and can be applied directly to, all the medical community. The handling of anyone suffering with and as yet, undiagnosed illness. For example, when the initial investigation has been found to be inconclusive. For anyone who has ever been treated privately, this would then require a doctor or consultant to provide an assessment of their findings to date. Not only to keep you informed, but also for the likely progression of the testing.

This is where the National Health Service deviates from standard procedures. Possibly because of time constraints, most probably because of lack of training and class. It's something that to this day really frightens me about these people's manners and their level of competence.

Some of the comments and conversations I have experienced over the last few years would make the hair stand up on the back of any sane person's neck. On the one hand I must concede that the individuals who wield their qualifications are far more likely to be able to give a fair and balanced opinion.

On the other I will tell you how it really is. It's an opinion based on my own experience with our health service and that of my mother and countless others who I have met over the years. It is aimed at every one of you who is given a diagnosis of Multiple Sclerosis. The truth is, in my opinion, the doctors and consultants are utterly toothless, inept and dishonest.

Their game face revolves around keeping control of the narrative. Pushing their patients into pointless trials and therapies. None of which are designed to cure, many of which are intended to appease and discourage. The worst are geared exclusively and entirely for Big Pharmaceutical Companies, sold like an Arthur Daley "used car salesman "type.

You know the kind of thing. Only one previous old lady owner, full-service history, reliable, etc.

guaranteed to break down in the next ten minutes! Even the language they use is non-committal.

Some of the conversations I have had with the NHS doctors have used the following words. 'Initial investigation requires further examination and testing", "initial assessment has been conducted too long after original appearance of symptoms".

On attendance for a patient review suddenly being informed that the appointment had been changed, or attendance for therapy drug unavailable because of failure to order the medication, symptoms "untypical" for suspected infection. Even illness dismissed as irrelevant.

Again, as I've emphasized, it all depends on who is being investigated.

For instance, I will bet any of you, somebody like Prince Andrew can allegedly molest or interfere with any girl he wants, or Boris Johnson can lie to anyone he chooses, or Rishi Sunak can quash any allegations of wrongdoing or impropriety of any kind in relation to his family or any parliamentary colleagues he wants.

Which is why I say... I am neither an A-lister, prominent politician or one of the privileged elites and I suspect nor are you, so we have to play a different game.

When you first present yourself with either symptoms or see blue lights in the rear-view mirrors. You need to get your strategy right. What this means and how it relates to my previous comments and comparisons is something that only you can decipher. But try to understand. If like me, you are lower down the pecking order it's crucial that you stay completely focused and don't get dragged into deliberate tactics and decision making by the closed shop that is "The NHS"

This for me, was my biggest failure. Not to take everything at face value. Thinking, erroneously that systems would be in place to protect me. I'm convinced the issues and maze-like navigation that I have encountered and endured, with the dead ends and false pathways, are all a direct consequence of not being vocal enough from the get-go. When I returned home and was feeling mentally exhausted and foggy, I should have gone straight to A&E instead of listening to my partner who suggested going to the village doctor's surgery.

It's comparable to a driving accident when you just do the exchange of details and particulars, instead of insisting on breathalyser tests and checking for worthiness of the other vehicle. I know and understand this now, because I saw how my ex, manipulated a traffic cop to make an unannounced arrest of someone who she wanted removed from her firm!

The fact the surgery proceeded to refer me to go to the local hospital was my second mistake. By rights I should have gone "blue light", especially considering I suspected it to have been a stroke. I self-drove and arrived at the hospital at 2:00p.m. On a Friday. A Bank Holiday Friday, which ultimately meant that nothing happened until the late morning of the following Tuesday. Ever seen the movie "Groundhog Day?" Because this is exactly how you feel in our health system.

The next comparison to be drawn between the wigs and the medical profession is something that I experienced in 2014. At that time, I was chasing around my local area and the city of Bath, visiting solicitors' offices in both locations. I was desperately trying to organise a legal challenge against my airline. I had recovered sufficiently from my suspected stroke in 2012, unfortunately I was forced to retire from work on the 31st of December 2012.

The details of which I have outlined in another chapter. It had taken me four months to recover from my initial bought of sickness, but I made another serious error in judgement when, under pressure from my base management at the airline company and because of a breakdown in a relationship towards my fiancée. The untimely death of my mother and the forced accommodation change in Somerset I rushed back to flying.

It was armed with all these complications to my circumstances that I began probing the beaks of the solicitors! I literally had a magazine full of implicating information and contributory factors.

For example: how was it possible to sign me off as fit to fly, knowing full well I had a spinal injury? Why did the company doctor who signed me fit to fly mysteriously disappear from the company records. Despite me having a full interview in Bristol?

Why did my attempts to get a grievance against the company always flounder? It was because of a deliberate attempt to shorten any meetings with me! (Dismissive & Deliberate Delaying tactics).

Why did the company, especially the base management not follow up with well-being health checks, following any kind of onboard incident? The reason why this is so relevant is because shortly before I had my health emergency, a trainee first-officer slammed the airplane into 'Bristol runway. In what I can only describe as an extremely heavy landing.

Other incidents that warranted further scrutiny and investigation were, that the airline operate with strict maximum working hours. Specifically, those who work on aircraft are subject to conditions that are set by the CAA. (Civilian aviation authority) but not if you work for easyJet. Because their crewing department plays hard & fast with the rules. Manipulating the data to suit their own agenda! I have the evidence for this but it's a conversation I was never allowed to air.

Then there were the questionable actions and blatant disregard for the health and safety of crew that I witnessed on quite an alarming frequency. withdrawal from employment in 2013 which meant navigating my way through a plethora of hoops and challenges.

Even the conversations I have endured with the administration and clerks at the solicitor's was an exact mirror of my dialogue with doctors and consultants, you allow them to control the narrative at your peril. Because for a legal team they only have one thing on their minds. Is this a winnable issue or case, how much money is involved or is it worth it.

Compared to the medical team questions. Is this an injury that can be successfully resolved. Has this person got the financial support and backing to achieve a good outcome. Do we have drugs or treatments and trials that could warrant further effort. Then there are the serious consequences for consideration when deciding to go on "the long haul" like taking a hospital bed or requiring one to one care and support.

Or perhaps there is the killer consideration for the doctors "Can we actually do anything useful" Which for anybody who was paying attention during the Pandemic, the answer is invariably "NO. So, for someone who has been exposed to this playbook all I will ask is. Again "is it worth it!"

My opinion is that the entire system is not fit for purpose. I will try to explain why. You see in many scenarios to do with healthcare it never really gets to "conflict zone" serious. Many people go through life without major medical complications or problems. The occasional breakage or flu virus is about the most severe illness we face in our first fifty years. I mean ok sometimes you can have uncommon symptoms or conditions, but I'm of the opinion that the majority of those cases are either self-inflicted or possibly down to poor choices. Which brings me nicely once again to the question of DUTIES OF GOVERNMENT!

I explained earlier how in the US constitution it is written that the citizens can expect the federal courts and government to take the necessary measures to protect them and their families and probably more importantly their property!

But let's be obtuse and deconstruct this belief. I am using the yanks, but it could just as easily apply to every other country on the planet. The biggest duty of your government is national security and the protection of its citizens.

Not like the U.K. where they have very different views. It's national security and the protection of the monarchy. It's something I don't actually think the majority of the people even understand, or if they do, they are unperturbed. Which then begs the question what does the average British person really want from their government?

The actual process of presenting yourself to a health professional is fraught with dangers. Let me give my simplistic assessment of the "what if's" against the "favourable outcomes". Let's look at what has emerged during my lifetime. Obviously, there was a great outcry about the safety of certain medications, have you heard of thalidomide, a tranquillizer that caused thousands of deaths and injuries in the 1950's and 60's!

Or the contaminated blood scandal of the 1960's to 1990's, turns out Britain was purchasing blood from convicts, drug addicts and other undesirable sources in the US. Thousands of patients were given unchecked blood and consequently were infected with a whole host of diseases. Including AIDS Hepatitis and haemophilia!

The other wider and perhaps more worrisome downside of conversing with the stethoscope brigade is a lottery if you will even get someone who can be described as competent! I'll give you a few of my experiences. Like my grandfather who went in for investigative surgery. Except he never came out. Or my grandmother who went in for an assessment after falling. Except she caught MRSA on the ward, didn't come out. Or my father who similarly was hospitalised after failing on the stairs at home. The hospital needed beds, so he was given the all-clear and sent home. He should never have been given the all-clear, got a severe headache after a few hours and had to be rushed back to hospital. Died that night. Or my mum who caught some bug in hospital and died from sepsis. Or my own catalogue of failings that I have mentioned in another chapter.

A hospital admission where they didn't get serious until four days later, because overcrowding meant they were unable to get the necessary beds and specialist needed to perform investigative CAT scan and MRI, plus it was on a Bank Holiday, so they didn't have any neurological specialists until the Tuesday. So, to nurses I say, pay them what they deserve. To the doctors "fuck off you greedy wankers"

Just letting a little frustration out there! Anyway, let me keep going with my deconstruction and critique of this failed project. Whilst doing my charity marathon to raise money and awareness of the Royal Marsden Hospital in south London, a specialist cancer treating clinic I got talking to not only some of the patients. But also, the doctors, who tried to make arguments for the treatment and the drugs and costs involved.

Just to give a personal perspective of this I should say that my ex-partner was diagnosed in 2005 with breast cancer, so I do understand the medical implications for dealing with illness. But what I have zero sympathy for is the papal infallibility syndrome which exists in the supposed help and support that gets offered to any diagnoses! As an outsider looking into this ultra specialised medical sector, I can't help but think that the "best solution" is definitely not the most efficient way to achieve (Successful outcomes)

Big pharmaceutical concerns are forever touting the benefits of their products and services, but what makes you think they are right? It's a quandary simply put, because the deck is stacked against the little guys. Just look at how influential the pharma-lobby was when deciding about mass vaccination! But what happens when you have valid reasons to question? If you think about it, it's the three monkey's syndrome. One can't see, one can't hear, and one can't talk. Which are you?

Anyway, let's get back to the British NHS a good way I have to describe it is from a commentary Michael Palin gave during his epic adventure. Around the world in eighty days. I don't have any idea what part of the journey he was on, except it was somewhere in China, he was discussing the number of Chinese workers being employed on the train and throughout the rail network. It is a strong argument for mass employment. With flag wavers every 250 yards along the track, or five chefs per carriage and then of course the train ticket collectors and managers. They even have a dedicated radio station with announcer for the journey. I believe it was 1986 but the point is to draw comparisons to the health service in Britain today. Where the exact opposite in terms of staffing is the key. In 86 China, the proportions seem excessive but look closer and you'll see that they are not. Only one person in any position of authority, lots of bodies doing the groundwork and crazily doing the work with a smile!

Today, I have read that 30,000 job vacancies currently exist for the NHS. The government is currently in dispute over wages for nurses, junior doctors and many other health professionals including ambulance staff. I remember a very poignant expression I heard recently which said that a democracy can be measured by how well it looks after its citizens and vulnerable. Which if you accept the expression as solid, level-headed thinking then you must agree the politicians in Britain have failed and should be rounded up and euthanized!

If you consider the fact that the country, or rather the government has underpaid as well as undervalued the workforce in the health sector for at least all my lifetime you will quickly see that pre pandemic it was a catastrophe waiting to happen, but let's do a little soul searching and find out how to address this issue. Something no government has attempted since my birth.

Point one, it's not the nursing staff, although I did have a few complaints whilst in the RUH Bath. Point 2, it's not the surgeon's, they seem very professional and competent. Point 3, it's not the peripheral staff (physiotherapists, hospital service providers like cleaners, caterers, porters) I think they like to be called ancillary staff. Point 4, it's not the specialist therapy teams. Or the scan teams and radiographers.

Which means the rest are the reason why the system fails so frequently and badly I'm talking about the administrators, wheelchair services, the doctors and worst offenders of all, managers and the ones who like to give themselves fancy titles and salaries! One of the most staggering things about my experience in different hospitals is how much of a postcode lottery it all is. I've been treated around the world in different countries and scenarios, and I have to say British healthcare doesn't even come in the top 20, oh my mistake, NHS healthcare doesn't come in the top 100, whereas British private healthcare does!

Maybe it was the junior doctor on my ward in Bath, Googling his symptom checker for a hint about my condition, or maybe it was the doctors who quite happily parked me off-site, for a whole Bank Holiday weekend, despite the fact I had demonstrated classic stroke like symptoms. Or maybe it was the doctor who was agitated talking to me about my health issues, unhappy about my questioning the suspected diagnosis. Which by the way I have never really accepted. Or maybe it was the junior doctor who woke me at 03:00 in my hospital bed to see what extent my dental issues were! I could go on with lots of crass unfortunate experiences at the hands of the muppets who like to be called DOCTORS.

Dictionary definition "a person qualified to treat someone who is ill." A very unsatisfactory description, so let me give you my definition, "a person who has spent hundreds of hours collecting the maximum number of qualifications possible to command a massively over the odds remuneration package!" The other day I was asked what a consultant was, or what a locum doctor does, or why doctors can determine what course of treatment or therapies are necessary or even preferable for a good outcome for patients who have been diagnosed with a condition!

Let me give some insight into my experience with health professionals and my family. Grandfather was not brilliant but had some discomfort in his abdomen. I'm sure that the surgeon believed the investigative procedure would establish what was wrong. Unfortunately, they killed him because they were not COMPETENT!

My mother was diagnosed with multiple sclerosis and consigned to the bin! Or put in real terms, she became a non-functioning skeleton of herself. Unsteady on her feet with countless daily challenges, including optic neuritis and very debilitating bladder and bowel issues. Muscle spasms and weakness, tingling in the extremities like hands and feet, then phases of mental decline.

I was in the front seat, passenger side of the car, when we had the accident. A motorcyclist lost control of his bike whilst cornering ahead of us. He slammed into the front of our car and flew off over the road. My mother applied an emergency stop. Hitting the brakes with intent and I was thrust forward and downward with the seat belt not providing any support. Now I realise that this is history and of no consequence or interest to the medical community. But it was only a matter of weeks after that event that she began her gradual decline and disintegration. It was also around the same period when I began to show classic MS symptoms, like insane tiredness and unusual sleepiness. So, there you have it, I've been living with all the stress, anxiety and restrictions that this disease is known to cause.

The clue is that last sentence, I've been living with it since I was about 9, when we lived in Holmbury St Mary's. The NHS obviously did all the testing they could for my Mum didn't however do anything for little old me. Because I am the middle child, the runt of the litter! I suspected of course because certain things were wrong with me, and nobody cared to talk about it. So being the affected I began distancing myself from the day-to-day difficulties that were emerging in me.

In certain atmospheric conditions and temperatures, I struggled to function normally. On a school trip to France, I got so fatigued from playing lots of football I slept almost the entire homeward journey from Narbonne to Guildford, most of it in the overhead luggage racks. I found concentrating on school impossible and my exam results are an accurate reflection of how I was feeling.

Even during some of my employment was stained with uncharacteristic behaviour. Again, with the tiredness and fatigue, or during certain temperatures that caused debilitation. I remember one occasion when we went hunting for the enemy in a forest in Germany and during a simulated attack and fight through, my legs stopped working and I was captured. It's probably the same reason why the body shut down during two of my marathons and one triathlon. But instead of crying wolf, I just kept going. So, you see it's not just the NHS that has failed me, so too the parents and also the military doctors. Who were about as interested as that old joke.

"Wire brush and Dettol ma'am." I'll let you figure it out!

What all the things both me and my mother showed and shared there is one constant. Which bearing in mind we're talking 50 years, this year. Gives a quite accurate appraisal of medical advancements! Which for me is summed up in one word. ABYSMAL. The nurses are the constant dependable and reliable. Surgeons are the hope. Which leaves the troglodytes.

Anyway, back to the evidence m' lard! I think I've already explained how the system killed my mother and father through the incompetence collective. But what Is staggering is how frequently the mistakes occur and how often the mantra "we're listening and always trying to improve" is marched out. Almost like a mistake isn't that serious!

We'll let me just say this. If you are deemed the cause of failure that costs lives. I'm sorry but for me and hopefully all of humanity. SORRY isn't enough. I think a stint in a correction facility like Alcatraz would be more appropriate. I bet this would make the "little mistakes" stop in any case.

I'll throw you all a few more bones now. Places to pause and think and places to understand how shit our health system has become. So let me chuck in the first curveball. Since I was taken ill, I've gone through lots of different kinds of treatments. Sounds good right?
Well, let me explain how utterly ridiculous and pointless it all is.

You see when you get ill in this country it's all about a tick box exercise. But even to get a meaningful diagnosis requires either a bottomless wallet or bank account, or a lucky break in the avenues of NHS Anti-care. For me it was 3 days before anyone did anything other than offer a bed and a sandwich. I was referred to hospital by my local GP, despite showing stroke like symptoms. But because today was Friday and it was a Bank Holiday, nobody did anything until the following Tuesday.

The ward I was placed in was unsuitable for any sane person and the noises and stupidity was unbearable. I ended up sleeping in the nurse's restroom watching the TV. I was wondering what the hold up to treatment was only to bear witness to the craziest episode in my life. I wondered over to the nurse's station to ask a few questions, when I suddenly noticed on a computer screen near me my details being loaded onto a symptom checker website. I was completely dumbfounded by this and thought I could have done that without having to wait around for 4 days

But it gets worse! I lost a gold crown tooth to a hospital meal. I put it on the table and went to the bathroom to clean my teeth and mouth, but on returning the broken dental work had been stolen along with my plate and drink!

On another occasion when I was still able to walk and drive, I was sent to see the hospital physio. Who got me walking again in 40 minutes. This is the last time I have ever walked unaided, and it was also the only time I have ever been given the neuro physio treatment I needed. WHY?
Well, I think it's because there are so few qualified and competent trainers in the system. But it highlighted to me how important a bottomless stash of cash is.

Next comes the distraction therapies, I have been given electric shock therapy, which means attaching several sensors around the spine and using a graded scale of 1 for light shocking to 10 for intense nerve stimulation. Well, they progressed very quickly to maximum without any serious effect. For me confirming the issues were spinal.

I have been given infusions of a MS therapy drug called interferon, or Natalizumab. All of which were ineffective, and the hospital also once again showed how utterly incompetent they are, by scheduling me in for treatment. I took time off work for the procedure and when presenting myself for the process, turned out that the drug hadn't been ordered.

Now bearing in mind every visit, appointment and procedure required driving, parking, taking time off work and scheduling a very full diary, you can see how much you lose faith in anything to do with the system in the UK.

I've been stranded in the home entrance hallway after returning from an infusion, phoned 999 for an ambulance, but was told I was low down the priority list. Luckily the central heating kicked in after a 5 hour wait and I was able to drive to the Frenchay hospital in Bristol. Only to be put onto another waiting list. When I did eventually get seen I was given the third degree about why I should not have presented at the emergency room. Despite being told by RUH Bath to do exactly that if I had a reaction to the infusion!

I have been in a hospital when the nurses were desperate for me to go into one of their specialist beds, the ones that supposedly prevent bedsores. Unfortunately, they are so noisy and uncomfortable that you can't sleep. Despite my protests I had to get the formal complaint procedure started before they backed off and allowed me to use a normal mattress.

I've been confronted by this insanity on a few occasions escaping the idiocy of the wards noise and procedures, by nipping out to get a bit of normalcy and a newspaper, when the internal hospital security has essentially arrested me for being out of bed. Honestly you couldn't make it up!

I've been in a side department of Southwell hospital in Bristol and whilst waiting for my appointment I was confronted with confidential patient records, documentation and private information that should never have been left unsecured. When I questioned the secretary on my way out, she just shrugged and said it's none of my business!

I'm one of the first people to say that they were admitted to Southwell Hospital. The nurses were great but I'm afraid much of my time was not! At the time my condition had deteriorated to no mobility, constant brain fog. I was able to walk with the aid of a walking frame the length of a corridor, which for anybody who knows Southwell will know that's about 100 m.

I was given another MRI assessed by a different team of doctors and neurologists. But quite by chance I had a conversation with an Occupational Therapist who confirmed my own opinion.
They were clueless.

Ok, I had the scan for a patient with MS, but the other symptoms affecting me were not consistent with that. Which means that they got lazy. I'm convinced it was too much trouble to discover what was going on, so they just decided to sign me off with an unwarranted diagnosis and save the potential consequences of a costly investigation and treatment for what was really going on! Once again, I have made a slight break from the narrative. But this is the troubling truth about distractions, they are intentionally placed to appease or deflect from achieving a proper kind of understanding and treatment for the injuries suffered.

One of the clearest and classic examples of this is the home adaptation policy. So far, I've been forced out of 3 properties. The first one by agreement with my ex-fiancée, the second out of necessity when my symptoms became unmanageable and the third, I like to call my Atlantis. A fictional domain I created by utilising a desire to escape the nightmare reality that was forced upon me during the first years of my 2012 stroke journey.

You see humans are very adaptable when confronted by illness. They learn what works and what to avoid. So, to escape the downward spiral I began following my instincts and choosing only those activities which I could perform comfortably. Hence the scuba diving. I'm unable to walk but give me a dive buddy and willing helping hands and I'm transported to a world where I can thrive! What does all this mean? It means that I realised early doors that I was never going to get the help I wanted or needed, because I didn't fit into the program mapped out by the healthcare professionals. Another very large and frequent frustration with our healthcare system is the perpetual shifting and changing appointments chaos. It was happening in the early days of my illness, where I would get neurological dates and times, sometimes to speak to the specialist doctor, or in some cases the eye doctor's or bladder and bowel services. It was never admitted, but I know it happens because whenever you attend an NHS department and are not sent under guidance from a Private Health Care or insurance provider, you immediately go to the back of the line.

I've attended hospitals for MRI, CAT, or purely X-ray investigations with fixed appointment timings to discover last minute changes have occurred and unfortunately the procedure has had to be postponed and rescheduled.

Which quite frankly is bullshit and highlights how much of a class driven society we aspire to. By the way it's also happened on numerous occasions with the dental services, who went AWOL during the pandemic. No surprises there then

I'm cross because I realised how crap British healthcare was from a very young age. I'm not slagging off the industry totally, because as I've explained and experienced there are some good aspects and some good people. But if I try to make a balanced judgement on things I find I can't because of all the unnecessary stupidity and stress that we as a family have had to contend with.

I'm cross because I assumed that your treatment today would be far better and more professional than the way my parents and grandparents were treated. I assumed that 50 years of learning the lessons of previous failures would have helped turn things into a positive and healthier experience I also assumed that the wrong uns would have been weeded out by now.

But guess what. They haven't and I believe that there are more Dr Shipton's or nurse Letby's out there desperate to find out if you can die like a good patient should.

I'll tell you how perverse it all is. I've witnessed a ward where call bells don't get answered because the shift is watching the World Cup. I've dated a nurse briefly while in the early stages of my diagnosis. Who wanted me to abuse her. I think it was somehow related to 50 shades of grey, but who can say!

Anyway, still not finished with distractions, I've been given lots of aids to supposedly improve my ability to function. Except that this is not true. The only reason I have been given the opportunity to use the apparatus like walkers, balance machines or frames is because it means they don't have to spend the resources and personnel necessary to make a difference.

I even have a hospital bed in the house in case I fall and require a means of getting back up to my wheelchair, all that investment plus I've had a few house adaptations like a wheelchair friendly shower and toilet fitted and a ramp installed out the back door to allow access to an electric scooter. I'm just one guy so you do the maths. How is this not the stupidest waste of money. All the scans, all the appointments. Ten years of going back and forth trying to get someone to listen and do something.

So, there you are, for anyone about to start on a health quest I really feel for you. I'm certain that you wouldn't be treated this badly if you were French or German. Definitely not if you were Canadian or American and dare, I say it. The Cuban doctors are leap years ahead of here. The government has failed us as a family for 50 years. But it's OK because the average person doesn't care!

But the difference between myself and the millions of other people who were practicing their state wandering skills is, I had one very lucky advantage. I knew I was ill, and I knew how to manage expectations. That might sound a little strange, but for anyone who carries an injury there is an unwritten and unspoken about rule. Something the Army taught me at the beginning of training. Any injury or weakness is something you must work on constantly. Which is what I've been doing since my first inclination of a problem.

So, for the sake of all you MS diagnosed here is my list and my solutions and self-help guide. I think the first indication that I was needing a bit of help, came with my incredible bouts of excess in the sleeping department. I can remember being told I had slept over 24 hours at grandparent's flat. The grown-up's put this down to "probably a virus!"

But the crazy thing was that these episodes have always awoken and debilitated me to one extent or another. It's something that you learn to recognise the warning signs of, like tired eye or migraines, with a very telling pain behind the eyeball, something which I have learnt to accept and train against by increasing my fitness and capacity to endure long hours of physical activity.

One quick warning though here. Be very careful about overdoing it while driving or on operations. I remember one drive I made from Chiemsee to Soest after a whole fortnight of helping with adventure training. I woke up at the wheel but heading towards an embankment. Luckily, I managed to swerve in time.

I've also been at a rock concert for "The Damned," at a club in Detmold called "Hunky Dory's," I had just finished a long week exercise and didn't want to miss the music, so I went inside the Smokey venue and guess what! I awoke in a toilet cubicle in the middle of the night. From memory about 04:00 with a missing memory of about two hours. I'm pretty sure it was 1985 because I remember watching Live-Aid on the television about a fortnight after that little episode.

Believe me when I tell you waking up stone sober on a toilet is not a good picture? I've done the sleep thing with one other exception; this goes back to my schooldays when we went on a cultural exchange week. Improving the language but also getting more comfortable with the sports teams. I shared a room with Alec Gravestock from the rugby team and I was put in goal for the football team.

Everything was fine until at the end of this tiring and action-packed week we were literally driven from Narbonne in the south of France to Calais without any real break. We also drove from Dover to our school in Milford again without much of a rest, and it was during that period of the trip that my body decided to shut down again. I climbed up onto the ceiling mounted luggage racks and pretty much slept through the entire journey. A feat I defy anyone not suffering with MS to undertake.

So next on the symptoms appreciation and dealing with tour I must go back to Busbridge first school. A pleasant little place in Godalming Surrey. I'm drawn to the sports day where everyone was encouraged to go faster, longer, higher and stronger in an atmosphere designed for the families. I've still got my certificates from this day, but the thing which stands out was the 800m middle distance race. I don't think I understood what was happening to me then but knowing the things I now know it was clear that me failing to complete this run was a direct consequence of the illness.

I just brushed it off at the time as an anomaly, a freak occurrence. I mean I used to run the dogs further than that on a regular basis. But I have been living with this problem since way back then. I didn't register that event as being an unusual thing until I was doing my basic training for the Army. The final test was a long run and March in full military gear, it was all going swimmingly until the sun and humidity arrived.

I felt and probably looked like a marathon runner struggling to get over the finish line, but I think from memory there were still 5 or 10 more miles to go. I decided right there and then mentally to never give in. It's another reason why I believe I've stopped the normal progression of the disease. I'm certain that the fact I have continually challenged myself has slowed my decline. I've had lots of events where the body has failed when the mind was willing.

My first marathon at Viersen, a run on the runway of our base in Canada, more recently the triathlon on the Mohnesee, or the 30km Hermanslauf across the hills to Bielefeld. But the worst one was the marathon in 2003 in Munster. I'm pretty used to these shutdowns now and I've found a little rest, cold on the skin and shade are the best way forward. On other occasions like swimming and sun worshipping I've learned to be very careful especially after falling asleep on Waikiki beach in Hawaii and waking up with 3rd degree burns and blisters.

After that episode I have always made sure I am rested before going to the beach! Another priceless tip for you all. The next major "Red Flag" experience with the disease I encountered was something which at the time I put down to petulance. It was a typical Sunday lunch with everybody ordered to follow the routine a bit like the classic German Television programme that gets aired religiously on virtually every channel on New Year's Eve. It's called "dinner for one," starring Freddie Frinton.

It's basically a humorous comedy sketch about an old woman who dines with her old friends and close confidants. Except that they are all dead and her butler has to pretend to keep the tradition going. With each passing course of the meal her butler toasts her health with the catchphrase "same procedure as last year?"

I won't spoil it for you, but essentially this was how our family conducted the Sunday meal. Except on that occasion, I tasted something that my brain started getting upset about. I'm convinced now that it was an alarm bell. Telling me "Don't eat the food," it was roast beef with the usual excessive portions of Yorkshire pudding and potatoes and vegetables.

Now because I refused to eat, I caused a massive fight which culminated in me wearing a plate of bread-and-butter pudding with custard. I didn't understand what was going on here. UNTIL many years later when the country went through the BSE epidemic, or in layman's terms Mad Cow Disease.

It was as if my actions had been justified. I'm also convinced that my actions that day saved my parents from a horrible fate. Because almost everything after that was changed to suit my palate, which incidentally mirrored my mother. But again, it was something that I never really considered until on one chance encounter with a friend from EasyJet. Alison told me about her boyfriend who was also diagnosed with the disease, nothing unusual about that I hear you say. Except she then informed me about his eating habits.

She said whenever he went out for a meal, he always ordered chicken, which is the moment for me comparable to Archimedes "eureka" moment. Allegedly when the Greek polymath discovered whilst taking a bath, how water displacement happened. Or for someone who has an epiphany. You see it all began to fit. For years in the house with my parents I would always choose either chicken or turkey. It's something I always did in the forces, well either that or salads. I even made a conscious effort, like Alison's boyfriend to only have dishes with chicken. Which basically means KFC, the chicken tikka masala, or roasted bird meat was my go-to food of choice.

Even when I was living with my own family, I would do non-sensical things like drive to WALMART in Dortmund to buy their roasted chicken, or wherever I did cooking duty it would be "the bird"?

So once again for anyone who is interested, an unusually high number of meals on the table that contain chicken is probably a key indicator and a good reason to get checked out!

The next warning sign I have had for the past 40 plus years is something that I am now able to rationalize and it's another one of those classic symptoms which most people would freak out about. But you see for me, in my denial zone it was a completely common thing that I had to deal with at my own pace. It's something I had countless conversations with my mother about even as I would be massaging her feet to try to alleviate the pins and needles that she constantly complained about. I've probably had it for the longest time, maybe even after the initial traffic accident. But here's the thing, boys don't cry or whine because in the words of my dad, "It's a sign of weakness? Well guess what?

I'm over that. It's something I first experienced at Guildford Dojo. Or judo club, where the Sensai was teaching a strangulation hold and basically letting the class experience the whole feeling of losing consciousness. An interesting experience, but one that left me with pins and needles in both hands and something which lasted about two days. It was also something which I experienced multiple occasions in my Army life. Forcefully climbing using ropes was one thing and whenever we practiced assault courses or doing drills that required you to leopard crawl, but this is where my ability to desensitize came into its own. I would just ignore everything as "Just a sensation!" A useful skill which I have practiced consistently for as long as I can remember. Which leads me onto the biggest "tell" I can explain, but again something I have consistently suppressed and something that explains a hell of a lot about my life story.

It's another of those things that I have pushed into the darkest recesses of my mind and is only something I stumbled upon thanks to Alison's boyfriend's recollections. It was also something I was staring into the face of for years with my mum. But never joining the dots.

I now realise how come I was such a failure with anything to do with the classroom. I'm not illiterate. I've always been a good reader. I'm not a lower level intellectual. Despite what some of my peers might suggest. Q. What do you think a peer is? No intellectually I can hold my own. I'm not a slow learner! Now if this was true, I wouldn't pass an R.A.F. computer systems manager course in three weeks, or learn to speak German, and pass a series of questions and tests in a couple of years, culminating in a qualification to be a cabinet maker, or learning to speak and write French in a few months or retraining to become a part of flight crew in a matter of weeks.

AND THERE IT IS: THE BIGGEST CLUE OF THE LOT:

During the few weeks I was at Luton Airport, retraining as flight crew I noticed that information was not sinking in. In the way I was used to. For example, the list of safety equipment storage locations was something I had difficulty processing. It was like attempting my exams in secondary school all over again. I really struggled with thought recollection and consequentially my results were not anything like what was expected.

I had seen that kind of behaviour in mum for years and years. But again, I never thought to link up the similarities. But here it was in me all over again. I'm happy to say I passed with flying colours (like the pun), and I worked on the aircraft for 6 years. Until that fateful moment after Amsterdam in 2012 when lying and cheating was finally solved, or was It?

Which brings me nicely onto the next level of the mystery that is my story and a quote which I think serves not just me but everyone in some way. "The greatest secret of a trick, is, what's in the magician's closed fist," and how I view this illness.

So, here's a metaphor. I'm going to give you a little trick which was used by the coalition during the Kuwait repatriation, after they captured thousands of Iraqis. They had tents full of prisoners to process and no way really of deciding the wheat from the chaff.

So, they let them stew for a day or so and simply announced to the entirety that the officers had been called forward for food and drink! Instantaneously separating the ranks and simplifying the interrogation process. Which as simple as it sounds is absolutely genius. It's how I view this disease being defeated. By some piece of inspiration. Something you all must believe in. It's like Alan Turing all over again.

It was a lovely Autumn morning on the day it kicked off. I was in my car, a boring Opel Astra, we had used it for about three years, and I was contemplating getting a newer one. I had driven off that morning with a multitude of different thoughts in my head and as I remember it, I had just finalized the team sheet for the day's football game.

The drive was very welcoming that morning and the roads were clear. I had a bit of the radio blaring into the car. Today was the first game of the new season, which basically meant clean slate. A fresh start for the team and the hope of improving on the mid-table finish in May. The weather looked like playing too. We had had a good downpour the previous night and it looked as if we might get a sunny kick off.

I was simultaneously optimistic and hopeful! I could see the ground could take a stud and sliding tackles would be painless. Then out of the blue I thought I had heard something about a tragedy for the world. I only caught little bits and pieces. The news was courtesy of German state radio. My language skills were not very advanced and anyway I didn't really think it would be something that would concern me, that was until I drove into the parking area by the pitch.

Everybody was huddled together around Dave's motor. I went straight to the changing room where one of our opponents said loudly "Paris," I began lacing up my boots and then I noticed Danny who had been looking for me. I began to get that feeling. You will relate to this feeling if you've ever lost a loved one! Danny just looked at me and said "Diana is dead"

Looking back on that moment I can honestly say I've only had this feeling on three occasions during my lifetime. The 9/11 live footage of the attack on the world trade centre. The realization that I was in a potential world plague and the third time is something which probably won't make people's top ten. It was when the German people started to tear down the Berlin Wall. This last one is something very personal to me. At the time I was dating a girl in the city, I didn't know what to expect because the corridor through the old DDR was quite intense, the towers were still watchful and threatening.

Reflective glass hiding what the border guards were doing. You could see lots of military movements whilst driving through places like Magdeburg and Dresden. I can even remember seeing the walls around Berlin with a sense of historical scene change. The trouble was nobody knew how premier Gorbachev would react. Oh, sure everyone knows it all played out peacefully but, in the beginning, we didn't know how Russia would react.

I always enjoyed the idea of one day meeting the great Princes Di, I had held a candle for her ever since the memories of "that dress" going into St Paul's. I don't think I can say a negative word about her. She always looked top dollar; the causes she championed were close to my heart. I remember feeling so proud of her when she hugged an HIV patient it was the first time I can remember anyone had ever shown publicly real empathy and dismissed any fear of infection, other moments I treasured were when she would go out into mine fields with troops, totally embracing the spirit of clearing up the explosive devices, in a strange way it gave me courage to be uninfluenced whatever situation I might find myself in whilst in the Army.

But there was one occasion which bonded me to her forever. It was the way she popped up in the audience at the greatest event of the twentieth century. 13th April 1985, Live Aid. It was another example of her ability to make faultless choices. I believe her endorsement was key to not only the success of this event but also every subsequent world disaster fund raising campaign.

It got people to understand that working together away from politics which are a force for evil, is the only way mankind can achieve any peaceful co-existence. By the way I don't want to contribute Live Aids success solely to her, because I think Bob Geldof and Midge (James) Ure might take offence. The success was also down to the incredible live performance put on by the rock group "Queen!" My only other connection to this great lady was a charity event I once organised and championed.

I ran and cycled 400 miles back to the Royal Marsden Hospital to get money for cancer research. The only reason I chose this goal was because Princess Diana was the patron. Occasionally I see old pictures of her, and it immediately reawakens old memories. There are lots of what ifs. What if the paparazzi didn't chase like rabid dogs. What if she had left the royal family much earlier. What if the public had been as supportive as Diana was?

I think we will never know the true story. But what is interesting is how different Harry and William have turned out. It's got all the intrigue of the grassy knoll in Dallas. Maybe it was arranged to prevent a union of Fayed and the Windsor's. Perhaps it was seen as the easiest way to restore faith in the royal family. Is it possible that someone has footage of the accident, and the government is being blackmailed!

So, you can see how conspiracy theories get legs? Let's get back to the story. When I checked the calendar, it was 31st August 1997. It hammered home to me why I had made the decision to leave the British Isles. It was corrupt on every level imaginable. Now I know what I'm about to divulge is going to be difficult for many of you to accept, but the truth must out. The very week I left the forces and headed for my new life I distinctly remember two things. I drove down the M4 to get to my parents, a short stop off to sell my car. When I noticed coming into the turn off for the M25 lots of smoke on my right-hand side. It was the perfect metaphor for Britain. Windsor Castle was on fire, and I thought, the idiots in charge were getting their just deserts.

The second thing, I got wind of during this drive, was how everything was only heading in one direction. It really was, "the race to the bottom." The service stations on the roads were unnecessarily expensive. The facilities were poor at best, the food was stuff from the 70's, also the number of loitering miscreants was disturbing.

It reminded me of a conversation I'd once had with Danny in Germany. After he'd been on a London Christmas shopping trip. He said the first thing that struck him after disembarking was how much of the trip up from Dover to the capital was filled by this architectural blight of rabbit hutch boxes for houses. With little space for gardens because the space for greenery had been turned into parking areas, everyone seemed to exist for their vehicles.

Not sensible family cars or fuel-efficient models but polluting gas guzzlers like SUV's. He also noticed how everyone was in a hurry to get from A-Z. With all manner of impolite driving behaviour. You know what, forty years later and it's still the same. If not worse. So, the question is Where is this going? I think it's probably best to start with why I left The British Isles.

When people take you 'under their wing' it is often used as a term of endearment. It somehow encourages faith that the world still has belief in your promise and potential. Now I'm not going to be overly critical of this much used expression, because I do accept that there are some occasions when mentorship works and that with training and experience it can make a difference. You can advance financially and in professional development you will learn important skills and behaviours. One thing it never does is promote ladder climbing skills, probably because the person under whose wing you are is usually a direct competitor for advancement!

I have first-hand experience how it works in this country! It's something which is not career specific or even performance and competence driven, it's what I like to call the triple bypass law! A metaphor for manipulation.

Essentially what happens is the surgeon circumvents the clogged arteries and allows things to move in an unnatural way, (hence manipulation) In Britain there are hundreds, if not thousands of different ways to move up the ladder. In certain professions there are clear career paths. A qualification attained is usual in some environments. In others there might be a change catalyst and there are the dark arts. Things like nepotism. Mafia aligned behaviour, sexual related promotions, old school tie, Masonic handshakes, hidden secrets, even the most mundane and obvious things like lying on the cv, police records etc...There are, spread across many gathering points in a business, conversation corners.

Places where gossip and skulduggery are prevalent. "Nods as good as a wink to a blind bat!" Sums it up perfectly for me. A classic piece from Monty Python's, "nudge-nudge" sketch. You see it's the combination of the double entendre and British humour that fuels everything that is evil in this country. The problem is most people here are too stupid to comprehend how they are being sidelined. But for me I experienced the worst part of sideways promotions and decided I had to go.

The only reason for coming back was part work related, part relationships related but mostly because mum was getting depressed about her home, (as in care home)! But we'll come onto that later in the story.

I'm going to start with the obvious "elephant in the room." It's Politics, which I hate myself for doing. But it highlights very effectively how shit Britain is!

So, here's the first juxtaposition why are economists and politicians playing off each other's failures? Or should that be why do bankers and senior civil servants always hide behind their policy guidelines and limitations to avoid culpability? This is going to sound wrong but the real problem with these government agencies, departments, political parties and banks. Is that they are entities that perpetuate bureaucracy just for the sake of it, to justify their own existence or for their own profit.

Whenever I watch Parliamentary proceedings, I find myself thinking that they are a bunch of utter bastards. For a start what's all that nonsense surrounding procedure and debate. I've been educated to believe that we are fortunate to have such a strong parliamentary democracy, with the proof being given that history has shown how dynamic and effective it is! Utter Bullshit.

I'm convinced that it was partly these historical formalities and traditions, whereby the Speaker navigates the discussion. Whilst all the while maintaining a faux pas' position during debate, supposedly showing utter impartiality when selecting ministers' questions, that resulted in Brexit! Or the "not fit for purpose," process of governance we have today.

When I say "today" what I mean is the system that we've endured for the past 75 years. Talking with a language more fitting of a bygone era. In so far that whenever anyone addresses each other it's preceded by "the honourable member" or "the honourable lady."

Let's get one or two things straight! There are no honourable anybody's in that place. I think the history books will bear me out on that, the fact that there has been scandal after scandal proves how corrupt and incompetent they have become. I could waste my time by listing all the occasions when they have been caught out. You only have to watch HIGNFY or read the front pages of the newspapers from the last forty years to get a measure of that. So, I'll leave that task in your capable hands.

Now I dare say some of you will defend the Palace of Westminster, pointing out the traditions, etiquette etc. I won't. Because I'm of the opinion it stinks, it's even worse in the House of Lords. I mean what does it say about this country when any old fart can take a place in the senior house by virtue of the New Year's honours list? Higher House my arse! Do we really deserve this shit storm?

Want a metaphor? It's part of the first Matrix film. "Neo" has just been told if he takes the blue pill he will wake up at home and everything will be normal. However, if he swallows the red pill, he will learn what's really going on. Basically, it's the same choices for British people whenever they go into a general election. In layman's terms, "a two-horse race."

Now obviously there are more choices on constituency ballots, but how come there are rarely more than blue or red winners? The answer is simple. The rich are blue and the less well-off are red. Talk about dumbing down!

In essence this is partly why most (intelligent and disenfranchised) normal people want to escape this godforsaken land. I'm convinced it won't change either unless the young take to the streets and behave like revolutionary France, because if they don't, I'm afraid it's going to be crumbs for your whole lives.

I don't know what motivates people to go to the polls, one thing is certain. I have lived all over the world, but nowhere I mean NOWHERE! Has such a pitiful lack of choice than in the British Isles.

Now, a moment of reflection, how many people do you know who are in the process of, or have actually made the decision to leave these islands? If you're similar to me, you will know of about twenty-five people who have left here for good. I think the most important question is. Why are the others still here? I'm no expert on the topic but I have a theory.

Everyone I know who has left wanted to get a life! Sounds strange to some of you I bet. It'll be the ones of you who have their own house and live in the pleasant-smelling suburbs of green belt countryside.

Quick question: what is that drives people away? Well for me it was the disparity between the levels in society. People like my parents were overstretching and living outside of their disposable income. It came crashing down when my mother became sick, and my dad invested badly into a business.

It was also a sign of the times in the early 80's. A period widely recognised now as the worst recession since World War 2. But who came out smelling of roses?

Pick up a few snippets, because it's all tied together. We are the generation that saw how certain situations never affect the entitled old money/families.

A big clue was dropped by the Conservatives telling people they should get on their bikes!

I personally experienced firsthand how the politicians and bankers squeezed and closed ranks on sections of the country that were deemed the expendables. Like the car industry, whilst simultaneously, council house residents in places like Durham were thrown bones and given a chance to own their property. A blatant bribe for disenfranchised coal mining communities.

What I would like to do next is go through all of the so-called pillars of society to get a better flavour of where we stand in the world.

I think the most effective approach would be to make a complete list of what we as a developed nation consider to be the columns. According to the internet we have governance, faith, health, education, family and arts and culture.

So, we've had a glimpse of governance, what about faith? I don't think I can currently name anyone of my social circle who openly advocates religion. Especially not with question marks over their pastors and bishops' improprieties. Historical abuse and inappropriate behaviour to name just a few. I have been very clear in this book about my feelings about this.

On the one hand I sympathize with anyone who might feel the need to talk about higher powers, but before you judge me, I have two very different thoughts on the subject. Firstly, what gives anybody the right to be ceremonial about anything?

Secondly why do humans need to feel they are the more evolved? It's makes it very difficult for me to understand why people are so desperate to get hitched. I'm certain it's not anything to do with whatever blessings are thrown around, it won't affect the interaction within families, so why would any sane couple splash the cash for the sake of tying the knot? Or is it massive peer pressure!

I am obviously not an authority on this, but I am and have always been an opponent of this wasteful, ceremonial stupidity. I'll give you a flavour of the things which annoy me. We'll start with the engagement! Which for me should only be a term defined in military parlance.

There is a difference set of circumstances for every couple obviously, but how did we get to where we are now? A brief or uninterrupted courtship which leads to a betrothal! Exchange of rings etc. An unchallenged exchange of views from both parties' families. What is then expected is a ceremony to commemorate the commitment and joining of the clans and then support for all concerned.

To which I say "fuck you"

For starters why do two consenting adults need anybody's seal of approval? It's your life and therefore your responsibility. I don't buy into the whole notion that it all benefits everyone in the community.

As someone who has never been included into any community, I stick two fingers up at the peddlers of this blatant lie. Because you will only be allowed into the inner circle of the community if you roll over and let your owner pet you, like the subservient gutter snipe that they think you are.

Just think about the money which changes hands to realise any marriage. It's not just conformity but also the equivalent of Masonic handshakes and ritual social ladder climbing, whereby every person invited to attend is a potential stepping-stone to opportunities and status.

That's the sad truth to all this. I'm convinced in the modern age it's never about love "whatever that is" is all about connections.

We next come onto health. It's obvious that you are happier with good health. The benefits are immeasurable, but again I have major issues with not just my own personal well-being, but more importantly the quality of life of the entire planet.

I am a doubting Thomas when it comes to modern medicine. On the one hand I think that pharmaceutical companies are manipulating data to justify prices for products. On the other I don't buy into the hype and arguments about effectiveness of their drugs.

I think that Covid and James Herriot are the key indicators for me. You see I used to be a prolific reader of anything and everything humorous. My favourite two authors for comedy being Tom Sharpe and Nick Hornby. But where I started, was with "all creatures great and small," a collection of anecdotal stories about this countryside vet in the Yorkshire Dales.

What has this got to do with human health I hear you clucking. Well, it's in the subtext of a story about a horse. Which caught my attention because of the implications it raised. I have forgotten the exact details about the case other than it was treated with an experimental drug administered by Tristan Farnham. (Vet)

The book told us how veterinarians were prescribing drugs which had unknown effects. What this meant was that unknown substances were being injected into animals without any evidence of their effectiveness or safety! Think this little tit-bit through and imagine two scenarios. The pharmaceutical drug is going into an animal that is essentially an agricultural product. It's going to have implications for the flesh of the animal, milk and any utilized organs and what do humans do with these creatures?

Secondly the animals will not absorb the toxins permanently into their bodies, which means at least some of the drugs will eventually become excreted onto the land, which logic suggests will eventually end up in your and my water supply!

Anybody still unsure about where mysterious illnesses originate.

I can remember years ago during one eventful Sunday roast lunch with my family. The beef tasted disgusting, and I offended my mother so much I ended up wearing the bread-and-butter pudding after a massive fight. (Always give the children the benefit of the doubt!)

Years later after the BSE crisis I got an apology from her, and she thanked me for changing her diet! I am convinced that most modern disease is caused by the pharma industry. It can't be coincidence that things like the prevalence of cancer incidence have increased by so much. But going back to normal health care. Let me put this in perspective.

I believe the British National Health Service is a broken system. It's one of those areas that no one wants to tackle, you occasionally read about policy changes and organizational improvements, but what do any of these headline making media bombs change?

The answer is, apart from tinkering around the edges, very little! Why? I'll be brief with my theory, and I want you to not just talk about it. But more importantly discuss it with your friends and colleagues.

You can substitute the NHS for any other public sector workforce. The police, emergency services, education and prison. Every administration on council or legal sectors. The sad reality is that we, (The public), have been playing their game for decades. The vast majority of these people are well educated and highly qualified, but they all shit out the same hole as you and me. So then how can they demand rock star remuneration?

It all starts off harmlessly enough post-graduation, with entry level positions on average pay. But fast forward a few years a few additional courses later and "hey presto" the money really starts to flow. It is this insanity which is killing the country.

Successive generations and governments from both sides of the political spectrum have failed to understand the "flaw in the plan" as Blackadder would say.

Topping up vast swathes of the electorate by offering inflation matching deals, is how the parties have managed to win over the two key groups in the population. The pensioners and the public sector. It's a kind of pyramid scheme on cocaine. The significance for playing this game is clearer when you look at the rank structure on display.

The public sector provides a clear promotion path. With financial rewards for achieving the next level, a comparison with the private sector is that. Private companies can offer a bonus depending on how successful their performance is.

Whenever I see or hear about Mr X buying a holiday home in Portugal, or Mrs Y owning a flat in Tenerife. I don't think I'm envious, as I have lived abroad since I was 18. What I find unpleasant however, is that most of the people who live overseas have done nothing remarkable to be able to afford this situation. In 90% of cases it's right place, right time. OR IS IT!

I'm going to annoy quite a few groups now, because the failures of this country rest squarely at the feet of the pensioners, politicians and the public sector workforce.

It's as clear to me now as early as the 1921 finance act and 1946 national insurance act were the driving forces. It was the post war mentality of rewarding whoever wanted extra support. I'm sure it was done with the best intentions, but it wasn't done properly, exactly like the NHS. Just take a one-hour flight to Germany and try to guess who lost the Second World War!

I believe that the major political parties are afraid to touch the public health system because of lobbying factions within the sector and because of the financial problems with public sector workers. So why the reluctance to engage? Why the reticence? It's because successive governments have failed to make it a priority to make quality healthcare available to everyone. I'm afraid is financial. The trickledown effect of NHS spending is swallowed up almost immediately by a money hungry monster that is like the character Oliver Twist in Dickens novel of the same name, "Please Sir, I want more!"

Except that the hospitals are not like the Victorian workhouses, but they do have deviants similar to the thief "Fagin." The modern-day thieves are the ones who sit in the administrative offices. They are everywhere in this world. With absolutely nothing to offer other than organisation protocols, (which incidentally is what every manager is, regardless of profession!)

Every single area you look you can find them hiding behind spreadsheets and statistics. I'm sure you could reach a fairer and more efficient solution to everything by simply withdrawing these middlemen/women and using any money saved to pay the nurses! The wards and GPs are micro-managed with their time, mostly so they can avoid litigation, but also so that their management can claim their bonuses! You also have an unworkable sharing arrangement, something I have experienced on numerous occasions. It's something which creeps up on you at the last minute and frustrates the hell out of you.

What do I mean by the "sharing arrangement" this is something I found out about the day I had a suspected stroke. As someone with first aid training, I recognised the symptoms and presented myself to my doctor. Who in spite of the dangers referred me to the hospital, not blue light oh no! I was just told to drive myself.

Because it was a Friday and a Bank Holiday weekend I didn't have the obligatory scans until the following Tuesday, by which time I would have had a chance to discover how serious it was.
I found out with a discussion to the radiologist that they should have seen to me straight away. MUPPETS.!

Other examples were, when I was still working, and I had to make multiple investigative visits to a neurological department at the local hospital. I had to arrange for my workplace to authorize the appointment, on a couple of occasions book transport to facilitate the testing safely and one time drop everything to participate at short notice a doctor's surgery to be able to talk to the specialist neurologist. So very much their convenience and not yours. To then discover at what can only be described as the last minute that they had to make changes and would send a rearranged appointment in the mail!

Next, I'm coming onto education:

I have written a few anecdotes a bit further into this book, for ease of digestion I'll give you a brief insight into where I stand with this pillar of our modern society. Hands up who supports and advocates the importance of a graduation, qualification-based system? You realise it's possible for individuals to cheat and flourish without being included in the state curriculum process?

I will concede that there are occasions when specialised skills and abilities can only be achieved by thorough training and examination but look at the internet. You can probably self-learn 90% of conventional methods, techniques and skills just by browsing.

Even occupational training is pretty much covered by useful tutorials and advisories. I'm confident that every able-bodied individual can learn any job. Which then throws up more questions than it answers.

If you can learn online by doing research and learning from alternative sources, why do we need a schooling program? I haven't done it myself, but I've read that the terrorists responsible for the trade centre attacks actually learnt some of the lessons of flying a modern passenger jet by using the dark web. It's also well documented that other malicious skills such as bomb making can be found on other websites, one of the reasons why ISIS was able to threaten the civilized world with their hatred.

So, thinking outside the box, the recent Covid lockdowns were probably good preparations for the next generation of exam takers. Which incidentally will all become obsolete when AI takes over the planet. Quick prediction. I think money will be phased out by 2035!

The next pillar is family. This is the most difficult one for me to tackle, you see I'm not able to align myself with any one entity. I have been trying my hardest to "fit in" my entire life. I have been a work in progress ever since my birth. I recently discovered that I was adopted as a baby in what can only be described as a crime against humanity.

Between the church and the state, I was denied my birth mother, and I think this is one of the reasons I utterly hate the British system. I can remember at least 5 times when I challenged my parents, grandparents or anybody who demanded my unconditional conformity. The biggest clue I had was at a very young age, I didn't look anything like my parents or siblings. I also didn't have the same taste in fashion, food, culture and music as they did.

I think it's the equivalent of being trafficked which we read about almost daily. The difference here though is I'm talking about state sponsored wrongdoing.

Britain loves to portray itself as the gold standard for behaviour and morality, well hang on a second. Let's delve into the recent history and examples of this country's deviant practices.

I could start with the slave trade and policies that were used during the stain that was the British Empire! It is a litany of abuse and neglect that completely runs through our occupation years. The most difficult thing for me to accept is how brazen and arrogant the old mentality was. You only must look at someone like Winston Churchill to gauge their utter contempt for others. During World War 2 he was still referring to countries like India and Egypt as if they belonged to the Westminster bubble.

Whenever conversations turn to the historical wreckage inflicted on populations like the aboriginal society in Australia or the Blackfoot Indians in Canada the narrative always gets squeezed to minimize culpability and avoid blame for the failures of the past.

To which I say this, right back to the time of a bygone age when Kings or Queens ruled in an absolute monarchy. It's not enough to dismiss forced land claim and capture as merely historical anomalies. I want every relative of those land grabs to be stripped of any asset they hold to be forced to pay back any money they've made from any illegal annexation, I also want anyone who has made shed loads of profit from the forced enslavement of peoples to be held accountable. I'm talking about old money conservatives who profited from the plantation's deposited around the globe, utilising their slave labour force.

I have no doubt that this could happen but there are a few big named families caught up in this. The major sticking point is enforcement. Oh yeah and I'm not an unpatriotic leftie. I just want justice for people who have been unceremoniously dumped on!

This section should be highlighting family, but that's the odd thing about British people. They accept their parents and the extended relatives, but they also include the royals as another extension. Which I have no idea why. They are Germans, originally from the House of Saxe-Coburg-Goethe. They changed their name late into World War 1. In 1917 taking the name Windsor from the Shakespearean play "The Merry Wives of Windsor." Which kind of begs the question, why? Though don't take my word for it though, just browse the web!

I've alluded to my family story. Substituted at the point of arrival, which effectively makes two families I'm supposed to have allegiance to. Then obviously I was raised to blindly support anything the royals did, which makes three and funnily enough I've got four more.

Anybody who has served in the armed services automatically belongs to this close-knit group. It's a bit like the masons except with guns and violence!
I can honestly say I enjoyed twelve years with this crazy family. It was like waking up every day in an episode of Monty pythons flying circus. Where we really did see, "The upper-class twit of the year show," on a daily basis. Talk about unsuitability!

In hindsight I think I can honestly say that only 1 or 2 % of the hierarchy deserved the respect they craved. It was a badly hidden secret that only the middle ranking leaders were able to command. The officers were paid lip service to, but never really respected. (Apart from aircrew, technicians, EOD and for the navy Captains and commanders.)

The other groups which I can throw into this mix are the colleagues and crews of the airline I have worked with. A fantastic mixture of talent, professionalism and great individuals with the best humour I have ever worked with. It's quite special to turn up at 05:30 for an early morning briefing and be rolling around with laughter. There are many similarities with the forces too, in so much as the focus and seriousness can switch from one second to another, it's quite special knowing that they have the skill set and tenacity to make any obstacle seem manageable.

My final two offerings for this chapter are firstly ones where my children reside. Incidentally my one big regret in life. Secondly, I've got to throw a plug to Arsenal FC, the one constant in my life. Sometimes amazing, other times just painfully embarrassing, but they have always been there for me, a very special little friend!

I now come onto the final pillar, probably my favourite too. Arts and Culture. I think part of my fondness for this section is because of my form tutor during secondary school, Mr Bailey. The schools only art teacher. He was totally unconventional, even taking the register in the morning. I remember him throwing the book at Pamela, who was a head girl. Telling her to get it right or she'd get detention!

I'm sure he was the reason I'm so laid back. I'm also sure he's the reason I love art in all its forms. I have visited the Louvre, and I've experienced live performances of Mozart during my visit to Salzburg, an opera in Milan, countless art installations, including one with my kids at Hans Christian Andersen's, birthplace in Odense Denmark.

I've watched many rock concerts with the jam, simple minds and Jules Holland & the millionaires to name just a few. I have experienced a ballet with the school, watched Peter O'Toole as Julius Caesar in the play by

Shakespeare. Which is not bad for someone who didn't appreciate the finer things until the jam. A concert trip organised by our PE teacher in Guildford. Something I'm eternally grateful for. They also introduced us to foreign travel. I do go into detail about this in another section, but this for me is the essence of culture.

Which brings me nicely onto the evaluation of the pillar system. I'm convinced that British people are the least cultured of all the European states. Our mentality abroad is without exaggeration, embarrassing, I don't want to tar everyone with the same brush but don't forget, I used to fly these muppets daily.

You would have the hens, the stags, the drunks, the druggies, the people of low moral decency, the spoiling for a fight section, that would sum up half the plane. Then you would get the space cadets, people of privilege, who would assume that they were somehow above everyone else. Even though they were on a low-cost airline.

Flights like Sardinia, Pisa, Madeira, Corsica and anywhere along the Adriatic Sea. The type of people who have prejudice as their raison D'Etre. I've seen some sit away from the children and employ a nanny to watch them? They are the ones who drink champagne on the flight and try talking with a condescending tone.

So, between the and the other, they are the reason why the reputation of Brits abroad is so bad. When I went on vacation, I would always distance myself from countrymen. The fact is that virtually nobody from the UK has ever tried to integrate on a foreign holiday, which is the biggest example of discrimination and double standards I can think of. I'm smiling while writing this. Because every whisper of binary Britain is laughable. It's also why I decided to leave in 1992.

So, let's do the forensics of this, analysing, dissecting and hopefully completing a comprehensive autopsy! We (the entire planet) have chosen a very dangerous path. On the surface there is cause to believe that things are going to change for the better. Except that we have failed to make the necessary adjustments to make things work.

The dictionary gives culture the following definition: manifestations of human intellectual achievement regarded collectively! This for me is a red rag to a bull.

It's basically giving Carte Blanche to regard anything and everything that has ever been produced by human endeavour as progress for mankind! Which I wholeheartedly disagree with.

We have become obsessed and blinded by history and growth, so much so that we have abandoned stability and achievable in favour of short-term profit.

Just imagine how we. In a cost-of-living crisis can justify the disparity between the haves and have nots! It never ceases to amaze me how people tolerate the differences but for the moment I'm going to focus on the UK. The highlighted sentiments could apply across the globe. In Gambia say or Buenos Aries. But as my old Sgt Major used to describe sunburn. It's a self-inflicted injury he would laugh. "I have no sympathy!" Just imagine how often you hear or read about a woman's right to have children! No, you don't.

You possess a biological vessel that has the ability to produce offspring! (Big difference),

So why do we pander to the demands and expectations that accompany any form of sexual relationship? It's quite time relevant today, more so than ever in fact. What with the war, Brexit, pandemic, cost of living crisis, energy costs and perhaps the two biggest challenges. Climate change and overstretched budgets. You see it's this last thing that people want to ignore.

There has been a sub-plot to pretty much everything that has been going on in Britain since the Thatcher years. If you browse behind the curtains throughout the country, you will get a feel as to how things have played out over the last fifty years.

For starters, this country has undergone a massive transition from being an industrial heavy economic society, to an economy which primarily is service sector based.

In some ways this has meant a transition from production to low level physical goods and services, like IT, the financial sector and travel and hospitality. We can't even provide our own food without massive subsidies and global deals. (Good luck Post Brexit!)

Of course we have retained highly specialised sectors, like aviation and aerospace, plus advanced technological industries like energy and power generation, but by and large the mass employment industries of previous generations have become obsolete.

Another punishing memory of the 80's is of course the miners' strike. It's not the fact that this industry has all but disappeared. It shows how shortsighted successive governments were. Pandering to failing and technically lacking players. Like the automotive sector.

I mean why would anyone want a metro or maxi! I remember Thatcher pounding the drum to get people to purchase British made goods. A Union Jack symbol on any product being sold was a guarantee that it would either break down or be of such poor quality and value for money that just the investment showed a total lack of judgment. Something which even we as schoolchildren couldn't understand!

Another example of the crumbling infrastructure of Britain was observed at probably the same time as the mining collapse. It was the deployment of the strong-arm tactics of the security apparatus. It was around that time that people became familiar with the SPG (special patrol group). I think this translated into (bunch of thugs).

It's curious how the British media are sensitive to the tactics used by other countries. But it is deflected and denied by our public opinion journalists. It's something I've experienced on countless other occasions. The policing of football games, the way protesters are marshalled, the worst of everything has become a reality in this country now. But it's taken two key events to finally bring about change.

The killing of Stephen Lawrence and more recently the rape and murder of Sarah Everard. I explained earlier how a traffic cop took a bribe to give my driver a free ticket home. It was for me, a young easily influenced teenager a pivotal moment. Because it gave me license to ignore any and every rule. So, let's swing this moment forward 50 years and do a litmus test.

We now have a government trying on the one hand to limit any kind of protest and framing things as being anti-social. Whilst in the same breath overseeing a staggering amount of internal criminal and detrimental misconduct allegations that have eroded once and for all the integrity of any public institution.

What with all the scandals and shenanigans that have surfaced over the last few years, how can we trust anyone or thing? I don't even need to do any research into the recent events. Everybody knows that we are in shit street! At this point I want the 8 billion of you to start panicking!

If the world unites and commits to the necessary actions required to facilitate the implementation of climate friendly solutions, diverts the resources to have one world one future. Then there might be a glimmer of hope. Unfortunately, the planet is run by multinationals, power hungry despots and billionaires with more money than sense.

As of today, Jeff Bezos is worth more than Zambia, Tunisia and Gambia, put together. In total he has the same wealth as The GDP of Ethiopia! Shameful?

ENTROPY: degree of disorder or randomness in the system!

But I think they will look at the squandering and vanity projects of the entitled, pensioners and private equity companies and individuals who really have been taking the piss! Not just Britain by the way. Also, everyone on team selfish.

Now I am not naive I realise that for the world system (globalization) to work there must be winners and losers. But after the pandemic and the economic crisis of Ukraine and Brexit. How about accountability?

Occasionally it's useful to drop into a narrative a little tit-bit to break up the monotony and not only ease any tension or frustration but also give an opportunity to expand horizons. So here goes with tit-bit number one.

Pernicious: dictionary definition, having a harmful effect especially in a gradual or subtle way.

Synonyms: detrimental, damaging, harmful, deleterious, malignant, wicked, malevolent, injurious, or we can cut to the chase and give it the real term meaning.

A political entity that purports to have the interests of the public in mind. Who upon closer inspection reveal that they are only interested in lining their pockets and the multinational lobbyists who are their backers! Let's move on to part two of word manipulation. Who hasn't heard of populism?

Dictionary definition:

The quality of appealing to or being aimed at ordinary people. Politically, an approach that strives to appeal to ordinary people who feel their concerns are disregarded by established elite groups. This is a convenient distraction tool, giving power wielding entities an opportunity to escape the scrutiny and consequences of media investigation. Just think how often a populist centric politician or government can manipulate a public opinion to make it seem like they are listening and making informed choices! Despite the fact they are actually lobbied by and in some cases funded and supported by the sector which is causing unrest and division!

Another example of British democracy in all its glory. It reminds me of my Union days, where companies employ union busting tactics "divide and conquer" (ring any bells EasyJet)

Alan Turing committed suicide June 1954
Pardon by QE 2 2013 ... 60 years too late!

It's interesting isn't it. It's taken countless decades of either blue or red governments without tangible impact on society or living standards for all of a sudden, a real window of opportunity to emerge. It's taken the boom or bust years of Thatcher in the 80's with her brand of wealth creation.

She used the social housing market to buy votes, or the insanity of Blair turning into Bush's lapdog, whilst throwing the door open for anyone or everyone. Then the more recent vandalism of the effects of a virus, a political virus and the impending environmental virus. With two or three wars thrown into the mix!

I'm going to try to sympathize with you... but I can't... over the past forty-five years most of my friends and acquaintances have left these shores. I know people who have gone to Canada, U.S.A. France, Germany, Japan even Denmark (my favourite country btw).

So, who here is surprised?

It's now February 2023 and here's the current situation. The country is in the middle of a cost-of-living crisis. People can't afford the basics. I have read that the average person can no longer afford utilities, council tax, groceries, petrol and diesel, transport costs like trains or buses, I could go on... but it's just depressing. So, what else do we have to look forward to? Oh yeah, the covid virus is still here. Apparently one of the Royals has caught it.

The Russians are desperately trying to take Ukraine by whatever means it can. Norway has today announced it will be sending the defenders eight tanks. To go along with US and British ones. Another reason why things could go pear shaped.

The Turkish people are still dealing with a series of devastating earthquakes, and most nations have deployed emergency recovery teams. Unfortunately, it looks like there may be more than one hundred thousand dead!

Then comes the silver bullet. In case you're completely asleep. We are going through a E.L.E. (Extinction level event) the planet is going through a climate emergency

I can honestly say that playing their game is not for me. It all started innocently enough with a frustrating failure on anything to do with schooling. I've highlighted sections of this in another chapter, but the point is I was too savvy to put up with studying. Reading, writing, box ticking, examining and qualification collecting never really floated my boat.

As I watched things unravelling around me at home and with my Saturday's work colleagues, my brother's friends and acquaintances I made at local sports clubs I pretty soon realised In England, it's not what you know, or how clever you are, or even how many qualifications you have acquired.

It's who you are friends with! So, I decided to take myself out of the equation. Let me do my impression of a dog owner, pretend you are my pet and watch me start throwing bones. An acquaintance of mine at Pepper harrow cricket club was someone who intrigued me. It's so long ago now that I'm not 100% certain of his first name.

But the point is, that guy (let's call him Tim) was a career university student. If I remember correctly, he was considering taking a course in ancient British architecture (the reason he and my brother became friends) but I think he had also studied language, history and ancient Britain!

He lived alone in Godalming around the Busbridge area, but the good thing was he played cricket and was very happy to take me along. We got along famously with the other misfits in the team. Like John o the one-eyed 2nd slip. He was ex forces (SAS I believe) but always had a funny anecdote and hated the old school tie brigade.

Then there was Ford Capri driving Alex and Motley like the character from "the Wacky races". But let's go back to Tim, because I used to pick his brains during our batting innings, when we were spectators in the pavilion. We were match scorers entrusted with the job of the doting and wicket recording until called out to bat. I once asked him why he pursued so many different degree topics. To my amazement he replied, "because I can!"

I was for want of a better word "gob smacked," and I also asked him about any jobs he had ever done or was interested in doing. His answer betrayed his private school upbringing. "None!" He was living in a one-bedroom apartment with kitchen, bathroom and lounge. He shared a laundry room with his neighbours and was totally reticent about details, I noticed his unusual taste for farming clothes and boots that I had also experienced from working on the tills at Waitrose, how Range Rover driving muppets, would haul around two fully laden trolleys and put it on plastic which was something quite different in the early 80's, the clientele also used a mysterious third language.

Again, this shop (supermarket) was 'Godalming centric, which means the pronunciation was Horse racing style, with slants on words. Yes, became Yah, excuse me became invisible or the use of belittling terms such as "boy and girl," and please and thank you metamorphosed into Watt and hmm okay Yah! The worn attire took on a different dimension too, almost all clothes were a nod to the top end fashion designer labels. Either that or military and horsey paraphernalia like Barbour jackets and tweed, normally paired up with chord trousers for the men and jodhpurs for the women. Don't you just love them!

But you see this kind of behaviour in every facet of modern life now. It starts with everything to do with camera work. Just look around at the headline maker's, every outlet for publication has an image. I don't think it's possible anymore to find obscurity. Even the nooks and crannies of the internet are not a safe hiding place. Everyone has their own social media platform. It's all about in your face loudness. Self-publicizing bloggers who are solely focused on increasing awareness and followers. Those who don't scream their lungs out are destined for tomorrow's vagrant spot. The corner of a shop front where you can cover yourself in cardboard boxes and hope to make it through the night.

It's all part of the next phase of "project control" look at what everyone has unwittingly subjected themselves to. I read a report recently that focused on identifying the occupants of our major towns and cities. Probably related to the passport photos and image collection of the state. The tube bombings of London were a major reason for this mechanism being implemented but I wonder if there weren't other factors why this was rolled out. Like money laundering or drug related.

So, here's a quick question. Who feels safer today than when we took part in Gulf War two? Oh yeah, granted we have all these improvements to surveillance and are constantly being told it's getting better. But who feels safer.

Underlying political subplot. something I really started to appreciate around the Lockerbie plane crash, or rather terrorist attack! It happened Dec 21, 1988. I was at work in the bar of the corporal's mess. The other guys in the bar shrugged it off. I watched it on the satellite tv and thought "it's going to kick off soon! "What was it about that attack which caused me to think about the doomsday clock.

Well, it's happened in the last few years hasn't it. Especially when Russia invaded Ukraine. I'm not surprised at how many times we have watched the major events unfold over the last forty years. To be frank I'm not sure what constitutes a major event any longer. I could be predictable and boring to list everything that has been a major incident or even just the ones that have been front page news of the telegraph or times. But that doesn't mean that much when you peruse the same period in global terms.

It's not just Britain that is selective when the agenda is being chosen. I believe it comes primarily from political parties and the plethora of lobbyists who stand to gain from favourable legislation and policy decisions. The other major factor is the little clubs that countries are signed up to.

Think free trade agreements or security arrangements like NATO. We are all aware of them but what purpose do they actually serve? Manchester United goalkeeper £250,000 a week! Dec 21 88, 26 April 86 Chernobyl nuclear accident. Time to Leave

Putting things into perspective, leaving, is for many one of the hardest moments of life. For the dead, it's often reported with a sense of irony. There are phrases that we use which have become formulaic. Just read the obituary columns in the newspapers. A loving father. A fine upstanding member of the club. A much-loved family man. An inspirational leader. etc. Now far be it for me to scoff and question such comments, but surely you can see the irony!

I remember my struggle to find something meaningful and original to use in the eulogy for my father, until I took a step back to compare examples from the newspapers and internet to question and judge. I must be honest it was only after plodding through 4 or 5 examples, that I finally reached an epiphany.

The Advisory articles say, pay a respectful tribute higher than a realistic and honest appraisal and also concentrate a massive amount on listing achievement, rather than showing human qualities like fun and humour!

Which is tragic. I mean, ok he's died, but isn't that enough sadness? Also why start listing crap! It's no secret that we are now able to educate and qualify ourselves entirely from tutorials off the internet. So why not just have a good laugh? What is this unhealthy infatuation with lists and qualifications anyway. From my own experience with people, one constant is abundantly clear.

The most highly qualified are not the cleverest. They are what I like to call paper clever. My punk/rock mentality was pissing down my leg, like a tartan covered argument waiting for the toilet. Anyway, back on topic, on one hand

I didn't want to disrespect anybody, on the other hand I wanted to make people laugh. Especially mum because she was a bit down.

In the end I went for the compromise version. Thanking him for picking me and my siblings from the other possible adoption options. Congratulating him for looking after mum for so long. As an unpaid carer. But most of all, reminding the small gathering that he was a daft Geordie. I mean anyone who can support Newcastle their entire lives are a few sandwiches short of a picnic.

My dad had many faults. Obstinacy, a love of cigars, pipe smoking and whiskey, driving even for the shortest distance, living beyond his means, stubborn beyond common sense, but also a belief that he was never wrong. Even to the point of utter failure to accept his responsibility for his firm going bankrupt. I will never forget how I received this piece of news.

I had literally just landed back in Britain from Canada. At RAF Brize Norton, got the train to Guildford and then on to Godalming. I had all my travelling luggage in my ice hockey bag, which was bloody heavy and quite difficult to carry, but eventually after a forty-minute trek from the train station, I turned up at my house, tried to put the key in the door of the porch and then nothing! I had phoned them a few weeks earlier to confirm my impending return.

This all seemed to be normal, but what I had overlooked was my father's habit of hiding from reality. I remember lots of doubts and denial regarding my mum's illness, I can honestly say that he never fully accepted the diagnosis given to him by the doctors. Which is poignant, because it's something that I don't agree with either. The fact is my house key didn't open the door that day. The old woman who answered the door was obviously worried because she had called the police. Who thankfully were linked into the going's on in 5 home farm road. I got dropped off by the two constables, at my parents "safe house" and was quite shocked to find the security guards around the building. So, Christ knows how much stress this was causing my mum. It reminded me of the barracks with shadowy figures stood in the tree lines.

Dad had not just lost his business but also our home. With death threats and all kinds of unpleasant consequences threatened. He had also lost our house and all his money. You could sense massive tension in the air.

So, imagine how it must have felt to have me turn up, swear at my brother, to then disappear down the rose & crown with my parents to have a drink?

I will never forget the first conversation. It's one of those life defining moments. Mum was angry and wanted my opinion. Should she just leave dad?

My answer to this question was what I think was the most important responsible decision I ever made for my parents. The siblings had already cast their votes. I was the deal breaker. But I'm not going to say it was a choice of right or wrong. It just makes sense of what being tied into a family is all about.

When I look at how people separate nowadays it's like a completely different story. Because there is loyalty and then there is the return to the zoo to watch the baboons! On this day humanity won. But now going back to the funeral, I think I should have just sucked in my contempt for everyone who was in any way responsible for my dad's death. But I had unfinished business with Guildford NHS trust.

Tell me, is there something perverse and comical about a health service which divides itself into trusts. Definition of trust. Firm belief in the truth, reliability, ability of someone or something.

It's probably my pessimistic nature but in no way shape or form does that definition mirror the realities of the British health service. But we'll deal with that in a little later.

Dad was many things, but never lazy, he cared mostly for mum, he also had two part time jobs, one was doing the bookkeeping for a pub, the other was delivering advertising books, things like makeup and clothing. I would help him whenever I was home. But what happens when you get older, having smoked all his life. You get niggles, he was extensively tested one day and found quite Ill.

Turns out he had to go onto dialysis, which because of him being mums only carer meant he got all the equipment he needed for home. So again, another situation which I only discovered during a flying visit on a weekend.

Anyway, back to the funeral pyre. Where the flames were growing higher.

The realization of what would be expected of my ramblings is something I never really identified with. It was also a moment of utter disintegration in my personal life. My family life was imploding in front of my eyes. My in-between job of the last 5 years was finishing, I had just had to cancel a job interview because of the funeral. I had been sleeping on a sofa for 2 years since my partner got diagnosed with breast cancer. I made all the sacrifices for everyone and when they phoned to give me the news of dad being Ill, I was struggling to get money for a flight home.

It was somewhere in amongst all these going's on, that I would make my decision. I suppose part fuelled by my mum not having anyone to rely on, but also down to a staggering number of contradictions and insincerities.

I am by character a very simple person. But I don't think anyone could have tolerated what I had to that week. My employers work partner had just thrown a petulant hissy fit a few days earlier. My girlfriend was doing her own thing. She was a different person with the chemo and treatments, she also kept disappearing on family breaks. None of which I was invited to, just the kids. The (her) family were not helping. Which meant I had the kids every weekend. She would use the car when it suited, but I was expected to fit around her treatments and take control of everything else. Which therefore meant travelling everywhere by train and bus. Not my best moments!

I took the call about dad from my sister, which got me into planning mode, trying to organise flights and travel. I would have driven but was told "not an option!" Then literally a day later I got the call saying, "it's all Ok!" Dad had fallen down the stairs and they had him in hospital doing tests etc. But he had been released a day later because he appeared fine. I was relieved by this as it was going to save lots of money, it also meant I could do the interview.

Well, bugger me, the very next morning, I was just about to leave for work when I got told to phone my parents. Louise answered, "dad has died."

So, you see, I'm of the firm belief, don't rely on others because they will always fuck it up. Whether that is incompetence, stupidity or a lack of judgment. The other X factor is the British healthcare industry. Because I can state quite firmly that the NHS are a bunch of incompetent idiots! What concerns me the most though is that nobody in Britain seems even remotely bothered or interested. Until like my father, it's too late.

But how can you say that. I hear you say. Well, I'm going to spell it out for you here and now. I am going to list all the deficiencies I have experienced since coming back to Britain. Then you be the judge.

NOT LINKED IN ANY SHAPE OR FORM TO MS:

Let's get to the crux of my argument here with this illness! The latest information sheet I have just finished reading is one of those flyers that occasionally gets sent out to all sufferers. I'm quoting the headline here. Multiple Sclerosis Trust. 12 October 2022, Entitled Co-Morbidity.

Co-Morbidity means having more than one disease or condition at the same time. Co-Morbidities are common among people with MS. One US survey reported that 77% of respondents had at least one other illness or condition alongside their MS. The most common co-morbidities included depression, raised lipid (fat) levels in the blood, anxiety, hypertension and chronic lung disorders.

This is the key to the pirate's treasure chest. Of course, your treatment and drugs don't work! It's because you (the doctors) have failed to understand the concept of what is going on. I have lived quite happily with my MS from the car accident on the drive home from Guildford. I didn't even know it was there on a normal daily basis. I had good self-management, I was also very fit for my age, I'm also clued up on first aid so I could self-identify the stroke symptoms I was experiencing that day when my legs started feeling heavy.

I even remember the conversations I have had with consultants, radiologists and other specialist neurologists. But the point is this. I also had a very revealing discussion with an occupational therapist in Bristol who confided in me that the doctors were divided with my diagnosis and with my concerns.

I suspect because they have strict guidelines about how much investigation they are allowed to do. I also believe that they code conversations with each other when someone is difficult, or like me calls them out for their utterly shambolic conduct and behaviour. It doesn't seem fair to me to put everything on hold for ten years because of some muppet's incompetence or lack of thoroughness. Do you know what the most significant injury I have is?

It's probably some minor virus or something like a mutating Epstein-Barr infection. Or the tick-borne virus. It could be cerebrospinal fluid leaking or even some innocent sub infection. But the point is, despite the US study on co-morbidity and despite me suffering 10 years of decline

The white coats don't want to look for what is actually affecting me! Because saying it is MS means that they don't need to have a look. Or in real terms "it's below their pay grades"! Financially uninteresting and too complex and expensive to unravel.

The MS trust article I have read points to (EDSS) expanded disability status scale. A collaboration between different organisations, groups and trusts to link the deterioration in people suspected of having co-morbidity symptoms and to try to identify the underlying affected areas.

In my case it appears I carry what is known as a cerebellar injury, according to the EDSS scale. Which means I suffer from ataxia, loss of balance, coordination and tremor. Which should lead me to my being assaulted in the public house at Leigh on Mendip, which is quite eye opening isn't it, if I follow up on this evidence? It means my secondary symptoms are outweighing the primary ones. Something incidentally that I have always maintained.

I'm also drawn back to the various aspects of symptom diagnosis which draw conclusions about the importance of certain degenerative occurrences. Now obviously I'm not a physician or medically certified doctor. However, I am in a position to realistically argue against this diagnosis, from a team of specialists. So, what is it that makes me want to scream and shout in their faces?

Something that happened recently when I was researching this book was, I stumbled on a bunch of inexplicable conflicting information about MS. The first one was in the "grey area" of massively differing levels of discomfort and suffering. With a wide-ranging variety of possible causes and symptoms?

Secondly was this confession made by the MS Society and the MS Trust whereby they accept that even the diagnosis of MS is a "difficult "concept.

Then thirdly and finally the old "golden ticket"! Where they wheel out the MRI scan imagery of myelin sheath demyelination as "PROOF!" For a positive diagnosis.

People who have all manner of co-morbidity problems might develop the symptoms.

People who are smokers can also show these kinds of lesions on their scans!

People who have a viral infection on their spinal column or brain stem can develop these injuries!

People who have damaged (CSF) areas with physical damage can develop these symptoms!

People who are infected with the tick-borne virus "Lyme disease" may have these conditions!

What I'm getting at here is that we need to forget about talking about MS as a thing.

The evidence suggests differently. I'm a believer that the reason so many people are displaying such varied injuries is because they **don't** have the same illness!

It's a very convenient little way of justifying the doctor's ineptitude and failure after 50 years of **second guessing**. The reason why they don't have a vaccine or cure is because they are knowingly barking up the wrong tree.

I remember way back when my mother was first getting sick, she was put through unimaginable pain and suffering. Not from her illness! No, it was from the testing, procedures and drugs that she was prescribed and told would make her better. Maybe it was the day she endured a lumbar puncture that I decided to keep quiet about my problems. "Who knows!"

What I do know is that she promised herself that she would go on a cruise if (WHEN) she got better. I think that this is my one big regret. Not being financially able to have filled that wish, so, to all of you who are diagnosed "don't put things off" do everything possible while you're still alive.

You see, I am like thousands of children before me. An anti-establishment believer. I am the one at the fringe, looking on with utter contempt at everything which our society scripts as being the norm, to coin a phrase. "I can't believe it's not butter! "

You see the great thing about this analogy is it's a reflection on our society. On the surface it has all the characteristics of being the thing you want to smear on your toast. It bears all the right indicators the same colour, same texture, same consistency, same taste. But let's transport this into conformity speak.

You see academic process dictates that children MUST spend a large proportion of their early life. Trawling through textbooks to achieve a good understanding of nothing of any significance. The college's offer a snapshot of understanding of something quite interesting but not important. Then despite what you concentrated on, you will receive a letter, a statement of access! What utter bullshit. You may have studied for three, five even nine years (for doctors) but you are still nothing special. You are over self-indulgent. Because let's face it. What with symptom checking websites and self-help web books I know everything they do. Or at the very least I have access to the information I need. You see it's all relative.

To put all these thoughts, together into a single passage which highlights the utter futility of collecting qualifications or even worse the obsession with certification. I keep one eye permanently on current affairs, (something an old aircraft technician advised) anyway I recently discovered Naomi Campbell received an honorary doctorate from UCA (university for the creative arts), so I had a quick peak on the usual search engines for similar events. This absolutely staggered my curiosity.

Go ahead and look yourselves. You can get all the qualifications and certifications you want. You are all still just HUMAN BEINGS! The biggest disease on the planet.

White lie:

During my brief but interesting flirt with England and being British, I have, experienced an emotional roller-coaster of an existence. To be blunt, every possible emotion has either been challenged or destroyed. I defy any average youngster to not go through a catalogue of mental health issues whilst navigating those difficult years from leaving primary school until about middle age.

For me it started about 1975. We had just moved to Surrey from London. Incredibly long bouts of boredom, interspersed with family interaction. As a middle child I found the dynamic at home challenging to say the least. As a family we were in a perpetual cycle of removal van followed by removal van.

No sooner had we finally unpacked than we discovered the boxes needed filling once more.

I gather the reason behind this procession of temporary housing was due to my parents slightly curious, continual changes of circumstance. My grandparents on my mum's side seemed to be the only constant. Dad kept changing job, mum had abandoned her brief foray into the workplace and our number had grown to five with the prospect granny might need rehousing with us, should her mobility deteriorate.

I don't keep many memories of my childhood, but I occasionally remember things like the candles and power cuts during the energy crisis of the seventies, or when the crabs escaped their buckets on the balcony in Hastings. Point is this. No matter where in the world you live or what your circumstances are, the recent pandemic has confirmed my long-held belief, humanity is the biggest disease on the planet!

The fragility of homo-sapiens to environmental changes (caused predominantly by us) or the poor recovery of our bodies, to things like disease, shows the futility of rooting for the home team. I mean let's start at the beginning. What does every independent people or nation demand? Bottom line is survival!

Unlike the modern, Westernised countries who are subservient to multinational corporations and whose stock markets are essentially interlinked domino trails, whose sole concern is a stable set of share prices. Or a set of good employment figures, healthy GDP etc, etc.

Our modern leaders are interested in one thing! ... Growth... Now this can be taken to mean hundreds if not thousands of things. Depending on which side of the fence you are sitting on. Each tiny little group, for example, the family, has a mixture of needs. Every family would wish for security. Of this I am quite sure. Shelter, e.g. Housing or at least a roof to protect against the elements. Food and drink. So now you see this is where people's needs stray!

Because let's start with the individual. Convention dictates each child has an unsigned agreement with not only the parents of, or the immediate extended family to, but also to a greater or lesser degree the local community, which taking the British example, can eventually mean answerability to 'The State.'

You are expected to complete education, become proficient at something, pay tax and conform. A large part of me thinks. This is a dystopian nightmare, because nobody would freely choose to play this game. It's as if you are in a poker game, holding a pair, when you know everyone else has better.

The journey starts with your mothers. A genetic disorder pushes them into listening to their hormonal clocks. Because despite logic, they are predisposed despite circumstance to creating offspring. Now I am by no means a misogynist but come on!

So, moving forward, the union of two, becomes three etc, etc. The combined wealth is then expressed either as a family unit of character or as a financial figure. Or in terms of land and property, or influence. Simultaneously we are forced into making changes which are governed by frameworks beyond reason.

For example, lets dissect the everyday status-quo decisions which the world's population subscribe to. We are all sold the promise of advancement. This is something which starts at home, it is practised the world over. Do your chores, this will result in some form of benefit. Even to those unlucky enough to have been born into slavery or some other similarly abusive existence.

This dangling carrot method is the norm. It continues throughout our meaningless lives I. Do this... Get that... Do this... Get that... And so, on... and so on... But think about it. Who is pulling Who? Ever wondered why virtually every person on the planet has become bank fodder? Slave to the banking system?

It is corporate bureaucracy at its most foul. I mean think about it! Where on Earth can someone escape the prying eyes of the big multinationals. They are in league with governments, so that once everyone is logged, it's like a total control thing. Global finance will soon be able to account for every single yen, dollar or euro. Big Brother is watching!

To me, this is part of every nation's capitulation to administration and conformity! I will use a sequence from the animated 1976 children's film The Twelve Tasks of Asterix to explain!

In which Asterix for one task is challenged to complete a Roman bureaucratic pro-forma. From one of those ridiculous self-important administrative arms of a local council. The sad truth is, the films exaggerated depictions of misdirection and hopelessness in obtaining said form, mirror perfectly how in modern life, a seemingly simple task is made frustratingly complicated.

Just look back briefly and consider in a day-to-day setting, how many service providers are playing these games? Now I can't speak for every organisation, in every country but I will bet, there are similarities everywhere. Done mostly on the insistence of a bureaucratic process, or unnecessarily complex regulation.

The elephant in the room whilst postulating or pondering these insane administrative requirements of form filling is the Club.

You know the type of things to which I am referring. The masonic handshakes or the wearing of school ties or jewellery etc. The sort of people who fly to New York or Milan to go shopping.

They eat at Michelin two starred restaurants and a long weekend takes in the Monaco grand prix or Mardi Gras. They are mostly exempt from filling, or they receive help in completion of some if not all sections, because blood is thicker than water!

Designed to intimidate, confound and even discourage. Digital paper trails are yet another example of Control. So, say, the forms are required for child support or housing benefit, The complexity and research necessary for completion far outweighs the maximum.

Sometimes embarrassing additional personal information or documentation is needed, like passports, bank statements and utility bills, all hurdles required to be jumped over. the hope of course is, for the unfortunate minority who are unable to produce these elements, a resulting denial of support will produce a verifiable saving, resulting in the administrators achieving a departmental bonus.

Truth is that many exponents or facilitators of such merry-go-round politics are upper class university graduates. In overpaid unnecessary positions. Jobs created for the sole purpose of perpetuating the line that education pays. Which is nothing more than a bare-faced lie.

In fact. It’s a kind of badge of honour, allowing advancement of some plum sucking privately educated son of/daughter of.

Irrespective as to whether they studied diligently and successfully or not and achieved the required higher-level diploma or grades, they must be

financially rewarded, giving hope for all future generations, who play the capitalist game.
So now, here is the thing. Education has morphed. For everybody not privately schooled. Your choices, like me, have been made, even before you were conceived. We live, work, earn and spend exactly as the corporations decide. Dancing to whatsoever tune the organ grinder plays.

But all it would take would be a minority of committed youngsters to think outside the box. Stop playing the pensioner's game. Play a different wealth distribution game

A chain letter for example is an exponentially increasing series of letters containing money or pledges, which when enough people join in, can result in vast sums of money changing hands. Away from the money grabbers. Stock markets or financial institutions, because this different method of wealth distribution flies in the face of conventionalism which we are actively discouraged from participation in.

Point is this, after over fifty years of playing the usual game of life. The alternatives are now more attractive than ever before. A friend of mine recently divulged another system of wealth distribution. Which kind of brings us full circle to the extended family, who contribute prearranged annual support payments, to designated family members. A modern age tribal behaviour, one which, I incidentally wholeheartedly can identify with, because trust me, anything has to be better than that which we have presently.

I will concede my thoughts are by no means original. The difference is this time feels right. We are in a world changing window of opportunity. The old brigades have failed us once too many times. I am not banging on about anything new but let us analyse the Status Quo. Throughout our lives regardless of nationality, sex or status, we have been given certain rules, values and aspirations. I want you all to think of yourselves as a new species. Forget the Before. Now just concentrate on what happens post-covsars!

Growth vs Pensions:

I recently caught the tail end of an interview between Greta Thunberg and the BBC. It was one of the usual lip service conversations whereby a seemingly impartial interviewer (BBC) would try to dilute the angst and fear of an environmental campaigner and all related minority concerns and opinions, as expressed by groups like Stop Oil, or fossil free, Greenpeace, WWF.

But what got me listening and focused was how ridiculous it all sounded, and yet how utterly realistic it was in truth. Greta backed up her answers with real-time examples. Which astounded me how hidden the reality appeared to be, when placed against the state of the planet.

Now I'm not a fan of the mainstream, I'm especially not a friend to politics or any of the world's economic models. But the one thing that this interview awoke in me, was the desire for change. even at the expense of human being's, I want the planet to live. Anyone who has children or even grandchildren must stop right now, hit the eject button. Because there is only one long term solution. We must stop this expansion madness.

Across the board in the western world, we are having two dimensional conversations about this level of pay or that inflation rate. The whole system and economic rules governing things like capitalism stitched together in a social framework, is flawed.

No, flawed is the wrong adjective, I think it's broken, and unfit for purpose, because it's geared towards helping and rewarding the least deserving people of society. Just look at football against surgeons. It's tragic. But no one wants to hear the arguments for objections! It's like the metaphor for humanity. Where the victors in war write the history.

Even things as basic as financial transparency and value, are meaningless. People's dollars and pounds are not worth the paper they are printed on. Which is quite revealing when you think how much power flows through the stock exchanges.

Human existence for the last two thousand years is nothing more than an illusion. But unlike the magician who saws the lady in half. What has happened is the sheep of this herd have been following the pied piper of Hameln. Like good boys and girls, investing objects of value in organisations like banks, with the hope of improving their tomorrow's.?

Well, I don't want to scare you, but this game is up. It's like someone who has bluffed whilst playing a hand of Texas hold-em poker. Someone has a good feeling and has gone all-in and is going to win everything. In case you want clarity, the human race is the one holding the losing poker hand.

So not wanting to drone on about environmental issues, let's highlight a few areas of catastrophic global influence made by the nations and companies of the world.

Our oceans, rivers and lakes are polluted. Filled with micro plastic's human waste and the consequences of flushing drugs down drains for a hundred years. Not just drugs for human use, oh no! Also, years and years of drugs used for agriculture and even pet animals.

Then we have the climate, which my generation has destroyed, despite being warned of the consequences of overuse of the combustion engine or systems like rockets and aircraft. Then comes the effects of industrial scale emissions like power stations, factories and other mass users of commodities, like car plants, plastic producers even clothing factories.

The choices were made long before I came along, but it is now we have to reverse that trend. I'm sorry to all the 90's children or later. But you have been left with solving all these things. The most obvious first step, is to kill the old.

Sound unreasonable! Well no. Because it's all of them who have caused this. So, it's payback time. Let's put all the issues of this generation in one basket and then use the joined-up thinking that I mentioned earlier. Because to ensure the survival of the world with all the necessary species getting the environment they deserve we need to start a process not too dissimilar to the badger cull performed in Britain in 2012.

As awful as that was, completely rubbished by the vets btw, it is the duty of the global population to drastically reduce our numbers. As a suggestion I am in favour of the enforcement of euthanasia for the over 60s and every infected and handicapped person. By my calculations this should reduce the overall numbers to roughly 5 billion. It would then fall on the remainder to work on global policy and possibly use the UN to enforce certain ground rules and conditions for prosperity for all. Sound too radical. Well, I'm sorry but it's what we need to do.

School Quandary, at what point do one person's private thoughts become a necessary talking point, an open letter, a source of compulsory reading? The clock is ticking and for all generations and all species on this planet, we must make a choice.

Personally, I Think it's too late. But maybe, just maybe, things can be reversed.

Because sometimes even the least suited have an idea, even an epiphany.

When someone as narrow minded and selfish as I decides to write, people should get excited. Because not since secondary school have, I had the inclination to put thoughts on paper. Even to this day, some 40 years later, I remember the event. Double English with Mrs West. Our homework was to pen a poem about nature. The first line of my effort read something like this:

Verily verdant vegetation upstream.

The use of alliteration purely coincidental. My dictionary had just happened to be open on the letter V, whilst I had searched for inspiration. Now this utterly meaningless, insignificant snippet of my past, should have faded into forgotten history and I dare say it would have, had it not been for what occurred in my next English lesson.

I will attempt to paint the scene on a bright March morning. The outside of the temporary school building or Annex was sparkling with the result of a morning's freeze. The playing fields still shimmered with a cold white glare. Around the edges of the sport's pitches the green was showing through areas which had begun to defrost. The pavement had a dull wet shadow, where footsteps betrayed the path students had walked from the icy spiders webbed football field.

Knowing what I do now, reminds me in vivid clarity, what happened next. The first order of the day was register, by this point I had usually become distracted. The morning sun was shining, but it was cold. My fingers were still numb from cycling.

Minutes earlier I had just arrived at school having cycled 5 miles after doing my paper round. The next event was the ritual of the return of student homework. What follows, can only be described in one way. "SHIT! LIFE CHANGING SHIT!" Because this is where I gave up with anything to do with conformity. The work in exercise books had, as usual, been graded in red ink.

The usual. B+ "could do better "kind of rubbish.
But not today, not me..........! @£$$
It said D- SEE ME.................! @£$

I had been singled out as a cheat. Even accusing me of getting my parents or some older person to do my work. Do you really wonder why students with access to firearms flip out, go on the rampage? I have just given you a hint.

Anyway, let's try to focus in order to avoid making a collection of unconnected ramblings. This work is directed to the young, innocent and awkward individuals, who like me was sick and tired of the human contradictions our parents and older generations created.

In the words of Monty..." vote none of the above! "

Why conform? Survival of the fittest. Darwinian theory. At what point do people trace our existence back to evolutionary theory. When do you think the next quantum leap should occur?

My answer is Never. We currently have a pandemic in the world. No-one really knows which way this is going to go.

Hundreds of thousands are dying worldwide. Governments are proving how inept and useless they are. We as a species always love to claim how clever we are. We are incompetent bungling idiots. Let us incorporate the survival of the fittest scenario into our world.

Anybody scared if things do not improve, we could descend into chaos? Who is quietly concerned how this might pan out? The problem is the warning signs have been out there for a long time. Did anyone know about using human foetus' cells to produce vaccines. The establishment don't want Mr and Mrs average knowing what is really being played out under our noses. Those foetus cells were extracted from abortions.

The Pharma industries have knowingly played hard and fast unethical games with health. This goes right back to anyone who peddled miracle cures or the elixir of life.

Let's not forget the company that swore of the health benefits of cocaine was also responsible for creating the poison which gassed the Jews during Nazi Germany. Now I am not trying to discredit all quacks, I just think people should read between the lines.

Do I think these thoughts might affect any future assistance I get from medical professionals?

I don't think... I know. But I also know a few home truths regarding healthcare. You can lead a horse to water, but you can't teach it how to drink. Let us explore the failings just in Britain.

Overcrowded healthcare. Young people need to open their eyes to this. It's your futures.

So, what are the options?

An extravagant increase in health spending with the burden carried by taxpayers. A private health insurance scheme but not just for wealthy or privilege but for everyone. An individual tailored system agreed by local authorities.

If this is not an appropriate time to put thoughts on paper, then I don`t know when is. For too long, speech or written works have lost their attraction, mainly because too much emphasis is given to publishing populist topics or having to listen to or read irrelevant spin.

Or worst still opinion is allowed to dilute a very simple binary choice. Its either Yes or No. Black or White, Up or Down.... What I am trying to offer is Order! Clarity on Every aspect of 21st century life. Or should it really be... 21st century Lie! I want to encourage Independent thought, I want change!

I want to share something my father told me, all those years ago. Listen to your heart! Or perhaps more fittingly 'LISTEN.'

Ever looked closely at your neighbourhood?

I bet everybody has more closely these last few months. Surreal isn't it. I bet everyone knows who lives around them now, you know, the elderly couple who have been self- isolating, or maybe a nurse or a care worker. Funny how circumstances can change people.

Did anyone understand, the seriousness of the pandemic? Or did we understand how fragile and utterly useless, all economic systems really are. First of all, I want to spell out all the failings, I'm not talking nationally I'm talking globally. Because now is the time to finally Stop the madness. What were the major concerns of the world's governments? Who really was watching, but more importantly who could you trust.

Remember all the initial discussion about where the virus originated? Also, and perhaps more importantly What kind of virus this was?

We had all seen the reports coming out of China, but did it really originate there, perhaps not wanting to overplay the potential seriousness of the virus, we all continued with a laissez-faire attitude, more worried about the weather or the football results. We even allowed The Cheltenham festival to go ahead. Did anyone predict or imagine, what was unfolding was a modern-day equivalent of 'The Black Death.' Actually, the answer to this question is Yes!

Interested how this plays out?

At the time of writing, no plausible answer has been offered to the question Why? What was going on in laboratories? Not in Wuhan. I'm talking worldwide. Familiar with the phrase the Jeanie is out of the bottle?

This can be traced back to the earliest civilizations', whether that's Roman Empire using poison to deny land, or early Egypt spoiling water quality. Whichever way you look you always come back to the Nazi's, and Joseph Mengele was one of the most well-known criminals against humanity. There have of course been many more. Ever wondered how many others slipped through the net? Pharmaceutical companies e.g. BAYER ag. This firm made the gas which was used to kill the Jews. Have you seen any public acknowledgment of this crime? Or regret? Of course not. Why? They didn't even have the decency to change the company name. Why not?

But this is not isolated, look at Britain, Russia, America, I could probably go on endlessly. The latest nation to use chemical weapons on its people is Syria.

So anyway, how many manmade illnesses have got out there since WW2? HIV AIDS, EBOLA, SARS. Now knowing how the medical profession loves to deny any involvement, who is suspicious?

Anyone who answers no, is either in denial or is so lacking in imagination they belong to a group of society I`m going to refer to as Zombies, because they may as well be the walking Dead! Right let's go back to childhood.

Our children begin life with such hope and enthusiasm. Probably like me start losing it around their first teenage year. The British schooling system is a joke. Because of political interference, subject choice or post code lottery standards, progress is rarely achieved. This is one of the Prime failures in our society.

Yes, the average student might gain some kind of education, but to transfer those skills in a meaningful way is virtually impossible. The system has also unnecessarily complicated hoops to jump through. insisting for every employment the job seeker has to hold a plethora of qualifications.

Students are sold based on an information trade off. 'Get good results and you will go far.' Absolute rubbish, the potential to do so is frankly minuscule. Unless you have the right school tie, or connections. I remember when I started working for an airline being asked to complete a City and Guilds customer service course. It served no other purpose than to reinforce politeness and common sense. Anyway, the company stopped the course half-way through, probably on financial grounds.

Just demonstrating once again how pointless education is. They dropped this compulsory requirement for 'operational reasons.' So, in other words everything which the ruling class said was 100% a requirement, turns out a 100% lie.

Throughout my entire academic life, I have been faced with 'face fits.' Prejudice, from selection for the cricket team, to placement into the class sets. But perhaps the craziest set of circumstances during my education was the conversion to decimalisation.

I thought as a child, how am I supposed to master something which even my teacher struggles with? Even the textbooks were geared towards Imperial measures...UTTERLY USELESS... Now consider this... Not only did I have to deal with the conversion of mathematical weights and measures, but my home life was imploding. My family had lots for a young guy to deal with Gran dying and also my mother being diagnosed with a severe illness.MS.

And we also moved house 4 times, from Cheam to Sutton to Abinger Hammer to just outside Guildford. You think you could stay focused on education, without common sense? What it did do was focus my attentions on the real world, and then everything became clear. They just want you to conform or disregard the pernicious behaviour of the state.

I can remember how the BBC used to mock the Soviet system and their communism, it was the height of the cold war, it was also unclear how dangerous things were, but you kind of wanted to believe our reporting was somehow better! It's Not!

The whole distractions created during Vietnam, Cuba, or Afghanistan provided the cover needed for western countries ruling classes to recover after WW2. But when they use the phrase 'time for countries to recover.' What they really mean is the ruling classes regaining their dominance. So, scroll forward 50 years and who now thinks we are any different than them? It's about mind control! If it sounds like it comes out of Orwell's book, '1984.' That's because it does.

Even the spin during the Thatcher years was biased. Think the Falkland's conflict. Convenient distraction? Or planned sub-plot. Intended or not, it highlights how easily swayed people are.

Remember the whole self-determination argument?

Now this information trade-off is just a cover-up, employed purely to deceive. The trick is to confuse not just in schools, but also daily life so that you do not have time to contemplate alternative lifestyles. Never mind the wisdom of playing a real-life game of Risk.

There are countless distractions to deflect your focus. Because for the average person We do not live ...WE EXIST... But let's not downplay the seriousness of this set of circumstances. We like to be seen as a nation that forged ahead with the Industrial revolution, are peacemakers or are known for their fairness or tolerance. Hmm Lets just examine the truth about our history.

We developed gunboat diplomacy especially during the Empire building years. We enslaved and killed as the governing classes saw fit, we used religion as a weapon. We caused wars trying to dominate and subdue for example the Mao Mao revolution in Kenya.

There we have one of the key words synonymous with being British... DOMINATE.... The truth is we are nothing more than a bunch of thieves. Now I am not saying we are the only ones who have behaved in this way.

Virtually all major powers are guilty of atrocities. So where are we as global citizens?

If humanity is ever going to evolve, certain conditions must be met. Firstly, Capitalism must be rejected or at very least adapted. This is not about jealousy of whatever company or country is currently having success. This is bigger and more radical than all of that. We need to re-evaluate our lives. All of us.

Why do we have money?

It keeps the powerful in power but more importantly it subjugates the masses to conformity. But guess what? Capitalism doesn't work! It just creates more admin etc. It is a device to harbour the offspring of the ruling classes in jobs created for the privileged private school plum sucking idiots. All of these university graduate positions are overpaid and ensure a society of them and us. Divide and conquer.

The systems do not work, After the Wall Street crash, the developed world suffered with bankruptcies. Repossessions and hardship, oh! hang on it happened again in 2008. So once again austerity! Hardship etc. Oh! Hang on it happened again 2020 Covid 19. So, What the Hell!

So, guess who comes out unscathed?

You guessed it. The institutions, THE BANKS, THE ROYAL FAMILY, THE RICH!

I daresay they will take a hit, but they are all self-supporting pillars. The average man on the street will bear the brunt. GUARANTEED. Those individuals are all better placed to weather any hardship. They also have a control over all state news platforms control the media, you win the war, or at least portray story lines, the way you want things represented. Did you ever wonder why the banks got out of these financial collapses without penalty?

As far as I'm concerned, all the bankers, financiers and families should have lost everything.

You want people to believe in a fair society. Then make it damn well fair. But they have no intention of ever doing so. It would upset the applecart. Do I accept it? ... What do you think?

Let's talk about the survival needs of man. short term you need shelter, water and a little food. If you look around the world these needs apply to 100% of the population. But human nature drives all of us to want more. But this could be the opening scene of a reality TV show called.

IN DEBT TO THE BANKERS! This time this IS a euphemism!

People are forced to live in one of Two ways. Hand to mouth. Or riding the credit train.
Actually, there is a third way, more about that later. Most people in lesser developed countries live hand to mouth. But in First world countries although a small percentage do live for the next pay-check it's all about the little plastic cards.

Imagine if everyone stopped playing their game? Let's revert back to basics. I would like to buy the new Toyota land cruiser please, what's that? It costs £25,000 ... OK... What about if I offer 3 goats and some beans from my small holding, I can give lessons in piano, and I'll teach French and German to your children twice a week for a year!

Far Fetched? Not in the slightest. We only use credit and money because we want things now. We have all got lazy. So instead of bartering on a transaction in a normal way,

We blindly accept the first offer.... MAD.... and then swap worthless pieces of paper in exchange. It's like the petulant child who wants an ice-cream RIGHT NOW!

No-one should live beyond their means but every single one of us is forced to play the lenders game. You hunt around for the best deal, but you end up paying extortionate additional costs.
Who has it in their power to prevent this? The national banking institutes. So, for example in the US, the Federal reserve in the UK, and the Bank of England, why does this kind of safeguard not exist? Because they are all too busy scratching each other's backs. Along with the politicians, business leaders, Chancellor of the Exchequer, Civil service etc.

I recently read about an experiment in a Cornish town where certain shops were trading goods in exchange for certain services like grass cutting or car cleaning. This is the direction we should be heading in.

When people become disenfranchised, they look for alternatives, which at the moment are centred around a couple of scams. No, I'm not talking about banks interest rates, although they are excessive and unnecessary. I'm talking about drugs, gang culture and all the vices you associate with their alternate lifestyles.

What worries governments most is not the fact they use violence to maintain discipline. No, they are most worried about the success these groups have.

The very fact people are quite willing to become drug mules show how much reward there is in taking these risks. Imagine how desperate you must be to risk a death penalty or life sentence moving drugs around.

Which brings me nicely onto the total control scenario. I recently watched a TV documentary concerning a banker. Now this man had done amazingly well. Studied long and hard in school and earned the highest qualifications. He got the job of a bank manager in Lloyds at a South London branch. He was subsequently investigated over his finances. His crime? He is BLACK... drives a nice car... and owns a lovely house. The police thought 'How is a Black man able to afford all this!' They wanted him to produce receipts not just for his whole life but also his wife's and his mother's. So, make sure you keep receipts for everything. And I MEAN EVERYTHING! Because that is the level of scrutiny they are now stooping to.

So how have police investigations become so detailed and intrusive? I think it's a combination of factors. The recruitment has become political and less selective. but I think the biggest factor is IT. They always plead poverty, we need this pension or that allowance. They have index linked salaried and get a good amount of free time and holidays, so don't give me that shit. They say we can't afford this or that, to which I say, rubbish!

If I have learnt one thing from this crisis it is just that. You choose not to borrow unless it is for ridiculous vanity projects or for more military hardware. The police are one of the elite enablers. The fact is the privileged are mainly weedy, insignificant individuals, like the child who got picked on at school. They need to surround themselves with protection, which takes the form of the police, lawyers, or bodyguards, amongst others.

So, who do you suppose has been responsible for the deterioration of their trust? Big business, supported by politicians. Thatcher during the miners' strike is one.

The trouble started when Unions started winning demands for different sectors of the economy. Such as higher pay and better rights. Well, this infuriated large groups of the elite until they changed or re-legislated Unions ability to renegotiate contracts. Until TODAY there are so many obstacles to be climbed before any leverage can be placed upon an employer. It`s almost not worth trying.

I was actually a union rep for 5 years, so I know how toothless and pointless they have become. You will note I have added two more cornerstones to the aristocratic cube.
The muscle power and intimidation of the Police and the legislators.

The police used to be over 6 feet tall and an authority. What we now have are 5ft 7inch and weedy, or females with an agenda. I hardly ever see them or if they are present, they are called 'Community Support Officers,' and they don't have powers of arrest. They bimble about acting as if they should be seen as some kind of decoy. If they do intervene you have to question their orders. Surely everything around the law is a joke. I was a military policeman for a while, so I understand.

You want justice? Then make prison so bad it makes people never commit a crime. But before you do, you must make a sensible quality of life. For everyone. Then once equality is achieved forget this whole pandering or worrying about human rights for sentenced prisoners. forget it.

I read the average prisoner has access to gym`s, outdoor sport, newspapers, television, most worrying though is mobile phones and the internet.

One idea I do have, is legalizing recreational drugs. It would free up the police and make money, which could be spent helping recovering addicts. So, who do you think would block this.? The governing classes. If someone is intoxicated on either drugs or drink, it creates a diversion to deflect away from the everyday problems, 'Smoke and Mirrors.'

So, let's assume we all figure out how much better local life could improve with fair trade.

Are the rich and powerful worried yet? No, but have you ever wondered how to spoil their day? Deliberately drive up their manor house. What about publicly being unkind, make them feel uncomfortable or deliberately speak to them. Never feel embarrassed about disrespecting them, they have done it to you, or your relatives for hundreds of years.

Overkill:

There is something quite endearing about people that want the best for everyone. It's all completely rubbish of course, but the thought process is a pretty noble idea. The trouble with equality is, it rewards mediocrity. Now I'm not going to make the case for either corner because I basically believe we should only encourage contributors! So, what exactly do I mean by that. I completely understand that not everyone will become a world statesman/woman or president or leader. What is achievable though is making a difference!

Let me explain, we are always trying to eke out an existence which both rewards endeavours, whilst simultaneously enjoying a feeling of purpose. So, using these as goals, it's possible to quickly evaluate what level of success you have achieved. Unfortunately, these are outdated evaluations. Modern aspirations have markedly changed things. In the current crises, what we are now seeing is the dawning of the Twenty-First Century reality. It's not in my nature to dress things up either!

For far too long we have all been going through the motions. Letting the systems and the idiots have the final say. I'm not going to do the embarrassing political speech here, because everyone is to blame for our historical failings. I'm going to let you fill in the blanks. Fact is: - we are a planet on the brink of death. Noticed how we always play the "spin" card? Dress things up to make them appear better than reality? Just ask Greta.

We can't do that anymore. You see irrespective of country or kingdom, throughout the world, we have always favoured a very select minority. It's the Alice in wonderland, rabbit hole analogy. Only carefully chosen candidates are allowed to chase the bunny!

The rewards for innovation or brilliance are always a double-edged sword. The initial pay off can sometimes be staggering, but ultimately the credit and usefulness of a discovery or development is always temporary, until it is stolen or lasting only as long as the patent, or the legal ownership is yours or you can achieve protection from the plum sucking brigade.

The Queen of Hearts, poised with executioner, axe in hand, waiting for the command "off with their heads," so you see, however well you think you are doing. One false move here or one mistake there. Then, like the video games of my era. Game over!

I have taken a 10-year sabbatical from life after my latest episode of relapsing and remitting and let me tell you, it's getting very predictable and insufferable (excuse the pun!) the list of grievances I hold are extensive. Just like a list of things I've had to endure. From heavy migraines and nagging pain behind the eye, to sleeping sickness which my gym teacher in school compared to trypanosomiasis (African mosquito transmitted disease.)

The neck injury I suffered in a car accident and emergency brake alongside my mother was never investigated despite my repeated attempts to flag up my concerns. (Seat belt failure).

Eventually things manifested themselves to focus everything on mum's direction, who very quickly began losing her balance, pins and needles in her feet and all manner of sensory changes. Especially with the bladder and increasing amounts of brain fog.

Interestingly enough, even before she was forced into early retirement and the withdrawal of her driving abilities, I also started noticing changes to my body. I also became aware of bladder issues, especially around water (which I just dismissed as being part of growing up) I was also noticing pins and needles whenever I was out on the push bike.

The point is, whatever you have read about the various symptoms and little idiosyncrasies that affect some or all NSD sufferers. I have experienced the lot. What this means is for anyone who is currently living with the onset symptoms, you are likely to experience the whole spectrum.

In my own particular case, I have discovered that lifting, vibration, sudden movement and weather appear to be my triggers. But for everyone else this is your homework. You must figure out what triggers any kind of reaction, followed up by total avoidance.

My experience with the NHS is a litany of failures from the outset. If I'm honest it's an embarrassment to even classify it as a service. Lots of overpaid mediocrity is how I would describe it. Where perception and box ticking are the course of the day.

Why else would they deny access to neuro physiotherapists or install utterly useless equipment other than to be able to tick a box! It's time for the closing of the circle. The NHS budget for the coming year is £162.6 Billion.

I've got no problem with the nurses, ambulance, paramedics, surgeons and niche sectors. But the rest of you I would cull like they did to BSE infected beef. Get over yourselves.

Interesting sub-section:

The entire lifetime of my mother's post infection or displaying symptoms, was primarily occupied with the intrusive application of a regime of nonspecific medications. None of which brought any relief. In fact, the majority were only good for helping the account balances of very influential pharmaceutical companies, so, my advice to anyone just beginning on their journey is, by all means try holistic remedies. Take any anti-inflammatory remedies that you can find and probably most importantly, stay as fit and healthy as you can, for as long as you can.

Just before I sign off, I need to get my own thank you letter out there. First one goes to my Caribbean caregiver Ashelle, and my latest one Lucy. Plus, everyone that has been my support. Including my little sister Louise. (not related) My two long term partners and fiancées and the people who I have shared laughs with along the way.

My first girlfriend was a diabetic, so I know what it means to be around people who have hidden illnesses. So just try to be patient with your acquaintances or colleagues, because you might be next.

To my neighbour and former Conservative councillor and her little spy (snake in the grass), Nazi, I say "fuck you, asshole," you are an insult to decency despite the image you try to profess. Drain blocking and peering around curtains. The epitome of CHAV with connections. Although for the life of me I can't think why you are desperate to keep a spare key for my flat.

Then finally to anyone who plays the ladder climbing game. I'm embarrassed for you. What are you going to do with those billions? My suggestion is to do what happens at the end of the Slumdog Millionaire film! (I'll let you watch and find out).

As a species we are a virus. The difficulty in trying to persuade otherwise is futile. I came to this conclusion in my teens. It was a period, dominated by the stupidity and selfishness of my, "so called peers!"

With all the institutions and multinational corporations given favourable terms, as opposed to inclusivity for everyone. Thatcher even had the Gaul to label the unions as a destabilising influence. Everyone is on strike. Call the police!

The majority just wanted a fare wage, as is today, so why was this so hard? I am convinced the only reason the police sided with Thatcher, was because of the threat to Police terms and pay. But we are now able to re-evaluate this error. I firmly believe that society has played the "animal farm" card once too often. A bus or train driver is just as important as a doctor or airline pilot. The coronavirus proves that.

Do you know what? I promised not to get too political. This is about MS. But hang on: - The utility company regulators are obviously not stringently controlled or policed. The effluent leakage into the sea proves that, and why are the wages for these entities being paid for by us?

In my humble opinion all the water companies, energy companies and so forth should have to pay the salaries and pensions for their regulators.

I mean if they are making so much profit that they can pay out dividends then they shouldn't have a choice!

It's just the same thing for the civil service. Things like the gambling regulatory body. I think that we could find so much money from these companies, that we could actually be able to force superb health and dental care for all. Not stuffing the bank balances and property portfolios of the entitled plumb sucking tossers! The idea that you can own houses throughout the world is a weird kind of rich arrogance. But surely as a nation we can turn this excess showboating and wealth into a sustainable care sector? "SURELY"

Because you have leeched funds and favours for all the post-war years and exactly what have you contributed. The answer is "sweet fanny Adams!" It is a given that certain groups ingratiate themselves into British society and are continually sucking it dry. But it all comes back down to who has the moral high ground? Is it the History Degree student or the aircraft engineer? For what it's worth, my money is always going on the blackie or greenie (slang for technician).

When I trained to become aircrew, a fellow student confided he had a PHD in Anthropology. To which my response was "why?" I mean seriously "the study of humanity" is it not obvious how fickle and insincere we are. What other species allows their brethren to suffer without so much as a backward glance?

Oh yes, before I forget. In this country there are over twenty (20) different regulatory health bodies. Which I dare say a class of kindergarten children could do a better job. Maybe we can completely rethink how an individual's skills are appreciated. The so-called experts, or elite professionals are very good at self-promotion. I'm aware most doctors, solicitors and financial advisors have studied for an extremely long period. Culminating in testing examinations and proficiency markers. But who believes that they do their job because it makes them feel fulfilled?

Of course not, they do it because they have a dream of becoming rich. Which for me is where the empathy drains away. They should become lumped together with the other failing institutions like the BBC, Parliament or the Sun newspaper.

All plagued by disgraceful episodes of incompetence, misogyny or in the case of the Beeb, a blatant attempt to manipulate the truth with contemptible bias reporting of current affairs and unjustifiable remuneration packages. They even have the audacity to host a program called "rip off Britain" in which they never investigate themselves.

So instead of playing this perpetual self-promotion game. Let's get some people in place who are actually interested and up to the task! Which in my case means getting to the bottom of some questionable decisions.

Like: the occupational therapist who signed me off fit for work, adding you've got a serious neck injury but that's okay, you can still go flying and the landings will have no impact on your health.

Or whilst getting discharged from the Army, you are aware that you have unusual lumps on your arms. I think it might be EBV lymphoma, but that doesn't matter because you have just run and cycled to London from Germany.

Or your mother appears to be suffering from whiplash injuries after the car accident, but you seem o.k. So, we won't waste time on checking you out.

Or the GP, who in 2012 sent me urgently to hospital for tests for a suspected stroke, not by ambulance but under my own devices. It was a Friday, and the hospital was shutting down for a Bank Holiday weekend, so I wasn't actually dealt with until Tuesday midday.

Oh, and finally the cherry on the cake. I'm sorry to tell you this but you were adopted at birth, from Harrow, so you are probably the bastard of some posh school student. Who knows you might even be the illegitimate son of a Prime Minister?

So here is the thing. I am not a wealthy, portfolio touting yuppie, or a property-owning well-off individual. If you have paid attention to the story, you'll notice I've never been more than middle class, the fact that my parents lost their house and business is something I've always connected with my mother contracting this illness, but what's important is to take the following message with you.

My father spent enormous amounts of time and money. Along with using his personal savings and resources to try to fix mum. They did occasionally travel. I was happy to invite them to Germany for one Christmas and to a villa I rented in Bretagne 'France. To see my first child. But what infuriates me even today, is that they never managed to go on a cruise.

It was mum's perpetual wish to be like the passengers on the Onedin Line, a British television series. So, in her honour and memory I did one to the Italian coast a few years ago. This is a beautiful, brilliant holiday option for anyone with MS looking for ideas. It would have been perfect for her. Unfortunately, the opportunity never arose. Which leads me nicely onto the other major factor in my recollections into the last fifty years. Also, one of my life mottos. Live each day like it's your last. Because as I can testify, events can change suddenly and dramatically.

On an unrelated note, I thought I would give out my advice on how to deal with the health system. I'm best placed and can talk of two generations living with the disease. My first advice would be to get private health insurance. A massive amount of my and my family's tribulations and expenses would have gone into a meaningful and productive conversations and therapies.

No wasted journeys going to hospital to discover the appointment had been changed or cancelled. Or for example taking time off work to attend a session to get the disease modifying drugs, only to discover that they were not even ordered! (A solicitor advised me that I had a case with this) but with the funds and insurer's backing you still have to make lots of unusual decisions. Do I need the treatment being suggested or should I try to inform myself first.

Whatever you decide, don't do what I did, which was to rush back to work. Get the scans and bigger picture about the extent of your injuries and work out something which I am thankful for my first aid training. Which states quite categorically on presentation of an injury not to rush in without checking to see what dangers to exacerbating the injury are present.

Something that the young doctor who signed me off "fit to work" either didn't understand or didn't care less about. (Another part where the solicitor said I might have a case)

Then finally once you have informed yourself, decide what your body is telling you. Your gut feeling is always a good indicator, but DO NOT, I repeat, "DO NOT TRUST JUST ONE DOCTOR."

My mother did this and because of that, she must have single-handedly contributed handsomely to big pharma.

I recently read a report on a Paralympian called Kadeena Cox, who has MS and competed at the olympics in Rio, Brazil winning gold in swimming and cycling. She has also starred in a television program called "I'm a celebrity, get me out of here" which proves you can be successful. So, there is hope!

But I need to draw on my experience and my mother's history to do something no medical expert or neurological scientist is prepared to do. I'm going to rubbish the standard form of explanation and description of the illness. Taking issue with everything that is spouted on MS charity documents and also the vast claims and counterclaims of neurologists and neuroscientists who have their understanding and interpretation based almost entirely on MRI results and the obvious Get Out of Jail Card throwaway remark, "It varies widely between every patient." Now, I am not a qualified doctor or radiographer, but I am coherent and conscientious. I have also over the course of my life discussed with hundreds of people who are MS diagnosed what their disease progression looks like. Not just out of polite curiosity or to give insight to my mum. I'm embarrassed to admit it was about me!

You see I wanted to know what to look out for and what steps or measures I could take to slow down the process. Well check this out, I want to propose my thesis on the progression of the disease and how to drastically reduce the advancement and severity of the symptoms. So firstly, let's destroy the textbook explanation and the dumbing down of the stages made by the white coats.

Clinically isolated syndrome (CIS), relapsing remitting multiple sclerosis (RRMS), secondary progressive multiple sclerosis (SPMS), primary progressive multiple sclerosis (PPMS).

Let's begin with how published publications supposed to inform and rationalize our injury are nothing more than convenient part explanations and simplifications designed to give a believable impression of what is going on in our brains and why we experience the symptoms that we have. I will give you an example of this in an internet document explaining the perceived impact of the illness and what to expect, titled, Stages of MS.

MS is a complex disease, it's difficult to diagnose and hard to pinpoint when it starts and how it progresses before symptoms become visible. Experts are starting to think about MS in terms of their phases. Imaging studies have suggested that a lot of background disease activity occurs before symptoms appear. This is called the sub clinical phase. Some experts proposed that there is enough evidence to describe the following three types.

I'm going to stop this right here. Because I am afraid that this is a fucking joke. 50 years of research and study and this is the kind of crap you feel will appease the afflicted?

To anyone who (like me) who has tried to raise awareness and funds to challenge the "incurable,' moniker, I have just got this message.

I've been to your meetings and fundraisers. I'm certain that the people who champion this project are well intentioned. But somewhere along those fifty years someone thought hey, "have some of this" guaranteed long term project with no pressure to make a difference, plus, it is a guaranteed free meal ticket.

And before you start to protest your innocence, I'll just say it as it is. J.K. Rowling was absolutely right about the ineffective apathy towards finding a cure. Because the gravy train is still in the station waiting for the next episode of trainee doctors to start the tour of blind alleyways.

You see the reason it's difficult to diagnose is because you aren't thinking outside the box.

The reason why I think it presents itself in many different guises because it is a central nervous system injury which means spinal column, brain stem and the individual elements of the brain.

Yes, the MRI can pick up on myelin sheath damage but actually you are missing the one key essential element of this picture. The damaged area is prone to further damage, whether that means an impact or some irritant like smoke from a cigarette, atmospheric pressure changes and even chemical reactions.

But for fifty years' worth of investigation and research, to write MS is "difficult to understand" in my eyes is a dereliction of duty.

So, all you doctors' currently earning ridiculous salaries and pensions I guess I want the world to give you the kind of treatment that you gave the Covid patients, YOU MUPPETS!

The difficulty I have with trusting people Is something that stems from my childhood. Constantly moving and being forced into situations that couldn't ever produce lifelong friendships. In some aspects of this constant tension and reluctance to make meaningful connections with others I sometimes wonder if I could or should have become a mass murderer. I mean the trademark signs were ever present. Isolated and insular, a preference for the odd and unusual. I actually thought I was going mad during my young teens, inventing a make-believe friend who I would talk to during my paper round or whilst cycling to school. In retrospect I firmly believe It was all connected to me being newly affected by the condition.

But back then I didn't really want anyone to suspect in case it might have the same consequences I witnessed affecting my mother. Which is something I'm glad I never revealed. Because I dare say I would have been another lamb to the slaughter. Spoon fed the lies and promises of doctors and neuroscientists who were doing their impressions of blind people. Tapping around in the dark. More than happy to sign over caseloads of drugs and other untargeted therapies or intrusive investigation and treatment. I'm confident now that I have figured out what 50 plus years of research and fund raising has failed to identify.

Yes, the scans and diagnostic process of looking for myelin sheath damage on the brain are a clear indicator of the presence of the disease. But they do not reveal the whole reason why we are so different. I am totally convinced that it's because we have different interpretations on this. The doctors always like to hold the moral high ground. Talking down to their patients in that condescending manner. Knowing what is best for them. When they are as clueless as the detectives investigating a crime. All bluff and posturing with no real understanding of what's happening.

I believe that we are all affected differently and in different ways because we don't just have the illness. I'm sure it's because we have multiple injuries, whereby one affects and influences the others. Take me for example. I know that vibrations and twisting of the spine. The thoracic area can increase spasticity. Or even when lifting anything above shoulder height can increase the likelihood of a jolt travelling through the limbs.

But does any doctor want to discuss that? Of course not, because it is far easier to label people and forget about them than to try to heal them.

Let me do one final analogy. Thinking about how the spots on a leopard make such good camouflage. When they can lie in direct view and yet remain undetected until they move. The complex layers of millions of cells are like those millions of neurons in the brain, each with its own unique ability or job. But instead of focusing on the intricacies of the big numbers of networks or data.

Which is how the neurologists like to confuse and justify their methods let's just focus on the big picture. The reason why the leopard hides so well is because it has adapted to blend into its surroundings. Whereas the doctors are doing the reverse, instead of tackling the anomalies in the MRI scans, they are looking too hard at the consequences of the myelin damage.

It's like the boy on the dyke in the Netherlands who prevented disaster by plugging a hole with his finger. This is where I am completely certain the solution to this disease is possible. We already know that the myelin can be bypassed and effectively replaced so my plea to anyone who is seriously interested in finding a one size fits all cure. FIND THE HOLE IN THE DAM!

My closing remarks are aimed at everyone. Including myself. Quick question, when you look at a picture of Venice, what colour do you most associate with it? The brownish tint of the roof tiles or perhaps the unusual greenish slush of the canals. It's difficult isn't it sometimes to accurately describe the depth of differences in a scene or landscape. I have used this example to illustrate how utterly ridiculous and stupid it is to define anything with the suffix "ish!"

Let's face it Brit "ish" or Scott "ish" are classic examples of lazy stereotyping. More accurate would be to just use the term him or her.

The reason for me to think about this, is its all linked into the worldly, economical subtext whereby everybody wants to express themselves with a title. For example, His Majesty or Lady so and so. But irrespective of the undeserving inequalities that this throwback to the Middle Ages promotes it annoys the crap out of me how, in the 21st century so many of those self-promoting titles are flaunted, that have nothing constructive to say about anything.

I say this because doctor (Dr.) is a classic example. I mean OK, they have spent a considerable amount of time studying medicine, anatomy and all the disciplines but aside from the specialists like surgeons and field medical professionals. Who does anything unique or useful, other than extending the lives of people? Even diagnoses although specialised, needing radiographers and other niche professions. Is something which the internet and pharmacy clerks can substitute for.

If I'm honest this argument also applies to professionals in law, like solicitors or barristers, judges and the police. You only have to look around the world to notice how utterly corrupt and inconsistent they are. I'm not just referring to the recent spate of scandals that have affected the U.K. this is far bigger than just a local problem.

The problem as I see it, is as follows. The over educated and qualified are essentially holding the whole world to ransom. They have created this framework of authority and power that they have no intention of giving back.

They all want a bigger and larger slice of the pie and when, like as recently happened during Brexit and the Pandemic they don't get their way they start behaving more and more like Sheldon Cooper, the spoilt little brat from the television series "the Big Bang theory!"

I mean honestly how can all these inquiries take so long. We all saw the Grenfell Tower disaster, so why is nobody in prison? We all saw Sarah Everard's evidence, why is the Metropolitan Police still an organisation. We all read about the failures in the health system. So why does nobody want to make the changes needed?

I AM EMBARRASSED FOR ALL OF YOU!

The only other little anomaly in my story goes right to the heart of what it means to be "ish" whether that is Brit, Blue or Flem. We are living in a dysfunctional shambolic joke of a world. Where everything revolves around the fixers. A shadowy Army of manipulators. Some in financial services and some in governments.

Their goal is to create the belief and confidence that has hoodwinked society since the word dot. Driving all of you to believe in currency and growth. Harnessing everyone into the "money-go-round" with the promise that it will all become better. Just keep producing more doctors, pilots and financial advisors. Keep getting married and having children. Irrespective of if it's affordable to your pocket or the planet. Because when we finally fuck up this rock we can always move on to the next one.

So Mr Bezos and Mr Musk I hope you are happy? Same for all the stock exchanges. At least Bill Gates wants to use some of his money to immunize the poor! Or would it be undiplomatic to suggest that he has other than honourable intentions?

YOU DECIDE:

Anyway, once again I have strayed off topic. The key factor In all things is how will this affect my/our situation and future? Because in countries like mine everyone has been living on borrowed money. During the Thatcher years great swathes of the country were sold off or used as bargaining chips for future projects. It's why so many people either left voluntarily or were forced to due to economic hardship.

So much so, that there has been a steady stream of migration to the foreign market ever since the conservatives told us to "get on our bikes" well guess what you narcissistic Nazis because of your mismanagement and every government in my lifetime the country is broken. You have only got yourselves to blame. The fact that we faired so disappointingly during the pandemic is just the start. But hey, WHAT DO I KNOW!

True civilisation is a confusing word. It's used incorrectly in a multitude of different situations and conversations. The most obvious example is when it gets paired with the human race! Because at no point in history has humanity ever displayed civility? I'm not here to write about the ups and downs of us. Or waste your time chewing over the big issues. Because you and me are never going to be able to tackle the big things. Constructions like capitalism, communism, or modern economics will prevent change!

This leads onto "being civilized?" What decides the definition for this? Is it possibly the dressing for different occasions? Or perhaps things like queuing for service at supermarket delicatessen counters. Or showing incredible patience at the post office.

The dictionary defines it as "an advanced stage of social or cultural development." so, let's jump into the daily routine of everyday life. It's multicultural around the globe. We all tend to share similar values and beliefs.

Oh, sure you'll be aware of the occasional intercultural differences and beliefs. Even across sections of this country I am constantly reminded about the small quirks separating regions. For example, did you know the people of

Cornwall eat scones differently to Devon? Apparently, it's all to do with what order to put the jam and cream on.

Even the way British people pronounce "scone" is varied depending on where you live or how you were educated. My parents always said SKOWN, whereas my Uncle Brian said SCONN.

Stupid isn't it. But just this little glimpse behind the facade is a real eye opener. It's also a very useful template which can be applied around the entire planet.

I'm going to list a few key words for you now! I want you to learn them completely including their definition's It will make sense shortly I promise. But without understanding these words you are always going to struggle with my thoughts! Ambiguous, Ambivalent, Equivocal, Double standards.

Let's do a quick calculation. How many obvious cases of ambiguity or double standards can you list in your immediate vicinity? Let's do the obvious.

Sorry to all the women and fancy (or not) male groomers, but get yourself worming tablets, because you are either an image obsessed cosmetics and fashion junkie, or you have a tape worm, which is constantly reminding you need to have a little bit more!

Personally, I think this is our greatest tragedy. It's not purely confined to this insane craving for image, smell or colour. It goes much deeper than that. Look at your own preferences. I dare say throughout the world most of you will have your "style! "It could be a hairstyle or a cosmetic. It might be a clothing penchant or something bigger, a manufacturer of high value goods like washing machines, or electric consumables like cars or the latest smartphone!

Point is modern life is controlled by dark forces and conglomerates. The average person is directly targeted by advertising! Who in turn are directly linked to financial institutions! Who want to get their hands on your money. The subtle nuances hidden in daily life are staggering. Even people who live here in the west have this naive blindness to control.

Up until recently I too thought I was cautious:

Let's wind this conversation back slightly. Who has seen the television aid advertisements, for example the young child is shown carrying a plastic container. She is barefooted on a drought cracked dirt track. The accompanying narrative describes how it's four miles distance from a water source, stones and a polluted stream.

Let's mimic a little bit of the sound of music. We'll start at the beginning because it's the best place to start. So, what makes a good person? It's very much an ethical thing. Some people are good and as we all know, some bad. The one deciding factor is who can be trusted with responsibility. Let me try to explain. One of the most perceptive pieces of television is from the film, Carry on Nurse. I'll do my best to outline the scene, Matron (Hattie Jaques) has just been doing her ward inspections, just checking the cleanliness and general orderliness of the inventory, patients included, when a patient (Kenneth Williams), makes a verbal protest at the ridiculous nature of this "by your beds" inspection, which completely throws Matron's normally unchallenged authority.

She is completely unable to accept the possibility someone is oblivious to social convention and refuses to kowtow to the command structure in the hospital. This breakdown of the status quo is resolved by a completely spiteful order to replace the bedding on the entire ward.

Now I realise the whole farcical nature of this is fictitious and purely used for comedic purposes, but unfortunately, it's something I have witnessed first-hand on a hospital ward in the town of Bath. Obviously not carbon copy bad. Nonetheless with the same detrimental intentions. I had been bed filling for what seemed like a week. Not getting any consultation from the doctors, or even any meaningful help with physio.

The most pressing problem I had to deal with was a broken golden crown (tooth), caused by hospital food. I asked for the dental service to get a look at it. But because I was being difficult, complaining about the lack of anything happening. I was woken at 3.00 am. by a junior doctor wielding a flashlight, she waved this around my eyes to blind and annoy me, then she left, leaving a bottle of mouthwash to fight off any pain or infection.

The craziest thing about this, was my golden crown, still with gold intact, disappeared that night and my protest about it was, frankly ignored. Another reason why I distrust all healthcare settings!

So why is this important in the grand scheme of things? I'll tell you. It's part and parcel of the system breakdown that is currently killing our country. Disenfranchised and disillusioned people who hold powerful positions. But have no moral backbone and definitely no difficulty in selling you or me down the river! But here is the cavalry, riding over the horizon sitting on a noble stead and just desperate to fight the battle that they brought up to.

No, I'm not talking about the Labour Party, or the Liberal Democrat's and neither is it UKIP, the SNP, Plaid Cymru, or even the Greens. In fact, I am avoiding all the political parties, because they are all incapable of one key motivation. None of them have got A PLAN! A few have ideas or something reminiscent of a game of Texas Hold-em Poker. But nobody has the guts to say it how it is. The biggest challenge here is not the economy or transportation, health or defence. Oh no, it's plainer than the nose on your face. I'm talking about HONESTY!!!

Just look around here and in the media and try this little exercise. Remember they must be British: Pick three people in Britain who you have admiration for and who you trust implicitly.

Pick three people of science who you believe have good general knowledge and are worldly. Pick three people who are local to you who you think is a great example of decency.

Not too difficult is it! So here goes I'll give mine: Stephen Fry (TV host), Tim Peake (astronaut), Ellen MacArthur (round the world yachtswoman), Professor Brian Cox, (TV personality and physicist and astronomer), Peter Higgs, (Higgs-Boson) Professor Richard Betts, (Exeter Uni & Met Office). Aargh...Big problem I honestly am struggling here. I would have to say Lucy (my carer).

So, we've established that this is not as simple as it sounds. Maybe it is something easier for you. The ones I could have selected are all very old or in some cases dead, I also wanted to steer clear of television personalities and politicians. The people of science were easier but again I found myself drawn to the dead or the dying.

For example, Professor Stephen Hawking the theoretical physicist (dead) or Francis Crick, biophysicist and discoverer of the DNA double helix. (Dead) As for the third section, I can't even list people like the neighbours as they are a weird mixture between the Old East German Stasi. (secret police), the weird cat-lady from the Simpsons or a bunch of CHAV's (council house & violence). But none of this would matter with the introduction of my ideas for Government.

The first one is something I have stolen from an idea I got from the television. It was one of those current affairs/travel programs. Which on this occasion was from the island of Jamaica! It centred around a revolutionary project that they have introduced to combat corruption and dishonesty. Mainly focused on their politicians and police force.

They've introduced the polygraph, or a lie detector to you and me. It would make absolute sense, preventing dodgy practices in parliament like those we have experienced the last 50 years. I'm talking about cash for questions, or the expenses scandal, the absolute scandalous behaviour of some politicians and their incessant attempts to bend the truth.

Just look at Boris and the Tories during the pandemic, but not just that, the lies that led to Brexit. The utter failure of the support organisations of government, even right down to the umbrella watchdog who should be out there keeping us safe, which I have seen firsthand that is not working.

I'm convinced that all these organs who should be overseeing the process and structure of society are failing because they are "excuse the footballing metaphor" the leaky last line of defence. Put in place, not to strengthen our belief in the institutions and democracy. But purely because they are an easy target when something goes badly wrong.

OFWAT and OFGEM have been in the news recently because of their failures. But that is too simplistic. It's like all the (Office for) nomenclature. The key is in the name. They are an extension of the government and civil service. Funded by taxpayers and answerable to no one other than (Select Committee's) a very convenient system that admonishes everyone during the blame game. The shareholders pocketing the dividends with a sense of impunity. Politicians smirking and getting their builders to go ahead with the house extension.

Introducing the polygraph to examine the honesty of all those organisations and individuals involved would guarantee a fairer playing field.

No more grubby backhanders in brown paper envelopes, or coppers deliberately misleading with dishonest politicians finally being held to account.

So then comes a must do moment. Dismantle the ceremony and stupidly surrounding the upper and lower house of parliament. I'm certain that the pandemic taught us many lessons. But surely aside from party gate or driving to Barnard Castle the big lesson is how modern technology should replace the antiquated and very expensive London centric culture.

So, what exactly does having the conversation mean? It's a variation on "having the talk "which is also not a million miles away from "whisper in your shell like!" You see, in theory anybody who finds themselves in a conversation with sub-text or ambiguous language, should really be able to navigate through and discover what exactly the truth or meaning or point is. But unfortunately, in England it's a constant minefield for the majority of straight talking and thinking people, when confronted with lawyer or political speak.

As a Child I can remember the constant lying. Or the blatant use of double standards. You know the type of thing. "Do what I say" "not as I do"

I remember travelling to school with mum. I was only about 11 because it was my first year of secondary school. Brother had already left on his bicycle, which meant I was the only passenger in the car. We were just outside Milford train station when mum suddenly turned and spoke.

Tying things together:

The final piece of my story is an attempt to make sense of my 58 years. I am, as I have recently discovered. The product of an unwanted/impossible pregnancy. Pushed about, like the cards in a top trumps game. Fortunately landing on the doorstep of a sympathetic and caring couple, who tried to provide me and my (adopted) siblings a little luxury and love.

I'm constantly reminded by chapters of my own life, of how things might have been oh so different! I tried to run away on at least 3 different occasions. But it wasn't until I walked through the cardboard city of Embankment just outside Charing Cross station in the early 1980's that I understood how important a place to call home really was.

I have always viewed myself as someone who is different from the mainstream. I am definitely not the proverbial sheep that follows the herd, or flock if you want! But I am fortunate because I have had the opportunity and breaks to pretty much, do my own thing. Not tied down with a need to constantly prove himself to some higher office. This is something I am truly grateful for. But simultaneously I feel I have to explain my motivations.

When you are growing up and constantly moving here, there and everywhere. Plus having to make sense of changes to your mindset and body. Not even realising how unwell you are. With the additional extra pressures of having a very poorly mother. A very unwell grandmother and having to navigate through a difficult period of British history and fundamental changes in the teaching structure of schools. (We had literally just gone decimal). It's a miracle I even survived that far.

So, imagine an insecure teenager who has just started to get the additional stress of secondary school education, whilst desperately hiding his imperfections and troubles. Desperately seeking to disappear into obscurity to protect his mother and simultaneously mastermind a future for himself that would be enjoyable as well as achievable.

The most important advice I can offer to any MS sufferers is to get thick skinned. I know from my mom's experiences that being a polite, rule following "yes" man. Is not going to do you any favours. You must become nasty and selfish. Only listening to your body and trusting your instincts. As I have already explained my mother was one of those people who trusted her doctors and swallowed all their ridiculous medical advice. None of which worked by the way!

Go outside and challenge yourself "EVERY DAY" because you only have one life, and you don't want to wake up one day with regrets? I personally have spent my entire life ticking off those Bucket List experiences. Playing against all the odds, practically every sport imaginable. Sometimes at a really good level.

Going back to the story of my taking music lessons. What I didn't expose previously was that I didn't achieve any qualifications or anything in terms of examination standards. But get this. Despite my body giving signs that I had coordination problems (possibly MS related) I stuck with it my entire life. Eventually playing electronic keyboards for a Christmas Pantomime. Singing Itsey Bitsey Teenie Weenie Yellow Polka dot bikini. Candle in the wind and horse with no name. In a successful production of Humpty Dumpty.

I played Golden Brown for my local football team, Christmas party, and on my 18th birthday party. I had a blast at playing New York, New York in a packed out 'Canadian Irish club. So again, I'm of the opinion that if you are having trouble with learning something. "PERSEVERE" because I am of the belief that to not try is to fail.

Put yourself out of your comfort zone. In 2017, I flew unaccompanied to go Scuba Diving in Cuba. A country I might add, that opened its arms to a wheelchair user. Where nothing was too difficult. I was even carried upstairs to a restaurant on one occasion to experience a Caribbean dinner. With Red Snapper and lobster. The hotel is. Melia resort. In Caya Coco. The diving instructor is a guy called "fat Tony" like the mafia character from "the Simpsons," and he does not even need you to show PADI or any qualifications! My kind of guy.

Even if you are still able to function with mobility and travel. Don't hide or give up because you will regret it at the end. I know my mum did. She made the effort on two occasions. Once to see her first Grandson in Brittany. On the West Coast of France. The second time was a longer journey to Germany to see the other boy. I know that those two trips made a huge difference to her. She suddenly realised that she was able to do something! I even got her walking in the sea in France, something that was great for both of my parents.

So, what is it I'm trying to dispense? I think ultimately, it's just a bit of self-belief. I mean OK, the entire history of my family and the NHS has been a fucking disaster from start to finish. From the way they put mum through invasive procedures and treatments. Especially Lumbar Puncture or (SPINAL TAP) like the band. To all the drugs that the pharmaceutical companies could charge the UK government for. Until the last occasions when she went in for something quite innocuous and contracted MRSA in hospital and quite unexpectedly died overnight.

The way my father was in hospital after being treated for a fall, got all clear and was sent home to free up a space in the ward. To then deteriorate overnight and have to be emergency readmitted, only to die the same night. In both cases I never got to say my goodbye. So, to all of you who might have been affected by Covid in a similar way. You have my sympathy.

To then my story, which I have tried to tell honestly. I'm not going to lie and say I think things are different now. Because I'm of the opinion that they have never been so bad.

Considering how many years the white coats, pharmaceutical companies and governments have been working on "BETTER OUTCOMES" they haven't really come very far have they.

To the MS Society, who have lots of influence and advice and any MS charity that is trying to help. I say this. 'During my mother's struggle' I volunteered as often as possible. Doing fundraising and on one summer I was responsible for a fairground ride at the Guildford County show. I was also responsible for organising local help for newly diagnosed in Bristol during 2014/5 until a bit more deterioration.

You all love to spout the variety of stages of the illness. Let me remind you... (CIS) clinically isolated syndrome. The first signs of neurological symptoms that might develop into MS. (POMS) Paediatric onset MS. First signs of symptoms affecting the youngest group of society. (ME!) (RRMS) Relapsing Remitting MS 70-80% of people who exhibit symptoms of MS have this. (SPMS) Secondary Progressive MS is what it says it is. (PPMS) Primary Progressive MS Progressive from when first discovered.

Well, I think that it's all fine and dandy putting individuals into categories. Unfortunately, your assumptions are flawed. Because you always talk about how everyone is different.

'WRONG'... The symptoms and pathology are the same for everyone. The reason why some people experience or exhibit different symptoms is because they are not all fighting just one condition.

In my case I have known I have been carrying an injury since the end of the 1970's. But it was never a massive problem. Occasionally I would experience an off day or odd set of symptoms. But you put those things down to cold or flu related. No, this thing that popped up in 2012. As something my first aid training taught me was Stroke related was something completely unrelated.

The fact that I was advised to go immediately to A & E by the GP. Made me realise something was wrong. Unfortunately, that particular Friday was a Bank Holiday. So, despite being admitted as possible stroke victim. I wasn't seen until Tuesday... Hey NHS, make you feel proud... I knew something didn't add up immediately. Mostly by conversations I had with people who occasionally went "the extra mile," an MS nurse in Bath Hospital actually asked me, "what do you think it is?" On another occasion after my second breakdown of 2013 an (OT) from Southmead Hospital in Bristol told me after another MRI that my medical team were divided on opinions.

Little Tip.... When a medically trained health professional tells you, "They don't know," RUN...RUN...RUN LIKE HELL...The other little tip is if you see a doctor on a computer putting your details into a "search engine" and then coming over to discuss the findings of the scans. Don't trust a word that comes out their mouth. Anyway, I'm just about done with my little project.... WAHAAY PROJECT ME!

It kind of reminds me about (anecdote) the time we were driving in a two-vehicle convoy and a French car pulled alongside trying to shout something to us. I pulled over and as the French speaking liaison officer I tried to find out what was going on.

Fortunately, I remembered the French word cambion from school. Meaning small truck. Realising the other vehicle in our convoy was missing I turned around and headed back into Lyon. On the other side of the road our vehicle lay in a ditch on its side. I remember Bob making the finger over the throat gesture and holding up two fingers. We thought two had died in their accident. When we eventually caught up with them. I remember Captain Darling asking. "Who's dead?" To which Bob looked up quite sheepishly and smiled and said, "no we broke two bottles of beer!" I'm a believer it's never as bad as you think.

After thought:

Something that I realise I have missed, writing this piece. Is how my mild manners have influenced my narrative. For example, I haven't highlighted the insanity and frustrations that I dare say 90% of British NHS patients experience on a regular basis. But which is also a contributing factor in my healthcare experience.

The hospital appointment system, whereby you adjust your personal schedule, in some cases like I had to. Cancelling work commitments, to keep to the hospital or specialist departments tight diary flow. It's a flawed process, with unbelievable amounts of administrative errors and double bookings.

Scandalously the responsibility of managing appointment and consultation sit squarely on the shoulders of personal secretaries. Something I find quite inexcusable. The Onus of setting the workload should sit directly with the consultant. Or head of department. Like the resident Neurologist. This way there wouldn't be excuses for any screw ups!

Because I have endured countless cancellations. Arranging a visit, to then receive a text or voicemail unmanageably late in the day, informing of a cancellation or rescheduling. A trademark procedure of all the healthcare providers in the Bristol and North Somerset area. I'm also afraid to announce that this is also true of private healthcare companies. An unacceptable practice of a crumbling system.

Something else that I have had to deal with, that I know is not an isolated incident. Was what happened when I still lived in Chew Magna. I was recently diagnosed and offered a (DMT) disease modifying therapy. An infusion of a supposed suppressant to the illness. Something by the way I haven't found any supporting evidence for. But anyway, I made all the necessary arrangements to get to the city of Bath to try this procedure. Despite being informed of the risks. Which for me included the risk of death because of a virus I was carrying.

The MS nurse explained I had something called (PML)Progressive Multifocal Leukoencelopathy Essentially the drug that they wanted me to take was Natalizumab. A drug which "Could" slow down progression of the disease. But the virus I tested positive for could cause serious complications and death.

Well before I got my first infusion, I had to make all those kinds of preparations. Squared away the situation with my workplace. Got a colleague to bring and collect. Made sure life insurance was covered and then got underway!!!

Well, bearing in mind only a couple of months earlier I was fit and able bodied, also understand that I had only recently returned to flying duty with the airline. So, I was quite apprehensive to say the least. But... GUESS WHAT... They hadn't bothered to order the medicine!

IT DOESN'T FILL YOU WITH CONFIDENCE DOES IT?

So ultimately armed with doubt around every aspect of British healthcare I did eventually start to trial the (DMT) thinking and most importantly hoping to get some kind of positive response to my symptoms.

After the second infusion I had what can only be described as a negative reaction. Losing balance and ending up in a hallway corner in my flat (coincidentally also a thatched building) I phoned 999 to ask for an ambulance to take me to hospital for testing. Something I had been advised to do, in case of any reaction.

I laid on the floor without any hope of an ambulance, until the central heating switched on. This seemed to rectify my inability to move, so, give or take a half an hour, I then drove to Frenchay hospital in Bristol. It took until about midnight to be seen.

I was literally explaining my situation to every Tom, Dick and Harry. Until I eventually spoke to the duty doctor. Who displayed bags of empathy and congratulated me for making the right choice to see if anything else was going on.

I got home at about two in the morning, totally exhausted and feeling unimpressed by the experience. So that was the journey that started the alarm bells ringing. Well, that and the stroke like adventure which got me into the hospital in the first instance. I have since, had many other hospitalizations and been investigated for lots of other problems.

Most of which are unrelated to the illness, but once they give you a diagnosis and label. It's how they justify all their actions! Trouble is I'm too old in this game. Having experienced the way mum was treated. I'm also disturbingly well-tuned to my body to know that my current situation is not directly linked to MS.

Also, I have had the conversation with an OT in Southmead, Bristol and other healthcare professionals like the MS nurse in Bath, which have fuelled my determination to get the truth.

So, to all MS sufferers just bear in mind. Co-Morbidity is a real thing. The Americans and Canadians have already made the link between "glandular fever" and MS. But I am convinced there are loads of other illnesses that complicate the situation.

So please take care. "Eat well (vegetarian is good)" Restrict any alcohol. NEVER SMOKE!!!

Pay attention to triggers and don't drive if you are experiencing optic neuritis. But most importantly go to MS functions and meet fellow members of our community. Enjoy your life and tick off the bucket list to do jobs.

In summary:

I'm conscious of how, during the writing of this book how frequently I tend towards the sublime or even the ridiculous! So, what I want is to have a realistic view of "BROKEN BRITAIN!" In many ways I have matured and endured over the last decade.

Whilst working on the airline I would frequently observe the emergency skills of paramedics and other first responder practitioners. A skill I'm pleased to announce that is mirrored around the country. With fantastic representation from the ambulance service, indeed every form of emergency response! Not just in Britain either. I'm convinced it's a worldwide phenomenon that supports the travelling public.

However, that is where the good news stops. As I have highlighted in my story. The second you are presenting anything that is unusual or unclear. The train comes off the rails!

Let me put that statement into context. We all understand the principle of emergency medicine. At the lowest level, this means using our own medical knowledge and resources. For example, a fall that results in abrasions or other minor injuries.

We get the antiseptic and cleanse the wound. Apply a bandage and administer any appropriate medication that we might have lying around the cupboards. In some cases, we may - with a visit to a pharmacist or doctor to ensure the self-applied treatment is effective. "No Problem"

What we're currently experiencing in this country is a complete breakdown in how our society and health system is failing. On a scale only describable by using the phrase "CLUSTER FUCK," from the movie heartbreak ridge.

The onus is no longer on us to make intelligent choices and decisions about accident care. Self-medicating or treating where applicable. Oh No! In today's Britain, you become a "Columbo! The TV detective who spends his days contemplating the autopsy of a coroner, or doctor, picking the details with a fine toothcomb. Eventually making sense of the tragedy and subsequently presenting his findings to shatter the failures of the previous investigation and the evidence provided!

So, let's see what has gone wrong. Obviously the first major mistake was made after I started to present with the unusual symptoms in the late 70's. Sleeping extraordinarily long periods. Mood changes, loss of concentration amongst other things. But because mum was newly diagnosed with MS, nobody was interested in the difficult child?

Any GP, or even the doctors and neurologists who were investigating mum, could, No SHOULD have done some investigating into this utterly disturbed juvenile. In my teenage years I was a thoroughly troubled young boy. I would go to Arsenal games to vent my frustration on the away fans. Sometimes even looking for trouble. I carried pockets full of fireworks and flares. Luckily the football team was always my salvation. Apart from one game against Spurs, when I fired a rocket at them, "Sorry!"

You see doctors don't want to perform spinal taps on children. They would rather be champions of big pharma. Pushing their narrative and drugs onto as many gullible and desperate people as they can. You see when you get a diagnosis of life changing proportions, you want a matrix moment! The blue pill is the cure, and the red pills are placebo with no benefit.

It's all mind games, reminding me of a tactic used during the first (legitimate) Gulf War. When all Iraqi prisoners were kept unfed and watered for 24hrs. Then told the officers would be fed first. Now obviously the captain's, major's and colonels all rushed forward to get their rations. Only to realise that it was a ploy to separate the lower ranks from the rest.

The junior soldiers were all fed straight away, whereas the senior commanders had a few days and weeks of interrogation lined up for them.

In a perverse kind of way, this is what the white coats are doing with sick people in western societies in the world. Picking and choosing who to give the expensive treatments to, or who gets the ascorbic "non active" therapy.

Now obviously, the medical community deny any or all these claims. Denying big corporations have any influence on what is happening in our health systems. Something however that is transparent to all who live and work in the industry.

Just Look at how quickly everything spun 360' during the pandemic. But it is also incredibly easy to spot in our city's major hospitals and other clinics and facilities. Where expensive MRI machines are popping up all over the place. With other specialty equipment emerging from seemingly unknown sources. Like the cancer treatment wards, or infusion centres with the really expensive drugs and other medical advancements.

And in a crazy kind of way, I'm incredibly grateful for the incompetence of the RUH hospital in Bath. Who screwed up my investigation and treatments, in a way so badly and across so many different parts of the NHS, it all reminded me of how much I utterly hate the medical establishment. From a routine self-admission on a March lunchtime in 2012. To the realization that the entire hierarchy is a self-focused and obsessed bunch of muppets who have no interest or desire to make a difference.

It's like the doctors and administrators, who are laughing at how easy they can steal our money. I think constantly of the morning when I watched the duty doctor entering my symptoms into an Internet, something they had waited for a Bank Holiday weekend to pass until trying.

Or when the duty ward doctor woke me up at 3 o'clock in the morning after my bridge (tooth) had broken on a piece of hospital food. The gold filling was stolen from my bedside, and I didn't receive any apologies or explanation.

Or when the drug that was supposed to be included into the (DMT) drug modifying therapy I was due to receive got missed by the MS Specialist nurse and therefore couldn't get given. Even though I had changed all my work schedule and family arrangements weeks before!

Now I'm extremely aware of what pressures exist in the world. I'm also extremely aware of how many other things are currently causing the UK to have a deep hearted conversation about what is really going on. But in terms of MS and the supporting infrastructure, things that should help all sufferers. Let's be really crystal clear... It's only a minuscule fraction of the conditions that affect the millions of sick people in the country. But I'm sick and tired of the same old arguments and conversations that are constantly coming out of people's mouths, whenever they talk about this illness.

Firstly, it's not ok to just use the throwaway comment, that everyone's symptoms are different!

Or secondly, oh yes, but everyone does not have the same pathology, the injuries are all different...or thirdly, no two people are alike, they all react differently to the various treatments available. So here is a revolutionary new approach... ITS BECAUSE THE DOCTORS AND PHARMACEUTICAL COMPANIES WANT TO CONTROL THE NARRATIVE.

They don't want you to know that they don't have time to properly diagnose you, and they also don't want to give you any personalized advice or treatments, because this goes against their training. I find this whole situation tragic if I'm honest. At a time when broadcasting has embraced diversity and disability. We have been desensitized into thinking that certain groups and illnesses are always going to be untreatable.

The current "BEST OPTIONS' being championed by the medical community are the so called "management drugs" a selection of toxic substances that are repurposed from supposedly being designed to treat one disease. To then miraculously being shown to offer a "benefit" to an altogether unrelated illness.

This type of "snake oil" politics was prevalent during the Covid pandemic. Do you remember? The completely dishonest practice of Big Pharma rolling out their whole array of pills. "Clutching at straws!"

I have a vivid memory of the kitchen cupboards at my mum's house. Filled up with dosset boxes of tablets all "offering" a potential benefit. What a crock of shit! The drugs were designed to keep the parents away from the GP. Asking uncomfortable questions. Or questioning the validity of the doctor's credentials?

Let me be clear. If a white coat talks about "potential" or "possible". They are lying... If they want to refer you, they are using distraction tactics, just like they did in the Gulf War.

If keep changing your appointments and specialist "team" including your neurologist. This is another mind games ploy. You see these people, including the MS specific charities are all part of a campaign of deception.

Now don't get me wrong. A lot of people involved with these things are well meaning individuals who have vested interests. Like affected family members or friends, but unfortunately, a lot are not. This is the great swindle of UK charity. Get a basic understanding of an illness. Like MS or Cancer or MND. Then spend lots of charity funding and donations by spreading the message (narrative) of the uneducated. With the goal of controlling the conversation. Never mind about devoting your time focusing on possible solutions to dealing with this illness, giving practical advice and information about ways for you to improve your situation!

For me it's always been fitness. Swimming, cycling and running. Something I know I share with Cadeena Cox. British Paralympic gold medallist. Or Stephanie Millward MBE gold medallist for swimming. 2016 Paralympic Games in Rio. I have learned to know the triggers and how to manage them.

But when you experience a life changing experience. For me it was a flying related incident. Was it the airlines use of oxygen reduction to the cabin. To pacify passengers. Or perhaps the impact of the landing itself? Who knows.... What I do know is that the health system is broken, just like so much of the UK. Just look at the energy sector, or the water sector, or British Mail, Rail or the government. Every aspect of what should be done is not. I'm writing this reading about, prison system, UTTERLY CATASTROPHIC. This is after changing the people in Westminster.

My best advice is to find a good MS group like I did in Salisbury and follow your heart... One final important thing. So here is the final missing link! I could obviously point to the fact that me and my mother both contracted the illness (MS) on the same day. Even though we were in no way related! (adoption). Or I could emphasize the failings of another government National Regulatory body. In my case. The C.A.A. (Civil Aviation Authority) for inaction over the airline's illegal duty rostering. Or the lack of follow up management displayed. When the crew are exposed to a heavy landing or become unwell due to the reduced level of oxygen being released into the cabin. Because it saved the airline precious pennies on fuel costs!

I could point to the failures displayed in the healthcare industry. From a basic lack of understanding. Or in my experience a lack of urgency to downright incompetence. (I wish to be clear here. In no way, shape or form do I blame the nursing staff!)

What all these things point to is what I want to call "THE BRITISH DISEASE" where failure is not considered unacceptable. No, it is actually rewarded!

Just look around the country and see how broken and useless 90% of the services are. Where most of the middle management and higher, are not sector leading individuals or inspiring faces. Happy to stake reputations on behalf of companies and departments.

Oh no, as we have witnessed with post office scandal, the water companies and even governments. Nobody is prepared to take responsibility for their actions. I know I'm not alone in thinking this. Because everyone I talk to in my coffee shop is of the same opinion.

We have become a country that rewards failure. I could cite hundreds of examples, I'll stick with just a few. How about the water companies, using their CEO positions as cash cows for shareholders. Whilst happily drawing remuneration packages worth millions!!!

We allowed the last government to fail on every level for the last decade. In which time, they did nothing to improve the lives of normal citizens, choosing instead to focus on internal politics. Things that lead to Brexit, a countrywide lockdown during the pandemic, an episode designed to make money for the health and pharmaceutical industry, as well as the stealthy imposition of a cash free society. (Talking About the necessity for people to be bank oriented) paying for things on-line or through credit cards! A massive win for the banks and the health sector.

We got through Prime Minister's on a weekly basis, and watching their deplorable conduct as a kind of soap opera. Forgetting that those muppets were earning nearly £80.000 on their wages alone. Knowing that most of them were earning a lot more. When you and I were facing the "cost of living crisis!" I'll just say Boris, Liz and Matt... enough said...But the third thing I want to touch on is something, some of you may find difficult to swallow....

I'm talking about doctors. Not the ones who do the effective treatments or procedures. You know the surgeons and the accident and emergency services. Or the areas in which the patient outcomes are being met or exceeded!

I'm talking about all those areas where they hide behind their qualifications. Most of the time showing a complete disregard for the needs of the patients. Handing out prescriptions like drug pushers on street corners and nightclubs hand out class A medications. I mean who really thinks this theatre will ever end satisfactorily?

Another frequently used tactic, is referral. Sending you to see specialists for illogical reasons. An exercise in falsehood. The killing two birds with one stone "analogy" and getting you out of the responsibility of a particular department or doctor, to then have to endure the consequences of new faces and new explanations.

In my experience and my parents, this practice is purely a diversion. It extends to every aspect of the neurological game. Where the answers are obvious lies and half-truths. But because they have the qualifications, they can do whatever they want to?

The answers to the FAQ's in respect to MS, MND, or even Cancer. Are tinged with unknowns. I defy anyone to go through an initial assessment and not hear "it's possibly! "Which to me sounds a lot like "I've got NO FUCKING IDEA!"

It extends to the nurses and administrators on these wards too. All of them complicit in the deceit, which in my case extended to being asked by the newly appointed nurse, "what do you think it might be?"

But the other completely unacceptable encounter that I have endured on my journey. Has been the misappropriation of the charity funds. Paying for monthly "expenses" and "services" for volunteers to meet up in lavish locations and "discuss" strategies? No wonder J.K. Rowling abandoned her affiliation to the MS society, when she realised how little they were helping her mother!

Controlling the narrative:

Once again, a few key things to consider, that all newly diagnosed, or even those who are left in limbo. With non-committal doctors' conversations are left to stew on. Find out from the "lead" doctor in your investigation or hospitalization. Exactly what they think you have for injuries! (Get it in writing and use it to help find answers) but be very wary of any attempts to medicate your situation with a selection of drugs. I've been told that there is no guarantee for any medicine. You have "to try them all to see what works! Utter Bullshit!

Once again, a distraction technique that doctors use to buy themselves a bit of breathing room without any need to explore alternative treatments and therapies.

What I found worked for me was frequent exercise on gym apparatus and frequent swimming sessions. Something the pandemic has prevented me from doing.

One of the most common arguments you will hear from neuroscientists, neurologists and in fact anybody who has any working function within this group. "Everybody is different" and "no two people have the same symptoms," or "no two people have identified injuries!"

Absolute nonsense... it doesn't matter if you have suffered a traumatic event of the brain. The brain stem, the spinal cord/column or even nerve damage. I'm of the opinion that we all get grouped together because of the financial cost of detailed research and investigation of our conditions.

My own injuries are similar to those experienced by my mother when she first started getting sick. The fatigue, pins and needles and cramps, spasms. With cognitive deficits thrown in for good measure. But I didn't want to let it win. I fought internally to ignore the situation and continue to live with the illness. Recognizing the triggers and adjusting whenever plausible.

Now I completely understand that lots of you will have different experiences. But here is the key... Ignore the sensations as much as you can. Stay active and SMILE!!!

I have made a journey these past 11 years, from able bodied to wheelchair bound and a shadow of my former self. But you have to always remember to find a positive in these times. I'm fortunate, because I've been able to live a good life. Travelling the world. Meeting lots of great people. But never really getting too close. (Something I learnt from mum) in a downward trajectory it saves heartache.

I am convinced that I have a co-morbidity, due to contracting the Epstein Barr virus. The illegal flying my airline made me perform. Or even the heavy landing I endured.

Whichever the second incident was, that has so badly affected me. I'm grateful to have been able to live pain free, for my first 40 years. Doing things my mum never got the chance to.

So whichever way my story goes over the next few years I have something that nobody will ever be able to take! A LIFETIME FULL OF PRICELESS MEMORIES.

If you have ever lost your way. I have the perfect solution! Take a few moments out of your day. I guarantee that after reading this you'll feel very happy and satisfied about your health, your future and perhaps most important you will feel more appreciative of your family!

These are the recollections of my personal battle with life. You see I know I'm not unique in that respect, because lots of people of my acquaintance and in my social group had doubts too. The crazy thing is, that I had somehow bluffed my way into a lifestyle which, whilst on the one hand felt like it was serving a purpose. On the other had left me unfulfilled.

Let me clarify, I was born on December 10th, 1965. Somewhere around northwest London. Exactly where, I have no idea. The only piece of documentation I have to celebrate this event is a kind of after-the-fact cover note. You see I know this now; but until recently, I had always passed this off as being a birth certificate! It was a reasonable assumption to make. It was after Mums funeral, when I started questioning why things were not as they should be. I was in the dark. When I say Mums death, it turns out now to be my adoptive Mums death! Confused? Because I certainly am too.

The only reason I now know my life is a fraud. Is this cover note. Because once we had settled the paperwork after her passing, it came up during a conversation with my siblings. It was during the accompanying drinks that I caught a glimpse of my sister's birth certificate. Which, after a visit to Google confirmed what my brother and sister new all along. Her birth certificate contained information blatantly missing from mine.

The actual birthplace, the actual address, i.e. street name and number, and the hospital, plus the delivering physician. Despite it giving approximate location, it says Edgware near Harrow. I have now seen a second cover note, which gives me a completely different birth name to the one I have used my entire life! So, if you think you were having a bad moment or even day! YOU HAVE NOTHING. My parents named me Mark, but apparently, the Sunday school I attended was full of other kids called Mark. So, I ended up being called Ross. Which I was led to believe was my middle name. But you see the trouble with this story is this is a different name to the one on the cover note.

Clear so far? I am 'David." WHAT THE FU@K! Not like the wonderful statue found in the Medici centric city of Florence in Italy. I don't even have a chance with my real surname. It's not Beckham or Bannister but something unintentional or accidental. The only thing that is certain is, it was just quickly thought through.

It's become quite a topical subject the last ten or so years. What with government and church involvement in splitting mothers and children during the 1950's 1960's and 70's. Well, I have watched this unfold in the media. Mostly on television programs where they focus on the mothers, it's a kind of typical British stable diet. A bit like the full English or fish and chips! But what all your moronic stereotypes foolishly don't appreciate.

Is this behaviour and the whole conversation is a metaphor for British behaviour throughout the course of the country's history. Every level of civil society is tainted by the failures and mismanagement of British life. To the point where any investigation and redress of cases is deliberately bundled and hidden away with a whole host of delaying tactics.

So that anybody who is ever unfortunate enough to become entangled in a state sponsored, sanctioned or even caused tragedy, must wait until they are either dead, unable or infirm or forgotten. Because this is one of the states favourite weapons of war.

Isn't it funny, how we are asked to be lots of forces for good? I'm of course talking about things like stuff you get from the classroom. They want you to be patriotic, diligent, hardworking!

It is the same thing with religious teachings, be a good neighbour, honour your parents, follow the commandments! Here in Britain, there are also other areas of conformity which is kind of a reason to doubt everyone.

Because of my opening thoughts about me. Let's start to unpick the whole disgusting truth about what it means to be a part of this island nation. The whole story is obviously something which revolves around my birth mother. She got pregnant during the 60's and was unmarried. Let me break here.

Who gives a damn! Oh yes apparently it was seen as an absolute disgrace to have a child out of wedlock.! Are you really that stupid? Apparently, yes you are! The whole tone of the conversation is flawed. To now say that the attitudes and values of their time were different. Is a complete lie. The only people who were holding the values were the government and the church! WANK@RS! and probably other agencies like the police or other academics like doctors and nurses of some opinionated doctrine.

The average going's on of the day, were a pretty radical step change of everything that was supposed to be acceptable. The whole system was imploding, and British people were trying to be human! Shocking isn't it. The Second World War had just been won. People wanted to go out and enjoy living! The state didn't approve. Because from what I have heard some of the birth mothers on Tv interviews say. Children were wrestled away from their natural mother as they were born. Doctors and nurses were rude and insulting to the women. The overarching message was that the act committed was immoral, unclean and blasphemous! HOW FUC@ING DARE YOU...

The very idea that I am now without knowledge of my natural parents and grandparents is unforgivable. I do not care about things like giving the agency a chance to apologize or even the possibility that it was done probably in my best interest? AGAIN FUC€ OFF... Let's look at the other things that this bunch of cocksuckers consistently and continually get badly wrong. Reading between the lines. So, here's the big question? What exactly does this little venture into my life story have to offer you the readers?

The people that you have around you are your true friends. Try not to become hateful of the people who make your existence harder. I could put the knife in here, but I'm aware of how my frustration would have a negative effect, so I will just finish by saying – try and be positive, or in the words of Peter Sellers...do you have a licence for your monkey?

I'm not sure how interested you can possibly be, for such a quirky outsider kind of person! I mean we, in the MS community are all painfully aware, of how different individuals process their situations and emotions, but that's not even remotely close to why I wrote this article.

You see I view myself as an important piece of the neurological puzzle that is MS. It's something that began to dawn on me during another one of those pointless neurologist appointments. Listening to a qualification holding muppet. Feigning interest and displaying a staggering lack of empathy and understanding of what is going on with sufferers. If I were to try to classify the general behaviour of these individuals and their administrative enablers. I would describe them as the ultimate snake oil salesmen.

Like all of the NHS services, they are administered and managed by a bunch of self-focused prima donnas. Every single consultation and assessment are tinged with their self-interest.

I always have the impression that I am the "elephant in the room" somehow an unwanted anomaly or a distraction from their real purpose! Which is pandering to the private healthcare concerns of their private patients.

I remember when my mother was beginning her medical journey. With lots of frowning and tutting, by doctors who were obviously no more qualified to help her than I was. For example, I can quite vividly recall the kitchen cabinet that housed her medication. I'm certain it grew on a. With lots of creams, tablets and other products. None of which ever worked by the way! But it was all geared towards the fantastic fantasy genre of the "incredible healthcare system?"

A completely fictitious world of lies and deception. With only a real goal of extending the treatment of MS sufferers and believability of the ability of neurologists throughout the country. I'm focused obviously on my illness, but what I've just outlined is equally applicable to the other conditions that have not yet been addressed.

Like Motor Neurons Disease (MND), or cerebral palsy. I have lived with my situation, alongside my mother ever since our car crash. But understand this.

In all these years, neither myself nor my mother have ever been given any kind of protection, support or, and probably most importantly any treatment that has ever given us any benefit in our physical wellbeing.

Incredibly though, and despite this fact and lack of progress. Qualification holders of "neurology" practicing in clinics throughout the country. Still charge a king's ransom for their services. I mean "COME ON! REALLY" what the heck. I personally blame the broken NHS. But people like the managers and administrators who have allowed this nonsense to continue should be held accountable!

I don't think they should have any influence over patients at all. In fact, I would go as far as to say that I trust the symptom checker websites and literature from MS charities, more than any "white coats!"

In the majority of cases an MRI showing lesions and tell-tale signs of MS are physicians' grounds for playing the Monopoly dream card from the community chest. i.e. "get out of jail free card."

I'm convinced this is the preferred option for the white coats. It automatically confirms the initial suspicions and simultaneously discourages any need for further investigation and diagnosis. I truly believe this to be the current situation in our healthcare systems. Oh, certainly as all the white coats will tell you, we are all extremely different! NO SHIT SHERLOCK?

If I had a pound coin for every time I had heard those words, I would be a millionaire by now, but I don't want to dwell on those pointless interactions with the doctors too much, because it would only raise my blood pressure, anxiety levels and general disgust for the health industry in the UK. The new evidence I have been gathering over the past 13 years has shown me time and time again, how unsafe my diagnosis really is. For example, I recently learned of a remarkable story of a parachutist who was involved in a serious accident.

His chute failed to open, and the force of his landing had caused massive spinal injuries. 'Not dissimilar to my two heavy impacts', one being a fall from a promenade in Dorset, the other being an extreme landing incident of my aircraft. A situation, caused by allowing a trainee pilot to take the flight controls, whilst making a passenger laden stop.

Something btw which is neither good practice (to my knowledge) nor legal! But once again the regulator is not vested in ensuring that these companies comply with the requirements laid down in law? The point of talking about the similarities between my situation and parachutist, is demonstrating how I'm living and playing a perverse version of top trumps.

It's the game we used to play as kids, where each combatant tries to beat their opponent by showing a condition of a card that shows superiority! Thus, winning the trick, but you see what I find unsettling is when you analyse the differences between us. I'm treated differently because I'm not a multi-insurance policy holder. Who has access to hundreds of thousands/millions of pounds worth of coverage... but hey ho, good old capitalism!

The chap who damaged his spine was given the opportunity to reverse the damage done. I think he was given surgery to repair the damage around his spine and then the rehabilitation and physiotherapy that he required to make a full recovery. Why is this important?

I'll tell you why this is important. It's because the jumper was getting private medical attention and treatment. The symptoms he shared with me and the things that mirrored his situation to me were almost identical. Even the bowel and bladder issues that he experienced. So, you see if you can afford it join a private insurance company, and preferably one that offers you comprehensive coverage and doesn't have to bill for any repairs outside of the ordinary!

BTW MS sufferers, if you are NHS only! I wouldn't hold your breath. Because you are at the back of a very long queue. One that is getting bigger and bigger, every single day!

The next giveaway I found that supported my theory, that I'm a co-morbidity sufferer was an appearance of localized discomfort in my right sided cerebellum. The area of the brain controlling balance, posture, coordination and fine motor skills. Incidentally the area of my body that experienced the full force of an unprovoked assault on me, by a misogynistic farmer.

A person who I had called out for his unapologetic sexual behaviour towards some women in my local restaurant/bar. But like all my changes it never really got taken seriously because the doctors had the trump/MS card to play whenever things got questionable?

Now some might question my thinking as being unreasonable or unrealistic behaviour, towards the medical professionals. But you see I don't buy into that narrative! It's something I have been watching my entire life. Firstly, through the eyes of my mother. Then quite suddenly through my own experiences. Which apart from being subjected to a spinal tap are almost exactly mirrored but separated by 35 years.

So What reasons are out there for the medical profession to be dismissive of the possibility of a potential second condition? Well, the answer for this is blatantly obvious!

I'm talking about money, because I truly believe that my situation (like hundreds) of fellow sufferers, is treatable. Let's not forget. My initial illness was probably triggered by a combination of a bad aircraft landing, an unprovoked assault and a combination of bad practice practices by my airline employer. But once I had overcome the initial sickness.

Remember stroke like symptoms and massive balance, posture and coordination issues. I have then taken 12 years figuring out exactly what is going on.

But you see the whole process of getting the scans, plus extensive deterioration and anxiety, caused mostly by the stress and stupidity that comes whilst focusing on your condition, is very debilitating. In the first instance you are trying to get well again, fit enough to return to work. The entire time worrying about your family and bank balance.

Now this is where I start to get personal with the "white coats" and the goddamn administrators. A healthcare system should be designed to serve its patients. But to my disbelief that is not true for the NHS.

It has been my experience that the whole system is not just broken, but in 90% of interactions the doctor/patient dynamics are totally flawed. In my case it started with the referral of a GP to Bath A&E on a Bank Holiday Friday!

A decision that meant that nothing was investigated for four days. Because you see the healthcare industry shuts down on the eve of a national Bank Holiday. All the areas of investigative reporting are self-serving, and the doors closed. So, I'm assuming that if you are admitted with life threatening injuries, this is the only occasion where a qualified MRI technologist, or CT radiographer, even for X-rays a trained operative can be found to perform the necessary work.

But it doesn't stop there with the inadequacies and failures in treatment. I'm 'old school' and have been trained through the military system! Where 5 o'clock Friday, doesn't mean that you close the doors and lock up?

It's where the excessively overpaid and underperforming guardians and architects of our health machinery are supposed to show leadership and commitment.

I'm of the opinion that this failure is the product of historic political and societal incompetence that we experience and expect daily. Remember my comment earlier about the possibility of removing people who are a liability? Or "sideways promotions!" Well, this is what you are left with. It's a daily occurrence in every walk of British life. Where incompetence and arrogance are rewarded.

I've experienced it in the military, but also on the airline and now in the NHS. A combination of poor or inexperienced position holders. I'm talking about a mass failing in suitability and ability. A sense that the holders of senior positions of responsibility and authority are completely out of touch with the reality that I call the "cluster fuck syndrome!"

It's something I have been struggling to put my finger on for these last few years. But I now have found the perfect analogy.

Do you remember the first television show broadcast on channel 4? It's called "COUNTDOWN," a quiz gameshow, involving word and mathematical tasks. Where contestants are pitted against the clock to find the best answers to solve numeracy challenges and untangling jumbled letters to reveal hidden dictionary entries. I'm not so much focused on the program, moreover it's the similarities between demonstrations of knowledge and problem solving that have caught my eye! You see it compares seamlessly with my health journey.

The acronym for reacting to a stroke patient is FAST. Something I'm sure many of you will be familiar with. If stands for "face, arms, speech and TIME." On the television show the contestants have to battle against the backdrop of an ever-reducing time element.

For me on my excessive delay for investigative testing, it reminded me, in so many ways of the Richard Whiteley fronted show. On the left side of my face, I had experienced a drop of contours. From my left arm I was getting an increase of "pins & needles," and the speech had been severely affected. With the clock continuing to reduce my chances of getting a satisfactory outcome?

Now obviously as I have explained, certain parts of my pathology were very much known and understood by me. I'm talking about the brain fog, the unusual sleeping patterns and the heavy leg thing. I was aware of visual impairment, weakness which I attributed to weather, climactic events. But the symptoms I was experiencing this day were completely different.

I was convinced about two key aspects of this deterioration. Firstly, I was convinced the impact of the aircraft landing was a very unusual phenomenon. Something that my body had endured hundreds of times before. But my fingers tingled like never before. It was more pronounced.

Secondly my head was experiencing the most intense sensation of "brain fog," I had ever experienced. The drive home was very challenging and every jolt from potholes in the road and also the vibrations of the diesel engine were giving me a feeling of sickness.

Hence my going out into the countryside to get some fresh air. There was still some snow on the ground and then just like that. I experienced the "straw that broke the camel's back" moment! I couldn't lift my legs, and it took an improvised tree branch crutch to get me home. On one hand I felt very vulnerable, on the other I was glad to have not been in the car, or worse still, in the air flying.

I'm now in a position of stability. When I can evaluate all the circumstances that have contributed to or caused my current position! Unfortunately for me, and for everyone who may have similar difficulties, I have got some key moments of my journey to share.

If you are ever confronted with the diagnosis of MS. Or are showing the classic symptoms. You are in a very challenging mental situation. Where things you used to do without a second thought, suddenly become more problematic.

One of the first changes I made was to get as fit as possible. I have found swimming helpful. This was something my body actually wanted me to do!

Being around smokers and smoke was a big "no go," but a vegetarian diet is a good cure for any bowel and bladder issues. But most importantly listen to your body. I'm convinced it can lead you in the right direction!

I'm in the unenviable situation where I have lost 2 families, all my colleagues and friends, except for two old workmates and I cat. A three-legged ginger called HARVEY.

Points to remember:

Some very important pieces of additional information. I have been battling with this issue for about fifty-five years, in which time health departments and industry have come up with zero (NO) tangible solutions towards helping people who are suffering. What this means is, for the organisations who claim to be helping people find solutions. They have achieved actually less than nothing! With a massive question mark over what they have done with the money raised?

I have met and spoken to hundreds of people enduring this same living nightmare. Where we are encouraged to share our stories and experiences, in the hope that somehow, we might find a distraction or therapy that might be beneficial or helpful towards managing our situations! Because you see the only improvement that has happened over 55 years. Is the explanation of what areas of your brain are affected.

The general level of effectiveness and ability demonstrated by the white coats and big pharma friends is at best "negligible," and at worst "laughable!" With a distinct degree of incompetence and failure that must be seen to be believed. I'm going to be quite honest here. Because frankly this scenario would equally apply to motor neurons or the other brain injuries. Anybody who is taking a wage from the supporting groups for these disorders is comparable to "A SNAKE OIL SALESMAN"

The reason why the majority of people who are diagnosed with MS and exhibit different symptoms is because we all have a variety of different illnesses! For instance, I myself have the classic MS injuries. But also, a spinal injury and head trauma. Mixed with the added complications of a glandular fever diagnosis in 2005. Unfortunately, the doctors are never going to agree to this, because it would throw up question marks over "competence"

I have attended meetings for affected people of all ages. I am always struck by the amount of literature spread around from the likes of the MS society or MS trust. But here's the problem. How much is actually going to be helpful? You see it's all about controlling the narrative! I want everybody to understand that the options available are extremely limited. At best offering a kind of placebo induced tick in the box. Where people assume they have options for a good outcome! Or at least some hope.

So, here's the question for all you affected out there. I'm not just talking about the diagnosed only. Because this affects everyone in the immediate vicinity. I'm talking about family, friends and relatives, the children and their friends and families. The directly affected through secondary relationships. Like the workplace of the affected. The schools of the family children affected. Even situations that become difficult, for example the elderly relatives or even the family pets and local sports and social club long before I started to dramatically deteriorate.

I realised through my mother's experience that the only people who you can trust are friends and family, followed closely by the care community, who believe it or not, I have total respect for. I have in my life personally pushed lots of wheelchair bound people. I got a dressing down from an Army officer for giving this young boy with cerebral palsy the wheelchair ride of his life one afternoon in Hampshire, during my short time at Middle Wallop, but you see "he was Sandhurst educated," and therefore knew better?

Incredibly the other sections of society who you know you can trust are community centred support groups. Which from my own experience includes a private therapy centre. A county focused social group. Which is a very hit and miss in terms of how well organised they are. I will compare it to the regional inequalities often associated to NHS performance. I assume you are familiar with the term "post code lottery!" Then finally there are the NURSES. A section of the healthcare system I utterly refuse to criticise. Underpaid, overworked and in many ways undervalued?

I would love to give out more glowing reviews and praise but honestly. I'm just unable to. I'm going to try another analogy now. Referring to Hollywood blockbuster movie "Men in Black." It's on some of the moments where the protagonists have to use a memory adjusting device to alter the reality of a situation complete and utter poppycock, I know, but there's a lot of similarities between those moments and the way that our modern-day neuroscientists are able to control the narrative of any discussion! You can see our illustrious white coats can be, and are, a force for good in many aspects of modern medicine.

The ones who are employed in A&E departments, or who deploy in life and death care, I absolutely can't fault them, the ones that scrub up as surgeons and (some) specialised areas of medicine too, but for goodness' sake, this is now 2025, with the diagnostics and advances in technology that an internet connected society has immediate access to.

I no longer have a need for twentieth century processes. I'm perfectly happy with the quality of "symptom checker" websites and the surprisingly simple ability to find the right people to contact regarding the problem and any questions that might be appropriate!

What I do not have any time or patience for is the "money-go-round" department hopping through hospital visits, clinics and endless doctors' appointments and consultations. The majority of which are totally futile, where you are directed into rabbit hole, just like Alice, except this is not a Wonderland. It's a doctor fuelled hell. Where you have to have your wits about you, otherwise you probably will get swallowed up in unnecessary procedures. I very nearly got talked into a surgery that was completely unwarranted. I luckily got away from taking an experimental drug that had no proven efficacy. yet could have killed me!

These are the considerations that you have to make on a daily basis. All the while knowing that you are under pressure from your employer the family or a million other factors. I'm fortunate in so much that I can draw on my mother's experience and knowledge. She was drugged to the point of being a zombie! Until we got her off all the drugs. I was really proud of her because after two hip replacements she got to walk with me and my kids in the sea. On holiday in Brittany, France.

Unfortunately, in 2014 she went to hospital for a routine check up on her condition and replacement hips, caught MRSA on a hospital ward and died two days later! Oh, NHS thank you so much!!!!@@%%!!!! This was why during the Covid lockdown I really didn't care who lived and who died. I know that last part is probably too difficult for many of you. But just like the doctors who I have had dealings with these past twelve years. I find you all a bunch of insincere tosspots. The epitome of a failed system. Oh yeah, you possess a qualification.... but to what ends? You are quite prepared to dish out your drugs. Aren't you? You are always happy to make spurious referrals to unrelated departments and specialists, because these are the things that help you to control the narrative. It's quite a comfortable position for the doctors and the pharmaceutical industry isn't it!

So, who do you think was laughing during the pandemic AND THEY ARE LAUGHING AT YOU RIGHT NOW £££££, so hopefully you can make the right choices.

The logical and illogical conclusion:

I'm going to try now to put all my little muttering's and posturing into a sequence that I hope will be easy to follow for everybody affected by a complex cerebral or spinal injury. For the sake of honesty, I have to inform you that you have nothing but bad prospects!

Let me outline a few of the most common and difficult conversations that await you. I am a great believer that our entire social system is based on a complete lie. For example. We are constantly looking for a supposedly better educated and more intelligent level of person to provide us with guidance on issues that we have no real experience or understanding of.

For example, we naturally assume that our political leaders and their advisers are best equipped to provide good judgment and leadership for our countries.

A situation over the past 50 years I'm sure you would agree that history has shown us how wrong we are! Or that the capitalist system we have been forced to accept is the one that has shown us time and time again, how utterly fantastic it works for everyone?

300 million expatriates living abroad is surely proof enough that the system is completely corrupt. I know this because I have witnessed it first hand from both sides of the divide. With my brother's merchant banker friends who were able to go from bankrupt to Spanish property owners in 24hrs.

To the 1970's/80' rough sleepers under Charing Cross station or today's cost of living victims who depend on food banks and charities to survive? Or the people who occupy the offices of outright authority in our society are beyond reproach and can be relieved upon to offer a clear example of wholesomeness and honesty?

Anybody who accepts that statement should be forced into euthanasia and put out of their misery because it is obvious they don't deserve to live any longer! Or how about the other staples of our daily culture. The gatekeepers of truths. Like entertainment or news providers? I'm talking about BBC, radio, our schools and businesses.

I mean nobody at the Beeb has been caught up in anything. Have they? The entire charade of our qualification system is not flawed, is it? Our financial system is a fair and fool proof method for dealing with transactions and trading, isn't it?

Our government and the responsible watchdogs for public services are a fantastic and important part of daily life. Ensuring water companies and energy providers offer a fair and acceptable service whilst also protecting the environment and public safety.

If this wasn't on your radar of areas where we are currently being cheated by scrupulous contractors and companies, then you might as well just give up. Because under your watch you have allowed the destruction of our country's infrastructure, and you have even unnecessarily rewarded failure by granting the payment of dividends and insane remuneration packages for the CEO's and board members.

So here goes with my modern day take on Billy Joel's "we didn't start the fire" song, except that it's not focused on American history, instead it's contemporary and very much British focused.

David Cameron, Teresa May, Brexit and Johnson shame. Liz Truss and stock market, Sunak and Black Lives Matter. Met Police caught again, BBC programmes, presenters or historical figures and acts of inappropriate behaviour. OFWAT OFGEM, or even the CAA. Post office and banks, closing ranks and using the legal community to do their best, to subvert the course of justice. Mr Bates and Grenfell Tower, but the public don't care?

We didn't start the fire. But the smoke is rising and King Charles is laughing. Diana is dead and the Coronation trumps the cost-of-living crisis, and even Coronavirus, but never mind because Cheltenham can still go ahead, and because the elderly have had their time, irrespective of what they contributed to society, but mainly because they are old!

The War in Ukraine, election following election, it doesn't really matter because the politicians still get in. Jews killing innocent and expecting sympathy. Controlling businesses, films and TV, Elon Musk and Jeff Bezos cornering global trade and space exploration. The danger of nuclear threats, and a Labour movement rewarding doctors and train drivers.

Whilst all the while Paralympic and Olympic athletes entertain. A distraction timed to distract the public from the inevitable reality. That is the race for the bottom!

Which leads brilliantly onto the health department failings and structural inconsistencies. I've mentioned it before but never really focused my story to this point. I'm encouraged today because for the first time in my life we are talking about how we need to change the narrative

I read this morning that Wes Streeting is looking at the massively excessive amounts of administrative posts, or management in the NHS. You should also add the executive directors of countless trusts and the non-functionary post fillers throughout the country. I mean be honest, which doctors are actually doing a good job?

From my experience you can take out function specific departments and then drastically reduce the "chaff" employing only the "wheat!" You can do the required section by using a little common sense. The A&E is a definite yes. As are, things like paediatric and birth centres. Closely followed by surgery and operation units. The dental service also counts as a must have with the main healthcare providers all moved to regional and localized facilities, which means that specialised services, such as cancer care, neurological care and the other many faceted niche conditions could and should only be treated by services that provide a real value or benefit to the community?

Now I realise that this paragraph is going to sit badly for anyone who is undergoing treatment or is even being investigated for potential serious health conditions. But why should we accept the failures of the medical profession?

Sure, we would all love all conquering pill, you know it's a bit like the fairytale with the magic beans. But unfortunately, it is a little more than a pipe dream. I mean just look at the numbers of successful interventions into all these difficult conditions.

I'm not going to say it won't happen! Because I don't want you to lose hope. But do yourselves a massive favour and view any claims of advancement in science or treatment. Even with the introduction of AI and all the possibilities this could offer.

Only believe it if you, or someone else who you know has actually tangible evidence that X, Y or Z works. Without the additional risk of being killed by "side effects," a situation btw that I briefly entertained in the past. Hopeful for an improvement.

Something that I didn't experience, or neither did anyone else who I spoke to, during this dramatic transition in my health. Trust your gut instincts. Plus remember why you have a "own body" oriented judgement ability. The white coats want you to be like Neo in the film "THE MATRIX." Swallowing the blue pill means you're in the fantasy realm of big pharma and you're only way out is through death!

Record every consultation with the doctors and administrators and play them back periodically to judge what level of assistance you have received. Periodically check your symptoms on "symptom checker websites" to gauge where you may have been misdiagnosed or at least have a secondary infection. You never know it could be something quite manageable, but the doctors are not interested, because they already have the results they want.

Just to clarify "SPOILER ALERT. SPOILER ALERT, SPOILER ALERT, SPOILER ALERT," I spoke to an OT (occupational therapist) during my investigation work at one of the hospitals I was assigned to establish the diagnosis and injuries. Who quite unashamedly told me that my patient team were split about the root causes of my symptoms. Confirming my suspicions that my injuries were not as black and white as doctors described?

An anomaly that opened the floodgates to my belief that I was experiencing another illness or injury, but that these muppets were unwilling or financially unprepared to investigate and treat.

So let me bow out by offering a little list of names and addresses that summarize my experiences during my lifetime. Bearing in mind that I understand how utterly inept and spineless this country and the corporations/bureaucracies are. With all Their flaws and idiosyncrasies. But you judge if I have a case?

Stolen at birth. Moved around the country like a gipsy caravan. So basically, denied the right to a childhood. Damaged by a car crash. Nothing ever reported or investigated. Neck injury probably caused by faulty seat belts. "The car was British Leyland Austin Maxi" enough said! Mother and I begin journey into MS. With focus purely on my mum. "Demonstrating ineptitude of NHS" fail school badly due to illness. So lied way to career and life. Army unit trained me for RAF system. 1985 got to watch "live aid" two months later my accommodation is destroyed by a fridge fire. Luckily nobody was injured, get rescued by dad at Dover ferry terminal after catastrophic car failure in Germany on the way home to prepare for deployment to Canada. Learn in Canadian forces base about death of a much-loved colleague Bill Johnson. A man who became face for MND (motor neurons disease"

Should probably mention that MS symptoms are mild and don't show up on many occasions. Few dodgy situations during cold weather extremes like snow or during a couple of sporting events. A failure during an attempted marathon about the 25km distance. Or a failed swimming section of my first triathlon because of cold water.

The snow fail was whilst playing enemy to a unit around the Hameln area of West Germany and my legs failed me during an ambush assault. After laying on frozen ground for about six hours. After training for computer programming and management course, left UK again to be deployed in N. Ireland. Then after the Michael Fish "no hurricanes" and Chernobyl was sent back to Europe to be treated in what eventually became Prince Harry's regiment. Watched the Lockerbie tragedy and then watched the aftermath of the Soviet Union.

Visiting a friend in Berlin while the corridor was still very much East and West. Witnessing history on a weekly basis, with trains loaded with Russian tanks and artillery waiting to be returned home, a very happy couple of years as I remember it. Spoilt by the insanity of Iraq's unwarranted attacks on Kuwait, but, of course, you have all probably got your own memories of what happened after those events.

I trained a group to run to the Royal Marsden Hospital from Germany to bring closure to my Army life and to raise money for cancer research. A guy at work was recently diagnosed.

I think that my fitness levels and general well-being were the best they ever got to around that time. I also began my exit strategy with the fall of the Berlin Wall. Made sergeant for a brief period and then that was enough for me. I left the day Windsor Castle caught fire. I'm convinced it was a secret sign.

The next twenty years are a blur. Living abroad again and retraining as cabinet maker. Continuing triathlon and endurance events, taking over as football team manager, learning about the death of Diana, then watching the UK make a sequence of crazy decisions and basically making every expat never want to return.

I think it started with Thatcher, selling off the country assets but thanks to Blair and everyone subsequently getting their two pennies worth your land has become a joke!

I'm talking about opening the borders to investors and scrupulous businesses. Putting everyone's lives in jeopardy by aligning ourselves with US foreign policy. I'm ashamed of the fact that our troops were deployed into conflict with no mandate, other than to follow the misdirection of foreign intelligence agencies. I look back at what I left in 1992. For the first time in a generation, we had hope! But now look at us!

The financial crashes and internal market shocks that we've experienced in the last twenty years have killed the belief in capitalism. The organs of society that are supposed to protect us are broken and we are now closer than ever to the breakdown of the country.

Yet, understand this, people who have illnesses like us, don't care about the daily self-inflicted injuries of the country. They are worried about the bills and the heating. They wonder if they will find somebody who understands what being a care giver really means! They wonder if they can get out and about, and if there is still a possibility of going out for a coffee?

And finally:

Just in case I have left a few things out let me clarify, you have probably already noticed how I have skirted around the edges with regards to certain areas of detail. So here goes a bit of disclosure. I used to fantasise about the railway. The trains and the feeling of having a good day out. The excitement of seeing some of the rarer locomotives. The independence of my journeys. Getting to know lots of different parts of the country and practicing my photography and occasionally breaking into the yards and workshops of the locomotives.

My favourite places to visit were the massive sheds and buildings of Swindon. The electric development and repair shops at Crewe. With the piece de resistance. The gigantic shops and repair facilities of Stratford, East London.

I'm actually quite convinced that it was during my illegal visits to British Railway establishments, is where I got my taste for the adventurous lifestyle.

The main reason why I tried to get qualified for working with computers, was because of my visit to the T.O.P.S, system in St Pancras London, but you see, that even though I qualified as a systems manager, I can honestly say that the day-to-day task was of data protection and security. With hours of backups, inserting programs to ascertain whether a specific helicopter piece is in stock is something which completely bored me.

I was a bit like (v sign) Malcolm the Sealink computer manager, who I met on the Cheshire Ring canal boat holiday. A person who was competent enough for the routine work but actually hated the computerization of his system. In a bizarre way it was a "full circle" moment.

Everybody who is a patient with a neurological condition will understand what I'm about to say next, or even the carers and support groups thereof. Whichever way you turn there is a plethora of information and advice about the illnesses! Stupid amounts of funding are being thrown at glossy pamphlets and literature with a supposedly comprehensive guide to all concerned, and designed to not just inform, but more importantly enable newly diagnosed patients to make informed choices when it comes to their needs. But here is the problem? Do you remember during the pandemic when everyone became slaves to our binary system of computing?

Our lives were revolving around PC screenshots. I personally used the time to do some artwork, painting a precious few water colours, and trying, badly to learn how to play the guitar until one morning I thought, let's write my journal.

My eyesight was really difficult to control during those years, but I have persevered and during my periods of self-reflection I kind of feel quite proud of what I've accomplished.

Those old days in the forces, when I stared at the computer screen, and found myself mimicking the character from "Little Britain," Vicky. You know the girl who looks totally indifferent and says, "The computer says NO!" Well, that was me! But just reflecting on all the interactions I have had with the PC, it's quite surreal to think about.

It pains me, especially with regards to the NHS. The nurses in Bristol, spending hours on screens, so I got thinking, "what a waste of man-hours," duplication and triplicating gone mad! I then realised the entire healthcare industry is deeply flawed, where doctors can access medical advice using symptom checker websites.

GPs can then blatantly use medication encyclopaedias in front of patients, or as recently became common knowledge, the questionable storage and treatment of private medical records. There are parts of me that want nothing more than a fully functioning medical system, but unfortunately, I have seen the failings of the NHS! Where we are jumping to give accreditation and qualifications to the lowest levels of competence, and where difficult questions and conditions aren't even being addressed, from the merry-go-round of studies surrounding certain diseases. Researchers are simply re-hashing 50-year-old data to justify their work to repurpose existing drugs, or to provide families and patients the erroneously stated evidence of potential breakthrough for an illness.

I'm absolutely committed with my belief that the illnesses can be controlled by a combination of hands-on therapies and changes to diet and anti-inflammatory medications.

I also totally believe that physical activity and exercise (especially swimming) can totally transform the lives of people who are struggling with their health issues. But that is a thought for another generation.

I also notice that recently the pharmaceutical industry has begun rolling out another "game changer" drug and electronic stimulus for Parkinson's disease? Funny how the long covid patients are getting physiotherapy isn't it. Enough said!

Finally, and controversially.

The final piece of the jigsaw has just been revealed. Not by some ground - breaking research discovery, or by some accidental drug use. I'm talking about the parameters of incompetence and arrogance that have fuelled the current failures and incompetence displayed by the global neuro community. Something which is totally transmitted and transparent during every consultation or appointment through a neurologist's office!

It's a mixture of indifference and total hopelessness. A knowing realization, that sooner or later someone is going to figure out their game. Well, bless my cotton socks. I'm a great believer in Karma but what happened today really did tie up the whole story. I was sat in a coffee shop when I flipped the pages of the morning newspaper. When I chanced upon an article about Lucy Letby. The nurse convicted of supposedly murdering a whole bunch of infants, I remember seeing the story when it first broke. I was naturally appalled by it, thinking back to the horrors of Shipman. The way that people of eminence and position were getting involved in another possible miscarriage of justice really got me fired up to include the story into my own.

You see, for all of us "patients" who are experiencing catastrophic failures in their healthcare. It really struck a chord with me.

Dr Shoo Lee, a Canadian neonatal care expert and the co-author of a paper on air embolism was emboldened to become invested in the legal case and subsequent 15 life sentence verdicts of Ms Letby, following up on the conviction. When discovering the prosecution had only used a limited number of potential methods to prove the untimely deaths of the babies.

Despite knowing, just like in my hospital treatment and investigation. That there had been countless instances of failures in the provision of timely care and intervention for patients!

A position which was subsequently supported and shared by 14 experts, including medical professionals from the US, Japan, Sweden, Germany and the UK. Also, a view supported by the veteran MP Sir David Davies amongst others.

Once again proving, if proof was needed. The UK healthcare, legal and probably hundreds of other supposed "organs of society" are not fit for purpose. So, what is the answer?

We've seen how governments love to use "public enquiries" to get the truth? Ask the victims of Grenfell Tower, or the sub-postmaster's how that

is going, or look at how much has changed 6 months after the installation of a new government? Two key mantras from my life have been.
"Answers people, is what I want!" Or. "If you can't make a difference, make an exit."

The latter belongs to over 50% of the boardroom sitters and almost everybody currently occupying the leading roles of the country, but I will let you be the judges of that!

Let's forget about the unhelpful terminology, the card the white coats love to play with the most. When your consultant or doctor starts using words like. Could, might, or possibly and potentially, this is your cue to get the hell away from them. Definitely never embark on a new drug when you are given those words of encouragement.

There's a more important issue at play here you have to be aware of. I wasn't even made aware of an underlying back issue, until months after my initial complaint. You see when doctors scan people without back pain. The uncovered disc bulging or degeneration the MRI reveals aren't necessarily the cause. Something that highlights the limitations of modern technology!

It also explains the utter failure of matching the current technology to symptoms. In a study published in BMJ Evidence Based Medicine, the researchers looked at 56 different treatments or treatment combinations available for back pain either of new onset or long term.

For new onset the only treatments found to help were NSAID's. Which included Ibuprofen, or prescription drugs like diclofenac. For long term the list was pretty low on options. But one thing was consistently championed. Namely "exercise," which ties in nicely with my own experiences. "You don't use, you lose!"

The findings came as no surprise to Professor Jane Ballantyne, anaesthesiologist at Washington University. She is quoted as saying "the majority of back pain doesn't have a generator you can easily fix."

The way that the doctors try to control the narrative, is nothing short of scandalous in my eyes. Not just on my behalf, but also every other MS MND or indeed everyone who is put through this process of "trying to get to the bottom of this," which is actually quite surreal in the scheme of things. Remember my admiration for the nurses and A&E doctors and surgeons? I totally stand by my opinions. The rest don't get my vote.

Q. How is it possible that a doctor with complete access to my medical history would have me returning to work. Knowing the impact, I would experience daily on my spine.

Q. Why would my employer think it would be ok to return to work when the company doctor was at best unsure if I would be placed in an unsafe position?

Obviously, I could go on. But this is where I let you decide. Bearing in mind the government wants to put disabled people back to work. Where do you stand?

**I know how difficult it can get sometimes with our illness. I lived my whole life with the condition. Watching how much it affected my parents and siblings. The biggest thing I have learned from my experience, is how important caregivers and nurses are. I always try to have the mentality that others out there are far worse off.*